GREAT EXPERIMENTS IN AMERICAN ECONOMIC POLICY

GREAT EXPERIMENTS IN AMERICAN ECONOMIC POLICY
From Kennedy to Reagan

Thomas Karier

 PRAEGER

Westport, Connecticut
London

Library of Congress Cataloging-in-Publication Data

Karier, Thomas Mark.
 Great experiments in American economic policy : from Kennedy to
Reagan / Thomas Karier.
  p. cm.
 Includes bibliographical references and index.
 ISBN 0-275-95905-8 (alk. paper)
  1. United States—Economic policy—1961-1971. 2. United States—
Economic policy—1971-1981. 3. United States—Economic
policy—1981-1993. I. Title.
 HC106.6.K35 1997
 33'8.973'009'045—dc21 96-53937

British Library Cataloguing in Publication Data is available.

Library of Congress Catalog Card Number: 96-53937
ISBN: 0-275-95905-8

First published in 1997

Praeger Publishers, 88 Post Road West, Westport, CT 06881
An imprint of Greenwood Publishing Group, Inc.

Printed in the United States of America

The paper used in this book complies with the
Permanent Paper Standard issued by the National
Information Standards Organization (Z39.48-1984).

10 9 8 7 6 5 4 3 2 1

For
Norma and Clarence

Contents

Contents

Preface

Not everyone agreed that the economic experiments proposed by Kennedy's economic advisors in 1961 were going to work. Their proposal to cut taxes and raise government spending simply to manage the economy was a novel idea. While critics predicted disaster and economists debated the numbers, Congress eventually implemented the entire experiment. This was the beginning of one of the most comprehensive experiments in American economic policy.

The Kennedy program in the early 1960s established a blueprint for future economic experiments. It also provides a stark contrast to another experiment that was based on an entirely different economic theory. In early 1981, President Reagan's new appointees moved with surprising speed converting conservative economic ideas into national policy. Once again the experiment was subject to heated debate but was eventually fully implemented as Congress approved the largest tax cut in history.

The supply-side experiment was joined by two other, equally risky experiments. The monetarist experiment, conducted by the Federal Reserve, began in 1979 and continued into 1982. Coinciding with these experiments was free floating, an experiment conducted by the U.S. Treasury from 1981 to 1985. Other books have been written about supply-side economics and some about monetarism, but most have overlooked the third experiment of the early 1980s, free floating. The benefit of looking at all three experiments at the same time, as this book does, is that this period in the 1980s then makes much more sense. Each of the experiments had a profound impact on the course of economic affairs. Attempting to interpret the results of any one experiment without considering the others can be a futile exercise.

The issues addressed in these experiments—tax incentives, Federal Reserve policy, and regulation of currency markets—are not going away. The public is still confronted with dubious tax plans, a secretive Federal Reserve Board, and daunting bailouts of foreign countries. By understanding this important episode in American economic history we should be better prepared to deal effectively with these issues in the future.

While working on this project I have accumulated my own debts. I would like to express my deepest appreciation to the Jerome Levy Economics Institute and to its director, Dimitri Papadimitriou, for providing generous encouragement. The Institute has created a unique environment for economic scholars to discuss their ideas and debate the merits of public policy. I especially benefited from my conversations with Wynne Godley, William Milberg, Hyman Minsky, Sanjay Mongia, and Francis Spring. The research assistance provided by Triveni Kuchi was invaluable.

A number of people read earlier versions of this book and offered valuable insights. I especially appreciated the comments by Paul DePalma, Lisa Brown, Juliet Skuldt, Tom Unrath, and Clarence and Norma Karier. I feel very fortunate to have received reviews from such thoughtful and attentive readers.

1

Camelot and Trojan Horses

In September 1979, the new chairman of the Federal Reserve Bank, Paul Volcker, announced that the central bank of the United States was adopting an experimental policy for managing the nation's money supply. By radically altering its monetary policy, the Federal Reserve intended to reduce the high rate of inflation without sinking the entire economy into a deep recession. For the next three years the Fed stuck by this experiment as it regulated the growth of the nation's $1.5 trillion stock of money.

In May 1981, a high-ranking Treasury official announced that the United States would not, for the first time in its history, actively buy and sell foreign currencies. The U.S. Treasury began its own experiment by adopting a self-imposed prohibition on intervention in international money markets. If successful, the dollar and other currencies would enjoy a spell of stability that they had never experienced before.

In August 1981, President Reagan signed a $750 billion tax cut dedicated to reducing the tax obligations of corporations and wealthy individuals. Never before had taxes been cut so much for so few. If all went as planned, the nation would undergo an economic renaissance and budget deficits would soon vanish. This marked the beginning of yet another experiment in economic policy.

With these actions, the United States embarked on three of the most ambitious economic experiments in modern times. Two were closely associated with the Reagan revolution, but all three were part of a conservative revival that began in 1979 and swept across the country during the decade of the 1980s. Economic experiments of this magnitude had been conducted before but never three at the same time. By adopting all three experiments the economy was deliberately exposed to more uncertainty and risk than perhaps at any other point in our history.

Risky experiments may have seemed justified given the serious malaise engulfing the economy in 1979 and 1980. Inflation was running in double digits and unemployment remained a chronic problem. Energy prices were soaring out of control for the second time in seven years, and energy shortages and the fear of future shortages had temporarily paralyzed the country. Average wages, corrected for inflation, had not improved much since 1973, and productivity growth was abysmal. On top of all this, the U.S. dollar was tottering on the verge of collapse.

Under these conditions the public was not only open to new ideas, they were demanding them. For many economists and politicians this was an opportunity of a lifetime—an opportunity to try out theories in the laboratory of the U.S. economy. Many of these experimenters had spent their lives under the shadow of John Maynard Keynes whose economic theories had dominated the postwar world. Keynes and his followers had provided a blueprint for economic policy that included a strong measure of government intervention, but with the general deterioration of the economy in the late 1970s, these Keynesian concepts came up short. The time was ripe for experiments.

THE NATURE OF ECONOMIC EXPERIMENTS

When one thinks of an experimental science, economics may not immediately come to mind, and yet it has been the source of some of the most important experiments of the twentieth century. These are not the kinds of experiments that rely on rats and mazes (although economists conducted some of these in the 1970s), but rather they are experiments that apply to the entire economy. In these experiments, the guinea pigs are the American public and the mazes are government policies and the nation's financial institutions.

Not all economic policies enacted by the government qualify as experiments. In order to be a true economic experiment, the policy must have a theory, a hypothesis, a test, results, and hopefully some conclusion. The deciding factor is usually whether there is an economic theory behind the policy that can be confirmed or refuted. If the government cut taxes in order to ease the burden on the rich, this would not qualify as an economic experiment. It is a simple redistribution of income intended to raise the after-tax income of the wealthy. If the government slapped a tariff on automobile imports in response to a foreign country's unfair trading practices, this would constitute retaliation, not an experiment. If the government increased spending on defense in order to enhance its military power, this also would not be an economic experiment. In none of these cases is there an economic theory underlying the policy action.

It was a different story, however, for the economic policies enacted during the 1980s because theories were involved. In the first experiment the Federal Reserve changed the way that it managed the nation's money supply. It decided it would no longer use interest rates, unemployment, and inflation as its guides, but would devote all of its attention to achieving a predetermined change in the money supply. The rationale behind this idea was derived from *monetarism*, a theory closely identified with the work of Milton Friedman. For years Friedman had complained that the incompetence of the Federal Reserve was the source of America's inflation problem. Friedman argued that the Fed could learn to avoid inflation if only it would implement policies based on his own theory, monetarism. When the Federal Reserve adopted his recommendations in 1979, it ushered in an important experiment to test the validity of monetarist theory.

The second experiment was conducted in the 1980s under the banner of supply-side economics. In this experiment, taxes were slashed a record-breaking $750 billion in 1981 with the expectation that the initial loss in tax revenue would be recovered rapidly in an accelerating economy. Supply-side economics was in many ways even more controversial than monetarism. Many economists considered this experiment premature because supply-side economics was relatively new and had not been subjected to professional scrutiny. Although this may be true, any theory, however improvident, can become an experiment as long as it wins the support of public officials. This is precisely what supply-side economics managed to do when it was adopted as official policy by the generals of the Reagan revolution.

The third experiment of the 1980s was based on free floating, a theory closely related to monetarism. The concept of free floating also dates back to the 1950s and is responsible for the proposal that the federal government cease active participation in international money markets. For many people it may come as a surprise that the government actually does intervene in these markets but this has been standard operating procedure for more than one hundred years. By intervening, the U.S. Treasury or Federal Reserve buys and sells foreign currencies much like any private bank or speculator. On any given day they may buy U.S. dollars or Italian lira and on the next day sell both. During the great free-floating experiment from 1981 to 1985, all this changed. Instead of buying and selling currencies with the intent of influencing exchange rates, the U.S. government stuck by its self-imposed moratorium on intervention.

In each of these three experiments an economic theory provided the intellectual basis for changing national policy. From these theories, hypotheses were developed and formulated more or less as predictions about the future. For monetarism the prediction was about inflation; for supply-side economics it was about economic growth and deficits; and for free floating it was about stability in international markets. Each of these theories produced a clear and testable hypothesis.

The need for economic experiments is obvious—the current state of knowledge about economic affairs is simply inadequate. Business cycles, for example, continue to defy prediction, even by top economists versed in the most sophisticated theories. The U.S. economy continues to experience booms and busts without any clear or consistent reason. Every expansion is followed by a recession, but other than that there are few other universally accepted truths. It is as though all the important measures of economic performance, including gross domestic product, personal income, and profits, are tied to some central, driving force that remains elusive. This is no small gap in our economic knowledge since business cycles could easily be considered the most important economic topic of the century. The mystery that surrounds business cycles casts a shadow on everything economists profess to know.

There would be a need for economic experiments even if business cycles were the only unsolved mystery, and yet they are not. Many other economic questions are still unanswered. The unexpected slowdown in productivity and real wages after 1973 continues to baffle economic scholars. Many of the original hypotheses have not survived the test of time, leaving even more questions than answers. Even the falling savings rate, a topic discussed later in this text, has yet to be properly accounted for. Anyone who professes certainty about these economic matters may be either a fool or an aspiring consultant. There is no shortage of important questions to be addressed by economic experiments.

To date, much of what we know about economics is due to careful observation. While some of these observations are useful because they cover long periods of time, it is the unusual event—the Great Depression of the 1930s, the world wars, or the oil crises of the 1970s—which makes or breaks economic theories. None of these events could be construed as an economic experiment because none were designed and implemented to test economic theories. They did, however, have a very similar effect by helping to weed out weak ideas.

One could have argued for years about the validity of the economic model popular in the 1920s. Did it make sense to assume, as this theory did, that a market economy would have a job for everyone willing and able to work? This was a dubious assumption even then, but it did not deter most economists from giving it a prominent role in their research and college instruction. Only the extraordinary unemployment of the 1930s, reaching 25 percent at its peak, finally settled the issue. Economists could no longer assume full employment in their models, at least not without appearing a little ridiculous.

There was also the once-popular notion that federal budget deficits would immediately undermine economic growth. A balanced budget, according to this argument, was the only way to instill confidence, and confidence stimulated economic activity. Throughout the New Deal of the 1930s the popularity of this belief prevented the government from creating deficits large enough to make much of a difference. Until World War II forced the country into spectacular deficits, it was unclear just how vacuous this idea was. Under immense deficits the country prospered as it never had before, putting an abrupt end to the Great Depression.

Another economic myth was laid to rest in the 1970s. In the early part of the decade, it was not uncommon to believe that the large U.S. economy was insulated from problems arising in foreign markets. After all, imports and exports together in 1972 were less than 10 percent of the gross domestic product, the official measure of the nation's output. How could something so relatively small, it was thought, have any real importance? But after the oil crises sent the U.S. economy reeling with inflation and unemployment in 1973 and again in 1979, foreign markets earned more respect, despite their size. The culprit in this instance, petroleum imports, was less than .4 of a percent of gross domestic product in 1972, the year before the first oil crisis.

Each one of these major events helped to dispel misguided notions about the U.S. economy. They were not experiments, but for the careful observer they provided a test of prevailing economic concepts and generated valuable lessons. Because these historical events were so extreme, pushing the economy far beyond its normal day-to-day operation, they were able to change the way people thought about economics. The Depression did not just produce unemployment, it produced unthinkable unemployment. World War II did not just create deficits, it created record-setting deficits. In the realm of economics, it is the extraordinary event that is persuasive. Unlike these earlier events, those of the 1980s were designed and implemented with a specific theory in mind, qualifying them as economic experiments. But what they share in common is that all three experiments in the 1980s were also, in some sense, extraordinary.

While these three events can legitimately be described as experiments, they should not be confused with controlled experiments. There were no controls and certainly no control group which, by scientific standards, makes them relatively poor experiments. They were in a sense *uncontrolled* experiments and, being uncontrolled, the results were influenced by all sorts of confounding errors. One does not have any appreciable degree of control over OPEC (Organization of Petroleum Exporting Countries) oil prices, the weather, or the aging baby-boom generation. Despite all of the obvious problems with uncontrolled experiments, the unfortunate fact is that we cannot do any better. There is only one U.S. economy so a control group is impossible, and to bar all confounding factors is simply impossible.

The fact that economic experiments are uncontrolled does not mean that they aren't useful. In the end, the results will either support or contradict the hypothesis. If the results support the hypothesis then this is as good a reason as any to accept the underlying theory. If the results contradict the hypothesis then at least the decision to reject the theory is based on something more than a whim.

Any experimenter, economist or scientist, still has to answer the final question: Would the results have been any different if not for confounding events? A laboratory scientist has to ask whether the equipment was sterile or whether all external sources of heat or vibration were eliminated. Economists have to wonder whether a spontaneous change in oil prices or a sudden shift in consumer tastes or any other myriad possibilities may have affected their results. The scientist can go back and clean the test tube or insulate the experiment, the economist cannot. At best, economists can speculate about whether the problems were large enough to make a difference.

If all of this seems offensive to the scientific purist, then consider the fact that there are no better alternatives. Macroeconomic policies cannot be *proven* on a blackboard any more than they can be *demonstrated* in a laboratory. The economy is not yet so predictable that it can be perfectly simulated by computer; our level of understanding falls hopelessly short of this ideal. It would be possible to avoid economic experiments by stubbornly adhering to traditional policies, ones that have been used before. But given our current slate of economic problems and the potential for new ones, I cannot imagine that relying on traditional policies will satisfy the nation for very long. The desire and the need to experiment is too strong to resist. Our best strategy may simply be to recognize new economic policies as experiments, choose them carefully, and evaluate them fairly.

Distinct risks are inherent in any experiment, even legitimate scientific experiments. The very least one would expect is for the subjects of scientific experiments to be volunteers, fully informed of the dangers, and if necessary, given the opportunity to sign waivers or accept compensation. The American public is seldom so well prepared for economic experiments. They may be so inundated with promises that they fail to appreciate the risks; a serious omission since the fallout from a failed economic experiment can be profound. At its worst, a failed experiment can cause the loss of millions of jobs, the accumulation of trillions of dollars of national debt, and the failure of thousands of businesses. The victims of an economic experiment may not all be volunteers, they may not appreciate the risks, and they are seldom compensated for losses. For all these reasons, economic experiments should always be taken seriously.

The reader should be forewarned that economic hypotheses are often disguised as facts. This is merely a subterfuge for winning political approval, without which no economic experiment is likely to ever be conducted. Who is going to let an economist with a hypothesis test it out on the U.S. economy! Instead, hypotheses have to be repackaged as confident predictions, sometimes even promises. In the 1980s, the promises were to resolve a growing list of serious economic problems including inflation, a slow-growing economy, chronic federal budget deficits, and volatile international money markets. One must be careful not to be deceived by the apparent factual nature of economic promises, they are often nothing more than hypotheses. Even when the promises are fulfilled and the experimenter claims full credit, it should not be forgotten that there was once uncertainty about the outcome.

Economic experiments can have an impact far beyond their immediate discoveries. There is a good chance that the economic experiments of the 1980s affected every individual and business in the United States as well as many in the rest of the world. At stake was the well-being of virtually every important sector of the economy including the stability of our financial institutions. It was much easier to be uninformed about these experiments than it was to be unaffected. While many people may have overlooked the significance of these obscure policy changes in Congress, the Federal Reserve, and the U.S. Treasury, they would have found it hard to miss the resulting changes in interest rates, unemployment, inflation, budget deficits, the value of the dollar, cost of imports, and trade deficits.

The economic experiments featured in this book were selected because they all had important impacts on the United States, and sometimes, the entire world. They all can be described as *macro-*

economic because they involved national issues like international trade, economic growth, employment, and inflation. Most important, each of these experiments provided us with a valuable lesson. Whether or not we as a society actually learn these lessons is another matter.

CAMELOT

The Keynesian policies enacted under the Kennedy administration in the early 1960s had all the hallmarks of a successful economic experiment. After winning a close election in November 1960, President John F. Kennedy and his advisors found they had inherited an economic problem; a recession had begun in the third quarter of 1960. By modern standards this was a mild and brief recession, ending in the first quarter of 1961, but it still alarmed Kennedy's advisors. The low growth rates accompanying the recession had contributed to raising the unemployment rate to 5.5 percent in 1960 and 6.8 percent in 1961. Anxiety about the recession was no doubt exacerbated by the memory of the Great Depression. Although soup lines, bank panics, and record unemployment were already more than 20 years old by then, any downturn in economic activity was still considered a potential disaster.

Kennedy's economic advisors readily accepted the challenge and came to play an important role in Camelot, the name supporters used when referring to the new administration. Kennedy made two quick appointments to the Council of Economic Advisors in 1961, Walter Heller from the University of Minnesota and James Tobin from Yale University, both leading Keynesian theorists. Other Keynesians would later take their turns on the council including Gardner Ackley in 1962 from the University of Michigan and Arthur Okun in 1964 from Yale University. The Keynesian revolution that had swept academia in the 1940s and 1950s gained access to economic policy in 1961.

Keynesian economics originated with Keynes's lectures in the 1930s at Cambridge University and was formally launched with the publication of his book in 1936 titled *The General Theory of Employment, Interest, and Money*. To its scholarly audience, *The General Theory* was revolutionary because it undermined the basic premise of conventional theory. Economists, accustomed to studying balance and equilibrium, found in Keynes's book lengthy discussions of imbalance and disequilibrium. This new perspective resonated with the economic realities economists saw outside their windows: unemployment climbing to 25 percent and national output falling by one-third.

As Keynes's ideas were read and absorbed in academia, they also attracted a coterie of devoted scholars. In many cases these were graduate students and young professors who were willing to let go of conventional theories and at the same time were able to appreciate the significance of this fresh approach. Some of these scholars, like John Kenneth Galbraith, would write about the merits of Keynesian policies for popular audiences while others, like Alvin Hansen of Harvard University, anchored Keynesian theories at the highest levels of academics. Still others were appointed to the Council of Economic Advisors in the 1960s where they directly influenced national economic policy. Each of these scholars made important contributions to the Keynesian revolution that swept the United States.

Keynesians in the early 1960s were likely to hold certain common beliefs. Among the most important was that economic recessions were not inevitable. According to the economic advisors in 1965, "No law of nature compels a free market economy to suffer from recession or periodic inflation."[1] Here was the belief that enlightened government policy could counter the natural rhythms of the business cycle. If successful, recessions could be delayed, shortened, or even avoided. The key was a well-timed artificial boost to the economy caused by increasing government spending or decreasing taxes. These actions, referred to as fiscal policy, tend to increase the size of the federal budget deficit. Traditionalists decried the lack of a balanced budget, but Keynesians insisted it was the only way to keep the economy afloat and pointed out that the deficits were only temporary. Once recovery was under way, the budget could be balanced or even allowed to achieve a small surplus.

Successful fiscal policy required careful timing and planning. Ideally, a fiscal boost should be timed to anticipate economic downturns. Too long a delay runs the risk of missing the recession entirely and giving too much zip to the recovery. If a recovery is already under way when fiscal policy kicks into gear, the economy may expand too quickly causing prices to rise and inflation to take off. Equal in importance to timing was the size of the fiscal stimulus. Too large a tax cut or spending increase could also push the economy too quickly, again causing inflation. Fortunately, Keynesian theory provided the tools necessary to calculate the precise size of the required fiscal stimulus; these were the so-called *multipliers* described in Keynes's book. If the multiplier was two, an additional billion dollars of government spending would ultimately create $2 billion in additional national output.

Keynesians may have had confidence in these tools but they also understood their limits. As powerful as fiscal policy was, it had to be used sparingly. If unemployment dropped below a certain level—the Keynesians believed it to be around 4 percent—inflation would surely increase. While fiscal policy was quite capable of pushing unemployment below 4 percent, the general consensus was that it should not be allowed to do so. The Keynesian goal of reducing unemployment stopped at the 4 percent threshold.

Keynesians were not, however, ready to give up on the unemployed and the poor, the ones who would be most seriously harmed by this limit. For them, Keynesians were likely to advocate social welfare programs, unemployment compensation, and other policies that would provide a safety net. These government programs were considered less onerous than the inflation, which in all certainty would accompany a lower unemployment target. To Keynesians, this approach struck an appealing balance between economic efficiency and compassion for those in need.

The perceived trade-off between inflation and unemployment was the subject of a study conducted by A. W. Phillips in 1958. He observed that unemployment could drop considerably after a recession without much change in inflation but only up to a point. Once unemployment hit particularly low levels, inflation became a serious problem. For each reduction in unemployment in this range, inflation appeared to move one step higher. Like a teeter-totter, every decrease in unemployment was matched by an increase in inflation. This was not too surprising to economists who were familiar with the shortages that were likely to arise during the later stages of a recovery. Businesses, in many cases, would respond to these shortages by raising prices and fueling inflation.

Perhaps Phillips's most original discovery was the finding that the trade-off between inflation and unemployment was repeated during each business cycle, mapping out a single, consistent curve.

In particular, the *Phillips curve*, as it became known, was relatively stable from one business cycle to the next. Because these discoveries were quite compatible with the Keynesian view of economic planning, they were readily incorporated into the theory.

Although fiscal policy was obviously at the heart of Keynesian policy, there was also a role for monetary policy. It is worth noting that monetary policy is not the same as monetarism. Monetarism is the theory associated with Milton Friedman. Monetary policy is whatever the Federal Reserve does to change the amount or availability of the nation's money supply. Keynesians believed that monetary policy should reinforce fiscal policy, as for instance when it became necessary to pump up the economy during a recession. All the Federal Reserve had to do was increase the amount of money in circulation and interest rates would fall. The lower rates would in turn encourage investment and consumer spending. Or if necessary, to slow the economy down to fight inflation, the government could reduce the money supply, raising interest rates and discouraging spending. The key to successful monetary policy, in their view, was to coordinate it with fiscal policy so that they either both accelerated economic activity or they both slowed it down.

These were traditional Keynesian ideas, much like the views that Walter Heller and James Tobin brought to the Council of Economic Advisors in 1961. The Keynesians were not in Washington D.C. long before they began drawing up plans to attack the listless economy.

THE KEYNESIAN TEST

The centerpiece of the Keynesian experiment was a series of tax cuts for corporations and individuals. The purpose of the tax cuts was to convert the federal budget surplus of 1960 into a deficit and if Keynesian theory was right, to accelerate the nation's recovery from the 1960–61 recession. The first of these tax reductions was enacted in July 1962 in the form of new depreciation guidelines allowing businesses to write off capital expenditures more quickly. In the Revenue Act of the same year, an investment tax credit was passed that established a 7 percent credit, primarily for new equipment expenditures for businesses. Together, these tax breaks were estimated to save corporations $2.5 billion.[2]

The second part of the experiment came in 1964 when personal income taxes were cut $6.7 billion and corporate taxes an additional $1.7 billion. What was unique about these tax cuts was that they were not intended to balance the budget; they were intended to stimulate the economy. This was a risky attempt to achieve a high level of economic growth without inflation.

While tax cuts were the most visible component of the Keynesian experiment, they were not the only part. In addition to cutting taxes, the Keynesians also supported an increase in government expenditures. During the first three years of the new administration, government expenditures increased an average $6.4 billion a year, primarily for defense, space research, technology, and various civilian needs.[3] As a percentage of national output, federal expenditures climbed from 18.3 percent during Eisenhower's last year in office to 19 percent in 1963. The combination of tax cuts and higher spending increased the likelihood that the federal deficit would grow.

While the appropriate Keynesian monetary policy in 1961 would have been to increase the money supply and lower interest rates, there was a problem. The U.S. government in the early 1960s was having an increasingly difficult time maintaining the price of the dollar. More dollars were being offered for sale than there were buyers, obligating the government to buy the difference with its dwindling supply of gold.[4] Reports about gold draining out of the United States were already beginning to ruffle financial markets. One way to reduce the gold drain was to raise interest rates in the United States, thus making dollars more desirable. The problem with higher interest rates is that they also tend to reduce consumer spending and business investment, which was precisely opposite the goal for Keynesian fiscal policy. The advisors were torn between a monetary policy that would lower interest rates to support their domestic expansion and one that would raise interest rates and alleviate pressure on the dollar.

Kennedy's economic advisors' solution to this dilemma was a creative compromise. They decided it was desirable to raise short-term rates to help the dollar and to lower long-term rates to support the economic expansion. Since both short-term and long-term rates often move together, this was not an easy task. To raise short-term rates, the Federal Reserve set an example by raising the discount rate, the interest rate it charged on loans to member banks. In order to lower long-term rates they attempted to increase the supply of funds to banks so that they would lower the rates themselves. If this monetary policy was successful, short-term rates would rise closer to long-term rates, effectively closing the gap between the two.[5]

There were back-up plans if this policy failed to rescue the dollar. For starters, the U.S. Treasury was pursuing more international cooperation with foreign central banks. Cooperation would prove useful if a massive bailout of the dollar were ever necessary. It was good preparation for the day when the U.S. Treasury alone would not be able to buy enough dollars to reassure financial markets. The United States also pursued policies through the International Monetary Fund and with individual countries that would increase its ability to buy more dollars on credit. And in two instances the United States attacked the outflow of dollars directly. It placed a tax on Americans who bought foreign securities, and it required recipients of U.S. foreign aid to spend those funds on U.S. goods. The latter policy was not only good for U.S. companies, it also helped the dollar.

One looks at the results to evaluate any economic experiment, and for Keynesians, the results could not have been much better. Between 1961 and 1967 the U.S. economy expanded at the annual average rate of 4.6 percent, much faster than the postwar average of 1.4 percent between 1945 and 1960. Even more astonishing was that the expansionary fiscal policy appeared to accelerate economic growth without setting off inflation. Over the same period, inflation averaged 2.2 percent a year, reaching only 3.1 percent in 1967. Here was the best that could have been hoped for—high growth with low inflation.

The Council of Economic Advisors also logged an impressive record of forecasts. In January 1963 the Council predicted that their policies would push gross national product (GNP) for the year somewhere between $573 billion and $583 billion. The final number for the year came in at $584 billion. The advisors had slightly underestimated what turned out to be an impressive amount of economic growth. Later revisions in GNP statistics would not alter this fact. In January 1964 the advisors predicted GNP of $613 billion to $633 billion for the year, that is, if the president's tax cut was passed. The tax cut did pass in 1964 and took effect immediately with a reduction in tax withholding. Actual GNP for the year came in at $622 billion, easily within the predicted range. In January 1965, the advisors predicted an increase of $28 billion to $48 billion in GNP. Once again the economy came in as predicted with an increase of $47 billion. Any modern forecaster would be delighted to achieve this level of accuracy.

One of the objectives of pursuing faster growth was to reduce unemployment. Success was also achieved in this area as the unemployment rate fell from 6.7 percent in 1961 to 3.8 percent in 1967. This was sufficiently close to the 4 percent target for Keynesians to proclaim that they had achieved full employment. Other aspects of the economy were functioning equally well. Productivity was up as were profits and wages. Businesses and workers were all doing better.

If there was one area of concern it was the international sector. The Council of Economic Advisors could only point to small successes in this area. The innovative monetary policy that attempted to raise short-term rates was relatively successful as the gap between short-run and long-run interest rates closed between 1962 and 1966. Short-term interest rates on 3 month treasury bills rose from 3.5 percent in 1962 to 5.2 percent in 1966 while longer-term mortgage rates hardly changed. But even this increase in short-term rates was too small to stem the rising tide against the dollar. At best, the government's policies reduced the number of unwanted dollars after 1960, but they did not solve the problem. As a result, the federal government continued to use its scarce reserves of gold and foreign currencies to purchase dollars. The stock of gold held by the U.S. Treasury fell from $17.8 billion in 1960 to $15.4 billion in 1964.[6] While these developments were foreboding to international traders and investors, they also were not disastrous. The problem was limited to the fact that the prevailing financial system was not working well and appeared to be in need of repair or replacement. The anxiety was that no one knew exactly what the new system would look like.

In every other respect, Keynesians could not have hoped for better results. In many ways this period was the apex of the Keynesian revolution that had begun in the 1930s. The experience of World War II was also important for Keynesians because it proved the corrective power of deficits, even when the problem was as big as an economic depression. World War II, however, did not demonstrate that Keynesian policies would work under more ordinary conditions, nor that they could succeed without creating inflation. Remember that the spectacular economic boom of World War II was accompanied by an equally spectacular outbreak of inflation.

The Keynesian experiment swept aside many of these doubts, providing strong support for active government intervention. In the words of the Council of Economic Advisors in 1965, "The lessons of 1964 will not be lost: Fiscal policy can sustain growth and raise spending power to the levels needed to use our resources more fully. Price stability can be maintained during a strong and balanced expansion. The balance of payments can improve in a period of prosperity." In their view, the experiment was a watershed, establishing once and for all "the economic measures that can best achieve particular objectives."[7]

Keynesians were more than willing to accept the results of the experiment as a confirmation of their theories. After all, the federal budget deficits had appeared to stimulate economic activity and did so without inflation. While the results were quite impressive there is still the possibility that luck played at least a small role. The expansion was successful for the very fact that it was not overdone. If businesses had been a little more optimistic they might have invested too quickly in new factories and equipment or they might have built up their inventories too rapidly. In either case the expansion might have progressed too rapidly, causing inflation to creep up and contaminate an otherwise exemplary expansion. The Keynesians were well aware of these dangers, and they continued to monitor the rate of the expansion quite closely. But while they could take credit for carefully limiting the size of the fiscal stimulus, they could not take full credit for the restraint shown by businesses. Business expectations vary widely and are only indirectly influenced by government policy.

The economic expansion of the 1960s ultimately did break away from the tight leash designed by the Keynesian advisors. By 1968, the economic experiment had clearly done its job, and it was time to remove the stimulus or even reverse it. Unemployment had dropped to 3.6 percent, well under the 4 percent target presumed to represent full employment. The Phillips curve was now clearly in effect, and inflationary pressures were growing. Inflation, measured by the consumer price index, rose from 3.0 percent in 1967 to 4.7 percent in 1968 and 6.2 percent in 1969, setting the stage for the next recession. In the pivotal year of 1968, every economic measure was signaling the need to turn off the fiscal stimulus but instead, the deficit expanded from 1.1 percent of national output to 3.0 percent. This year marked the end of the Keynesian experiment.

The deficit of 1968 has generally been blamed on increased spending for the Vietnam War. This was an important part of the story, but it is worth recognizing that there was also no effort to curtail domestic spending or raise taxes. The influence of Keynesian advisors had waned sufficiently by 1968 so that their policy recommendations were being routinely ignored. Despite the resounding success of their experiment, politics regained control of the federal budget.

Although Keynesians would never quite recover the power that they exercised from 1961 to 1964, their ideas remained influential into the 1970s when they confronted a new set of problems, the energy crises. It became clear rather quickly that their theories were not designed to deal with these problems. In all fairness, this was not a unique deficiency of Keynesian theory. To this day, no known economic policy could have rescued the nation from these particular crises.

THE MODEL EXPERIMENT

In a way, the Keynesian experiment served as a prototype for all future economic experiments. It was designed to solve a particular kind of problem. The solutions were risky but derived from a credible economic theory. It produced promises that helped win the political power necessary to be tested on the American economy. And of course, the successful results earned the experimenters a certain degree of respect and esteem. Keynesians could be proud knowing that any future experiment would do well to meet the same standards and achieve comparable results.

The remainder of this book describes how three subsequent experiments were conducted. It begins by exploring the theories behind the experiments and then describes the experiments themselves. Later chapters compile the results and provide a conclusion. The closing chapter takes a look at the legacy of these events and speculates on the next economic experiments. Although this book is organized on the basis of the scientific method, none of the experiments described in this book are scientific experiments. There are similarities between economic and scientific experiments but there are also important differences. In order to appreciate these distinctions it is worth exploring the details of these three experiments.

2

Origins of Monetarism

Like most social scientists, economists devote much of their time
to answering questions, some inconsequential but others of profound importance. One of the more important questions concerns
the amount of money the federal government should place in
circulation. Given that the government can alter the amount of
money, how much should there be? Too little money can cause even
an efficiently operating economy to grind down into a recession or
worse, a depression, while too much money is inflationary. These
dangers set limits on the primary U.S. monetary authority, the
Federal Reserve, but they do not eliminate all room for discretion.
A wide middle ground remains in which the money supply can be
changed without accelerating inflation or a debilitating depression.
Which strategies or goals should guide the Federal Reserve as it
maneuvers between these twin perils?

One possible answer was voiced by Milton Friedman and eventually incorporated into what became known as monetarist economics, or more simply, monetarism. Friedman's answer may have
remained purely academic, buried in economic treatises, if it hadn't
been embraced by the top officer of the Federal Reserve Bank in
1979. But this is getting ahead of the story.

Friedman insisted that the Federal Reserve should fix a target
rate of increase in the money supply and stick to it at all costs. But

what would be the target rate of increase and why should the Fed stick to it? What would be the dangers if the Fed failed to stick to its assigned task? The answers to these questions are deceptively simple. In order to fully appreciate their significance it is necessary to explore the fundamentals of money and monetarist theory.

FRIEDMAN'S INVISIBLE HAND

If Milton Friedman didn't invent monetarism, he at least reinvented it. In fact, monetarism without Friedman is impossible to imagine. He worked out the major principles of the theory in the 1950s and 1960s and then set out to persuade the rest of the world of its wisdom. Because monetarism is synonymous with Milton Friedman, no injustice is done to the theory by focusing exclusively on Friedman's contribution.

One should not forget that Milton Friedman's primary calling within the economics profession, which is the source of both his fame and notoriety, has been as a champion of free markets. This is neither a new avocation nor a particularly unusual one. Following in the footsteps of Adam Smith, many generations of economists have taken their turn at defending free markets from the corrupting influence of the state, a sentiment that undoubtedly harks back to the construction of the Coliseum and aqueducts in ancient Rome. One of Friedman's more noteworthy accomplishments was to distinguish himself from this rather competitive field by taking extreme and dramatic positions, even by the standards of contemporary conservatives. As a purist and a zealot, he succeeded in attracting attention.

In their popular market manifesto, *Free to Choose*, Milton and Rose Friedman contrasted a romanticized vision of market capitalism to a bumbling and corrupt modern government. Their book described the operation of markets in much the same way Adam Smith did 200 years earlier in the *Wealth of Nations*, but far more efficiently. Where Smith required more than a thousand pages to explain market mechanisms, the Friedmans thoughtfully condensed the discussion into a single chapter containing precisely 28 pages. The two works differ in other respects. The Friedmans replaced Smith's reverent depiction of a pin factory with an equally inspired discussion of pencils. So many individuals have had a hand in its production, the Friedmans marvel, it is "astounding that the

pencil was ever produced."[1] There are other markets more central
to the operation of a modern economy, but they may not correspond
as well to their notion of an idealized competitive market as pencils.

The one-sided picture emanating from *Free to Choose* has become
Professor Friedman's trademark. The state was discussed in terms
of "tyranny" and "maladies," while the market was allowed "to
flourish" with "prosperity" and "freedom." Such black and white
images were used to mobilize support for an antigovernment
agenda—abolishing the minimum wage, health, and safety regulation, Social Security, and public education. In fact the goal was even
more comprehensive: to eliminate the role of government in all but
a few essential activities. Where public functions cannot be eliminated, he advocated specific rules to constrain the autonomy of
public officials.

What is the source of Friedman's unwavering devotion to private
enterprise? Others, like Adam Smith, emphasized the practical
benefits: the efficient use of resources; the responsiveness to
consumer demand; and the rewards for innovation, risk, and
self-sacrifice. Friedman clearly endorsed these arguments, but for
him, the justification for private enterprise can be found at a more
fundamental level. He writes:

> A person like myself who regards freedom as the major
> objective in relations among individuals and who be-
> lieves (itself a scientific not a value judgment) that the
> preservation of freedom requires limiting narrowly the
> role of government and placing primary reliance on
> private property, free markets, and voluntary arrange-
> ments—such a person will resolve his doubts in favor of
> policies relying on the market.[2]

Filtered through these values, it is no surprise that Milton
Friedman's professional inquiry into questions of economic policy
so often resulted in a condemnation of government. It seemed that
no matter what the question, Friedman's conclusion was always
the same, the situation would be vastly improved by limiting the
involvement of government. Friedman's critics have complained
that he is likely to write the conclusion before the arguments, as
this quote so candidly reveals. The danger with such ideologically
driven conclusions is that in some instances they may not work.

Pure ideological positions may look fine on blackboards and in university seminars but can prove dangerous in the real world.

DOLLARS AND CENTS

Much of what economists know about money is not new but still may seem a little surprising. The obvious purpose of money is to pay wages and salaries and to buy things. A modern economy could not begin to function without it. Can you imagine having to rely exclusively on barter? How would you trade your skills in book-keeping or art for a new car? The existence of money allows you to sell your labor one day and buy a good or service the next, in other words, to carry on transactions. Money is obviously essential in the modern economy, but this raises some important questions. What is money and who creates it? After settling this question, it is possible to consider how changes in the amount of money affect the economy.

Our economy uses money in a number of different forms, none of which are exactly equivalent. Purchases are relatively easy with cash, checks, or travelers checks.[3] There is little question that each of these is considered money. But if a checking account is money, what about savings accounts, time-deposits, or government bonds? The answer depends on the concept of liquidity. Cash and checking accounts are highly liquid in the sense that they can be spent almost immediately, while savings accounts must first be converted into cash or transfered to a checking account. Recently, the small delay in converting savings accounts has become even smaller with the advent of phone transfers and the ubiquitous bank machine. The delay involved in converting a time-deposit or government bond is expected to be somewhat longer.

This illustrates a point that is a little disconcerting: There is no single objective definition of money. Money is merely a continuum ranging from highly liquid assets at one end to highly fixed assets at the other. Where money begins and ends on this continuum is not so much a technical issue but a matter of preference, one that government statisticians resolve by calculating a series of meas-ures, each with varying degrees of liquidity. The most liquid measure, M1, is comprised primarily of cash, currency, and check-ing accounts. More encompassing is M2, which combines M1 with savings accounts and a few other types of accounts.

If the first surprise about money is that it is not represented by a single number, the second surprise is that the federal government does not have complete control over it. Of course the Federal Reserve exercises considerable influence over money but this is not the same as absolute control. How then is the amount of money in circulation determined?

First consider an imaginary situation where cash is the only form of money; the amount of money would then depend entirely on how much the U.S. Treasury printed and spent. If a billion one dollar bills were printed and spent then this would constitute the money supply. The government could increase the amount of money available in any year by spending more than it collected from taxes or from buying bonds.

Printing money like this has been used most spectacularly by the United States to finance major wars. When the patriots needed money to finance the American Revolution they resorted to issuing notes known as Continentals. At one point during the war, when the future did not look especially promising for the revolutionaries, merchants stopped accepting these notes, giving rise to the expression, "not worth a Continental." There was also a proliferation of currency by both the North and the South during the Civil War. The North not only bettered the South on the battlefield, but they did so with relatively less reliance on the printing presses at the Mint. The North, because of its superior credit-worthiness, was able to raise a greater proportion of its funds by borrowing. The South, on the other hand, flirted with financial panic by its excessive creation of money. The possibility of the government flooding the economy with money in this manner is much stronger during wartime.

In reality, not all money circulates as cash and in fact most will be deposited in checking and savings accounts. This would not alter the amount of money if banks simply held the cash but of course they do not. They turn around and lend out some fraction of deposits, keeping enough on hand—called reserves—to cover daily transactions. The fact that initial deposits lead to loans, which are simply additional checking accounts, illustrates how the banking system itself creates money. A deposit in one bank will lead to a loan that is then spent and deposited in another bank. With the second deposit, the process starts all over again. The total value of money in bank deposits at the end of this process is much larger than the original deposit.

When banks are concerned about sudden large withdrawals, they typically lend out a smaller fraction of their deposits, thus shrinking the quantity of money. For example, as the U.S. Civil War progressed, Southern banks became increasingly pessimistic and increased the relative size of their reserves. By 1863, several major banks in Virginia, South Carolina, North Carolina, and Georgia had all increased their reserves to at least 50 percent of total deposits, a high level by historical standards.[4] At this point in the war the future of the Confederacy was less than ensured and banks wanted to be prepared for the possibility of large withdrawals. The approaching Union forces evidently created a strong incentive for sound banking. Due to the precautionary measure of increasing reserves, the amount of money available for loans declined, which in normal circumstances decreases the money supply.[5] As this example demonstrates, the banking system itself can alter the amount of money in circulation as banks decide to either augment or deplete reserves.

Perhaps one of the greatest impacts of the Federal Reserve System, created in 1913, has been to change both the ability and the inclination of the banking system to alter its reserves and, consequently, the amount of money in circulation. First, the Fed, as it is called, requires banks to hold a minimum amount of reserves for different types of accounts. The option of throwing caution to the wind is limited by this decree. On the other hand, especially cautious banks are still free to increase their reserves above the minimum. But banks may not feel the need to be cautious if they trust the Fed to back them up during periods of duress. Deposit insurance, passed in 1934, had a similar effect. By reassuring depositors, it all but eliminated the potential for bank runs, further relieving banks of the need to hold particularly large reserves. In summary, banks are free to hold as much reserves as they desire as long as they meet the minimum requirement.

Savers can also affect the amount of money by choosing the form in which they hold it. For example, you can individually contribute to a decline in the quantity of money by cashing out your checking and savings accounts and putting the money in shoe boxes at home. While you retain the same amount of money, your bank now has smaller reserves on its books and is forced to reduce its lending.

The money supply will tend to fall as a consequence. Of course to have any noticeable effect on the economy as a whole, withdrawals must be immense. Something like this happens every December as shoppers withdraw large amounts of cash for the holidays. While this tends to shrink the money supply, the effect may be short-lived as businesses quickly redeposit the cash into their own accounts.

Central banks in foreign countries can also change the amount of money in circulation. Buying dollars with another currency and holding those reserves for the future can take dollars out of circulation. At various times in history, foreign banks have accumulated enough dollars to make this more than a mere theoretical possibility. The diversion of dollars to foreign banks reduces the amount of money in the national economy.

Although banks and savers can change the amount of money in circulation, it is the Federal Reserve that exercises the most visible influence. In addition to setting minimum reserves for the banking system, the Fed can directly increase bank reserves by buying Treasury bonds from banks. In exchange for bonds, banks receive money which can serve as the basis for more loans. The Fed has a third means of changing the money supply: it can lend reserves directly to banks. While the Fed cannot force banks to borrow additional reserves, it can entice them by lowering the interest charge, specifically defined as the discount rate.

How does one go about changing the amount of money in circulation? It would be difficult if not impossible for Congress or the president to persuade the public, domestic banks, or foreign central banks to voluntarily act in some way to effect a change in the money supply. Therefore, responsibility for monetary policy has by default fallen to the Fed and its relatively small group of governors and regional bank presidents. It is this role of the Fed that so disturbed Milton Friedman and the monetarists.

MONEY MATTERS

To a monetarist, central banks are at best a necessary evil. Although they are seen to provide some valuable services—clearing checks between member banks, holding bank reserves, and buying and selling foreign exchange—they also wield great power because they alone can increase or decrease the money supply. Milton Friedman may concede that the Federal Reserve must manage the money supply, but he does not approve of giving them wide discretion. In fact, when a government function is unavoidable, as in this case, Milton Friedman advocates assigning the government a very explicit goal. It just so happens in this case that the rule is a monetarist one. Friedman states:

> Certainly, the monetary policy I have come to favor—a steady rate of growth in the quantity of money—is highly congenial to my preference for limited government so far as possible by clearly specified rules.[6]

While Friedman consistently advocated a steady rate of growth in the money supply, the magnitude of that growth has fluctuated. Prior to 1969 he was inclined to believe that 4 to 5 percent was appropriate, but in an essay written in 1969 he reached a firm conclusion that 2 percent was ideal.[7] He attributed his prior ignorance to the fact that he "had not worked out in full the analysis presented in this paper."[8] The analysis consisted of mathematical equations, punctuated with incredible assumptions including, "members of this society are immortal and unchangeable,"[9] and "Money rains down from heaven at a rate which produces a steady increase in the quantity of money."[10] By 1979 Friedman appeared to have forgotten the 2 percent rule and reverted to a wider range of 3 to 5 percent.[11] In summary, Friedman advocated a strict target increase in the money supply somewhere between 2 and 5 percent per year. But you have to wonder about the wisdom of a rigid target for the money supply if Friedman himself had trouble pinning one down.

Why should the Fed attempt to constrain the increase in the money supply between 2 and 5 percent? Friedman claimed that at this rate, prices would remain essentially stable, that is that the inflation rate would be approximately zero. In 1968 Friedman stated "that a long-term rate of growth in M2 of about 5 percent per year would be consistent with roughly stable prices."[12] By 1979 the range necessary for price stability was widened only slightly to 3 to 5 percent.[13] This constitutes one of the key hypotheses of monetarist theory.

Friedman offered both a theoretical and historical justification for his money rule. The theoretical argument is derived from an identity familiar to economists as the equation of exchange. This rule maintains that the quantity of money must be related to the total value of goods and services purchased. For example, an economy that has $1 trillion of money and sells $7 trillion worth of goods and services must spend the average dollar precisely 7 times. Now what happens if the amount of money increases? Either the value of goods and services increases, or people will spend the money more slowly. Since Friedman found it hard to believe that more money could cause actual production to expand or the rate of spending to slow, he concluded that more money causes higher prices or inflation. He did, however, recognize that a small increase in the money supply was necessary in order to accommodate the growth in the real quantity of goods and services. This is the origin of his 2 to 5 percent rule for increasing the money supply.

The equation of exchange by itself does not actually support Friedman's money rule. All it shows is that a 2 to 5 percent growth rate in the money supply could coexist with zero inflation or any other inflation rate for that matter. Friedman's other argument for his money rule was based on the historical relationship between money and prices. Summarizing the results of an extensive historical study he conducted with Anna Schwartz, Friedman claimed that the quantity of money and prices were "closely correlated."[14] But much of this correlation can be attributed to three distinct historical periods, the two world wars and the Great Depression. During the wars, both money growth and inflation reached record levels. Alternatively, the Depression was characterized by a record reduction in money and falling prices. From these findings, Friedman concluded that "substantial inflation is always and everywhere a monetary phenomena."[15]

"Substantial" inflations must also include the hyperinflations that raged across Europe between 1921 and 1946. A study of several of these by Phillip Cagan was included in a book edited by Friedman. In each case, Cagan found that the increase in prices was roughly matched by a comparable increase in "hand-to-hand currency," essentially cash. During the Austrian hyperinflation of 1921 and 1922, prices rose 47.1 percent a month, while cash increased 30.9 percent. In Germany, prices rose 322 percent a month during the hyperinflation of 1922 and 1923, while cash increased 314 percent. Hungary experienced hyperinflation of 19,800 percent a month in 1945 and 1946, and its cash and bank deposits increased at a rate of 12,200 percent.[16] The Hungarian experience is almost beyond the realm of comprehension. An egg that cost 1 pengo at the beginning of the month cost 20,000 pengos by the end of the month! In every case, these "substantial" inflations were associated with "substantial" increases in the money supply. These were of course extraordinary events and not necessarily transferrable to normal times when inflation tends to rise and fall more gradually. But inspired by these historic anomalies, Friedman proclaimed, "Inflation is a disease, a dangerous and sometimes fatal disease, a disease that if not checked in time can destroy a society."[17] Friedman's solution was enticingly simple, "a reduction in the rate of monetary growth is the one and only cure for inflation."[18]

KEYNESIAN COLLISION

Milton Friedman and his monetarist prescriptions met stiff resistance from the economics profession during the 1950s and 1960s. First, because he was selling a cure for a disease that was already in remission. From 1952 to 1967 inflation in the United States, measured by the consumer price index, never exceeded 3.5 percent.[19] In this regard, his theory was premature since the major inflations did not recur until the 1970s, at which time they hit with a vengeance.

The second problem was that Friedman was paddling against the current created by a revolution in economic thought, a movement he referred to as the "Keynesian virus."[20] Beginning with the 1937 publication of Keynes's treatise, *The General Theory of Employment, Interest, and Money*, many in the economics profession had invested considerable time and effort mastering the more arcane details of his theory and were not about to reject it without good cause. While Friedman engaged the Keynesians in esoteric debates over economic theory—the nature of the demand for money, the relationship between interest rates and inflation, and the formation of inflation expectations—the most important debate focused on the Great Depression. After all, it was the Depression that crystallized support for Keynesian theory and legitimized fiscal policy as an anti-Depression measure. If Friedman was going to gain more than a foothold within the economics profession, he would have to challenge Keynes's interpretation of the Depression, and he did.[21]

The Depression was not a controlled experiment. There were no major changes in national economic policy in 1929. In fact, for much of the 1920s, the economy had performed quite well, providing few excuses for the government to change anything. The origin of events that transpired in 1929 were almost wholly rooted within the private sector.

The problem began with an economic downturn in August of that year, by itself not a spectacular or unusual event. The same cannot be said about the ensuing stock market crash of October 29, 1929. The Big Board (New York Stock Exchange) collapsed, shedding 21 percent of its value in a single week and 72 percent over the course of the next four years. The Crash, as it became known, brought an abrupt end to years of highly lucrative speculation.[22] If one were inclined to believe that the Depression had to be caused by a single profound event, the Crash would be it. Billions of dollars of wealth dissipated for lack of demand, and a cloud of uncertainty blanketed the entire country. In short order, business and consumer spending soon collapsed, culminating in the worst crisis in American economic history.

All this fit quite well with the Keynesian story that focused on the unreliability of business investment. The initial reduction in investment spending followed the pattern of a typical business cycle, but the ensuing collapse was blamed on the profound uncertainty created by the stock market crash.[23] Outlays for new investment fell every year after 1928 until the bottom was reached in 1933. Adjusted to 1929 dollars, investment spending fell from $11.7 billion in 1928 to $5.6 billion in 1933.[24] The pattern was not unlike those of previous business downturns, although the severity was unparalleled.

In many respects, the bursting of the speculative bubble, symbolized by the Crash, stands out as a unique and decisive event. Decisive both because it occurred early in the Depression and because its origin was never in doubt. While the initial economic downturn may have been a factor in the timing of the Crash, it was clearly not the major cause. A sound financial market could never have been brought down by the mildly depressed economy that existed in October 1929. The failure of Wall Street was clearly due to its own precarious condition, one that was created by the wild speculative boom of the 1920s. For example, during just three summer months of 1929, June, July, and August, the stock market rose by an astounding 25 percent. Stock prices for General Electric were up 46 percent, Westinghouse climbed 89 percent and AT&T

jumped 94 percent.[25] Much of the demand for these stocks was financed through credit with an expectation of even greater price increases to follow. From a typical Keynesian perspective, it was the speculative bubble that created the Crash that in turn exacerbated the evolving economic decline.

BLAMING THE FED

As the Depression got rolling the distinction between cause and effect began to blur. Crisis conditions created by the rapidly deteriorating economy pulled down several weak sectors, such as agriculture and banking, and pushed many economic indexes into an unfamiliar range. Unemployment reached a high of 25 percent, corporate profits fell 75 percent, 9 million savings accounts were lost, interest rates on government bonds fell to one-half of a percent, business failures increased to 3,500 a month and 4,000 banks closed their doors in the single year of 1933.[26] When it comes to grim economic statistics, the Depression holds most of the records.

The search for an alternative explanation for the Depression led to an intense scrutiny of public officials whose actions may have otherwise passed unnoticed. In this group there was no shortage of potential culprits. Congress, for example, panicked in 1930 and passed the Smoot-Hawley Bill, which raised average tariffs to 60 percent on those goods covered by customs duties. The ensuing collapse in international trade was quickly pointed out by defenders of free trade as conclusive evidence of the futility of protectionism. To be fair, world trade declined steadily throughout the Depression due to the worldwide economic slump that began well before Smoot-Hawley.

The federal government was also blamed for not running a large budget deficit soon enough. It wasn't until World War II that the deficit reached a sufficient magnitude to jump-start the economy. For Milton Friedman, the problem was not a lack of government spending but a lack of money, a blame he placed squarely on the shoulders of the Federal Reserve. The idea that the Federal Reserve caused the Great Depression was anathema to Keynesians since it contradicted their belief that the Depression originated with private enterprise and could only be remedied by the public sector.

Like many of the presumed causes of the Great Depression, money problems turned out to be exceedingly difficult to classify as either cause or effect. The money supply, measured by M2, fell every year from 1929 to 1933. In fact the loss of one-third of the nation's money supply in four years was unprecedented. Under normal circumstances such a rapid decline would wreak havoc on financial and business sectors, but during the Depression it was just one of dozens of extraordinary events.

Why exactly did the money supply decline? Whatever responsibility the Fed deserves for this development must be shared with the Depression itself. From 1929 to 1933, banks attempted to increase their reserves, a precautionary step motivated by the deteriorating economy.[27] But in order to raise reserves, banks curtailed loans, which meant a reduction in the money supply. A second reason why the money supply decreased is that many savers drew their money out of the banking system after 1930.[28] A loss of confidence in the economy and the banking system prompted savers to cash out their accounts, depleting bank reserves and further depressing the money supply. International events did not help either. Britain's departure from the gold standard in September 1931 precipitated a literal panic as foreigners unloaded their dollars for gold. It was anticipated that the pound and perhaps eventually the dollar would lose value making gold the safer way to hold money. The United States watched its gold stock plummet by more than $600 million in a month and a half.[29] Because money was then backed by gold, these losses put further pressure on reducing the money supply.

But the most devastating impact on the money supply had to do with bank failures. As banks by the thousands suspended operations from 1929 to 1933, hundreds of millions of dollars worth of deposits simply vanished![30] All told, as many as a third of all commercial banks disappeared during this time.[31]

The historical evidence seems to suggest that the decline in the money supply was more an effect than a cause of the Depression, making it difficult to pin the blame on the Federal Reserve. But Friedman insisted that the Fed could have prevented the rash of bank failures, which would have stabilized the money supply and saved the economy. Based on this argument, Friedman claimed that the monetary collapse "originated in large measure from the Federal Reserve policy, and it unquestionably made the economic collapse far worse than it would otherwise have been."[32] He even speculated that, "If the Federal Reserve System had never been established, economic recovery would very likely have begun in early 1931, just as it had in early 1908."[33]

The Federal Reserve, like Congress and the president, was at a loss as to how to revive the economy. Many at the time accepted the prevailing wisdom that tight limits on the money supply and a balanced budget were actually useful. In a letter to president-elect Roosevelt, Herbert Hoover insisted, "It would steady the country greatly if there could be prompt assurance that there will be no tampering or inflation of the currency; that the budget will be unquestionably balanced even if further taxation is necessary."[34] The Federal Reserve was not immune to such thinking. Although the Fed took a few steps in the right direction of increasing liquidity by decreasing the discount rate in 1930 and buying bonds in 1932, it also took a step in the wrong direction when it tightened up on the money supply in 1931 in response to Britain's departure from gold.[35]

In hindsight, the Fed could have done better, but not a lot better. To claim that the Fed could have prevented the Great Depression is like saying the captain of the *Titanic* could have missed that iceberg. If the problem is not apparent, how can it be avoided? Certainly the Fed could have done some things better, but this was equally true of other government officials, business leaders, private investors, and even consumers. But since most of them had no idea that a Depression was even remotely possible, how could they have been expected to prevent it?

Although the banking system in 1930 was clearly in need of government assistance, this was not something that Friedman could easily acknowledge. His devotion to free markets is so complete that he just cannot admit that there are instances when free enterprise fails. Even in this case, he did not admit that banking was turbulent and unstable, but only that the government was at fault for not bailing it out in a timely manner. To this day, banking would probably continue as a volatile industry with an inherent propensity for panics except for the assistance of government regulation. Deposit insurance, passed in 1934, provided the only stability that banking has ever enjoyed.

THE KEYNESIAN-MONETARIST DEBATE

Friedman disagreed with the Keynesians over the cause of the Depression, but he was especially hostile to their views of monetary policy. Though Keynesians were initially skeptical of the importance of monetary policy, most came to appreciate its potential contribution, especially in combination with other macroeconomic policies. By their thinking, tight money (slow money growth) could be useful during inflation by driving up interest rates and forcing a reduction in investment and purchases of consumer durables. Alternatively, during recessions, loose money (high money growth) could reduce interest rates, thereby stimulating investments and consumption. With this understanding, monetary policy was gradually incorporated into the broader Keynesian agenda designed to moderate wide swings in the business cycle.

The intentional use of monetary policy as a countercyclical tool clearly violated Friedman's vision of a benign, unobtrusive government. As he mobilized his arguments against interventionist policies in general and monetary policies in particular, he was forced to articulate a more precise description of his theory. The useful result of this was that the distinction between monetarism and Keynesian theory became slightly less ambiguous.

One important area where this occurred was related to interest rates. Keynesians argued that the immediate impact of tight money would drive up interest rates. Just as a decrease in the supply of anything tends to raise its price, so too with money. This idea was not particularly appealing to Friedman for the simple reason that it challenged his vision of an ideally competitive economy. In such a world, real interest rates—corrected for anticipated inflation—are supposed to be relatively constant.[36] The one sticking point was that real interest rates are seldom constant, appearing to respond to changes in the money supply. Friedman could insist that these movements were only temporary, but Keynesians never claimed otherwise. High interest rates for even a short time can have a devastating impact, such as causing a major recession. This dispute was directly tested during the monetarist experiment in the 1980s.

There was another, equally important area of contention between Friedman and the Keynesians based on the Phillips relationship between inflation and unemployment. In all but a few extraordinary times, there has appeared to be a trade-off between the two. As unemployment falls, inflation tends to gain momentum for the simple reason that people with more income and more job security tend to buy more. It is not surprising that when consumers want to buy more than what is produced, businesses respond by raising prices.[37]

Keynesians took this Phillips trade-off seriously. They resisted the temptation to reduce unemployment below a level that they thought would lead to unacceptable levels of inflation. They conceded that some people would be left unemployed, not because of any personal deficiency, but to protect the rest of society from inflation. Seen in this light, unemployment compensation is more than a charitable donation; it represents the cost of providing low inflation.

Once again, such practical views contradicted Friedman's ideal of perfect competition in which unemployment is essentially non-existent. In his more pragmatic moments, Friedman viewed unemployment as a "desirable" outcome of a dynamic economy in which "new products emerge and old ones disappear, demand shifts from one product to another, innovation alters methods of production, and so on without end."[38] The idea that unemployment could be a permanent side effect of fighting inflation, however, was irreconcilable with Friedman's model of perfect competition. In his words, "We have been misled by a false dichotomy: inflation or unemployment."[39]

Friedman's academic reasoning collided with the basic facts; the trade-off between inflation and unemployment is a widely observed historical pattern. Time and time again, increases in unemployment coincide with a drop in inflation. Friedman offered the period 1865 to 1879 in the United States as a counterexample because there was a "rapid rate of economic growth" and yet prices fell "over 5 percent a year."[40] However, Friedman conceded that "the decline in prices was especially sharp from 1873 to 1879," which just happened to coincide with a major economic recession.[41] The Phillips curve would have predicted exactly this: falling prices and rising unemployment.

There is even less reason to dispute the trade-off during most of the twentieth century. Any historical correlation is going to support the Phillips trade-off if only because of the two world wars. During both wars, unemployment sank to record lows, while inflation went through the roof. The only clear exception to the trade-off appears to have occurred during the 1970s and is easily accounted for by the oil crises. It is much easier for Friedman to call the Phillips curve a "false dichotomy" than to actually prove it is one.

Despite dismissing the trade-off between inflation and unemployment as a false dichotomy, Friedman nevertheless proposed a solution to it. In fact he proposed a solution to all unemployment. The solution was to eliminate inflation. Once inflation was conquered, Friedman promised, unemployment associated with the Phillips curve would also disappear.

Recall that Friedman's solution to inflation was a small 2 to 5 percent increase in the money supply. All the Federal Reserve had to do was to fix a slow, steady increase in the money supply and not only would inflation be eliminated, but so would unemployment. All of these incredible results would take time since, according to Friedman, "The benefits appear only after one or two years or so, in the form of lower inflation, a healthier economy, [and] the potential for rapid economic growth."[42]

In addition to the cyclical trade-off between inflation and unemployment, the United States has experienced a gradual increase in average unemployment rates. Over the past 40 years, unemployment rates have been creeping upward—the average for each succeeding decade higher than the previous one. Friedman attributes at least some of this to the misguided application of monetary policy: unnecessarily stimulating inflation with excessive monetary growth and then curbing it with monetary restraint. The result is "a roller coaster along a rising path,"[43] culminating in "higher inflation plus higher unemployment."[44] All of this would be eliminated, Friedman promised, if only money supply growth met his conditions.

THE MONETARIST HYPOTHESES

We have reached the point where it is possible to summarize the key monetarist hypotheses. Obviously not all monetarist hypotheses are included on the list, only the ones that are relatively unique to monetarism and are related to the macroeconomic experiments of the 1980s. Of all the monetarist hypotheses, the following meet these criteria:

1. Only stable monetary growth between 2 and 5 percent can eliminate inflation;

2. Unstable monetary growth by the Federal Reserve leads to higher inflation; and

3. There is no trade-off between inflation and unemployment.

Keynesians debated the merits of these monetarist hypotheses for several decades without winning a decisive victory. Over the years, arguments on both sides of the debate became increasingly arcane, often reinforced by elaborate mathematical equations and conflicting statistical evidence. But as Milton Friedman noted, "The true test of a scientific theory—is whether it works, whether it correctly predicts the consequences of changes in conditions."[45] His opportunity came in 1979 with the conversion of the top officer of the Federal Reserve to monetarist economics.

3

Gambling at the Fed

In order for any economic theory to be tested in the real world it must capture the sympathies of those in positions to implement it. Since most economic theories never find a following outside the musty halls of academics, the world is usually spared from becoming an economic guinea pig. An important exception was monetarism, which broke loose from the ivory towers in the 1970s.

Because monetarism is fundamentally a theory of monetary policy, it had to be adopted by the central bank in order to receive a fair trial. This is exactly what happened in the United States in 1979. The actual announcement that the Federal Reserve Board was planning to give monetarism a try was met with some surprise. Not only did this constitute a dramatic policy reversal from business as usual, but the new policy was highly controversial. Monetarism, as already described, was closely associated with Milton Friedman, who was widely perceived as something of a zealot, preaching the gospel of free markets.

With the benefit of hindsight, one can usually produce reasons for any historical event, and the case of the Fed's monetarist experiment is no exception. Economic conditions in 1979 were more than atypical, they were dismal; inflation was high despite a sluggish economy. The year would close with a 13.3 percent inflation rate for consumer goods and services and an average unemployment rate of 5.8 percent. Conventional wisdom was equally grim. The application of monetary and fiscal policy could tame inflation, said the experts, but not without threatening a serious rise in unemployment.

Looking back at this period, it is easy to wonder why the second oil crisis was not given more credit for the unusually high inflation rates. The import price of a barrel of oil soared from $14.57 in 1978 to $21.79 in 1979 and inflation rates reached a postwar high.[1] Moreover, the response was nearly identical to what had occurred five years earlier during the first oil crisis. The fact is that hindsight has made all of this much clearer than it was at the time. In 1979 there were so many competing explanations for high inflation—including unions, big business, inflationary expectations, misguided monetary policy, and of course, the oil crisis—that the issue remained unsettled, if not a little confused. In the midst of this turmoil, monetarist policy took hold at the Fed.

WHY MONETARISM?

The unexpected inflation of 1979 created the opportunity for change, but it does not explain why the Fed settled on monetarism. The simple answer is that as a challenger to the dominant Keynesian theory, monetarism had few rivals. Students taking economics courses in the 1970s would have believed there were only two macroeconomic theories, Keynesian and monetarism. Authors probably figured that focusing on the Keynesian-monetarist debate made otherwise dull economic textbooks a little more interesting. It is certainly understandable, given the prominence of this debate, that the Fed would see monetarism as the only real alternative to its prevailing Keynesian approach. But there are other reasons why the Fed should have been drawn to monetarism.

The role of central bankers was hardly revered by rank and file Keynesians. One group of Keynesians insisted that monetary policy was largely incapable of having any significant impact on the economy. But most of them granted that tight monetary policy could retard economic growth, but the reverse, loose money, would not necessarily restore it. The metaphor for this view was a string, because a string is effective in one direction when pulled but not in the other direction when pushed. The string metaphor simply meant that tight monetary policy could choke off rapid economic expansion, but a loose monetary policy could not create economic growth. Expansionary monetary policy was no more effective than attempting to push on a string.

A third group found merit in monetary policy only when it reinforced fiscal policy. Since the correct fiscal policy was to restrain growth during inflationary expansions and boost it during contractions, monetary policy was expected to follow suit, or "accommodate." A chair of the Fed once described this function as "leaning against the wind." What each of these viewpoints shared was the belief that monetary policy was a weak tool, and at best, complemented the more important work performed by fiscal policy.

In some ways, monetarism was the perfect foil for Keynesian theory. Where Keynesians demoted monetary policy to some minor role, monetarists elevated it to the highest level. No doubt both sides were inclined to exaggerate their positions, rallied by the fervor of the debate. But still, there is something suspiciously human in the fact that central bankers exchanged one economic theory in which their role was either irrelevant or subordinate for another in which their position was preeminent. The adoption of monetarism was more than a change in operating procedure, it reflected a change in the board's sense of self-importance.

While it may be useful to speculate on the motives of the Federal Reserve Board, it should not be forgotten that it is comprised of seven individuals with potentially different interests and viewpoints. Although the seven may nominally share power, the convention has evolved in which the chair is "first among equals." Besides being the most publicly visible member of the Fed, the chair is also more likely to establish contacts with Congress and the president. Whether for this reason or simple force of personality, the balance of power at the Fed frequently favors the chair. This was certainly the case in 1979 when the evolution of monetary policy closely mirrored the views of the Fed's chair, Paul Volcker. Volcker brought to this position a long history of banking experience, a generally conservative outlook, and a certain sympathy for monetarism.

MR. VOLCKER

On July 25, 1979, President Carter nominated Paul Volcker, then president of the Federal Reserve Bank of New York, to head the

Federal Reserve Board. The *New York Times* endorsed the decision, describing Volcker as "the logical choice for the job." According to the *Times*, his nomination to the Fed would ensure "moderate, independent leadership" and was a "sound appointment."[2] David Rockefeller of Chase Manhattan Bank praised his former employee as "eminently qualified" and able to resist political pressures in shaping monetary policies.[3] A retired chair of Manufacturers Hanover Trust Company was quoted as saying, "Seldom has President Carter used his appointive power so well."[4] Bankers and financiers, in this country and abroad, responded positively to the announcement. With brief rallies for stocks, bonds, and even the beleaguered dollar, it appeared as if financial markets had voiced their approval for the appointment of this "sound-money" banker to head the nation's central bank. Paul Volcker later confessed his pride in this brief show of approval from the market.[5]

Outside of the banking and business community, however, there were reasons to worry about Volcker's appointment. His reputation as a staunch advocate of tight money even in the face of high unemployment was well known. The *New York Times* took it upon itself to try to calm these fears by claiming in its editorial that the "Fed isn't likely to make any sudden shifts" under Volcker's leadership. Instead, the board could be expected to continue its "cautious, and pragmatic stance." They went on to predict that if Volcker did inspire any changes at the Fed, they would be "largely symbolic." They could not have been more wrong!

The editorial writers would have been better informed if they had paid closer attention to the article by Leonard Silk just a few pages earlier in the same edition. Silk pointed out that the Carter administration well understood the risks posed by Volcker's appointment. The commitment to Paul Volcker was a commitment to tight money, and while tight money may mean lower inflation, it also means higher unemployment. According to Silk, the "restrictive monetary policies likely to be favored by Mr. Volcker in efforts to bring inflation under control could exacerbate unemployment and worsen President Carter's chances for nomination and reelection."[6] As things turned out, this was an accurate forecast. Volcker's Fed was anything but business-as-usual.

Volcker earned a bachelor's degree from Princeton in 1949 and a master's degree in political economy and government from Harvard in 1951. From there his career followed a steady progression from junior economist at the Federal Reserve Bank of New York, to Chase Manhattan Bank, and Treasury Department official under Kennedy, Johnson, and Nixon. When the world monetary system collapsed from 1971 to 1973, Paul Volcker, from his position in the Treasury as undersecretary for monetary affairs, assisted in burying it. He returned to head the New York Federal Reserve before returning to Washington as chair of the Federal Reserve Board.

Volcker's affinity for Milton Friedman's theory, monetarism, was no secret. In an important speech delivered before the American Finance Association in September 1976, Volcker addressed what he considered the major contributions of monetarism. He granted that in the long run "an excess supply of money contributes not to real income or wealth but simply to inflation." The capacity of governments to "fine-tune" consumption and investment he claimed faced "real limitations." And the experiment in "practical monetarism," in which the Fed reported its targets for monetary growth, he deemed most useful. But his endorsement of monetarism at this time was less than complete. While he praised monetarism for "emphasizing old truths in modern clothing," he also warned that it could be taken too far, as for example, in the monetarist saying, "only money matters."[7]

OCTOBER SURPRISE

Before Volcker was sworn in on August 6, 1979, the Fed had already begun an effort to shrink the money stock, symbolized by an increase in the discount rate. Higher rates are intended to discourage bank borrowing, thus reducing their reserves and consequently restricting their capacity to make loans. This action was followed by further tightening in August and another increase of half a percentage point in the discount rate in September.

As Volcker recalls it, the failure of the September action to produce any tangible evidence of lower inflation was a turning point; the markets appeared to place more importance on the close vote in the Fed (four to three) than on the substance of the vote that was to raise rates. Volcker was concerned that the Fed's determination was not being taken seriously, a fact that jeopardized its effectiveness.

Volcker later insisted that his primary motivation for encouraging the Board to accept monetarism as its official operating procedure was a desire to be taken seriously. In 1983 he said he merely wanted "to get people's attention," and in 1993 he said the strategy would tell "the public that we meant business."

After consulting with the secretary of the treasury, the chair of the Council of Economic Advisors and foreign central bankers, Volcker prevailed on the Fed to adopt this strategy. The bombshell, at least in the financial world, was dropped on October 6, 1979. The announcement by the Fed contained three components. First, there would be a significant increase in the discount rate from 11 to 12 percent. Not only was this a large increase from an already high level, it was unanimously approved by the board. The solid vote helped to project the image of a united and determined board, avoiding any doubt about its intentions.

The second part of the statement included an increase in reserve requirements for several sources of bank funds, other than deposits. While banks have traditionally been required to retain a specific fraction of demand deposits and savings accounts either in their vaults or on deposit with the Fed, reserve restrictions for other sources of funds have often been less stringent or nonexistent. Motivated by relatively high interest rates, banks were increasingly drawn to these underregulated sources to finance an expansion of loans.[8] It was widely believed that tightening down on traditional sources of bank funds would do little good if these nontraditional sources were allowed to mushroom. Therefore under the Fed's new policy, any increase in these nontraditional sources would face an additional reserve requirement. With this decision, the Fed extended its ability to control the money supply.

The third and final action contained the monetarist experiment. Although the Fed had reported targets for growth in the money supply for many years, it had a poor record of hitting them because of its preoccupation with interest rates. For years the Fed conducted *open market operations*, meaning the buying and selling U.S. Treasury bonds, with the explicit purpose of smoothing out short-term interest rates. Monetarists believed that if the Fed was serious about actually hitting its monetary targets that it would forget about short-term interest rates and focus on bank reserves, the funds held by banks to cover daily business and emergencies. In its October 6 announcement the Fed proclaimed its intentions to adopt the monetarist recommendation and focus on bank reserves. Under these guidelines, the New York Fed, which actually trades government bonds and changes the money supply, would be guided in its daily intervention by reports on bank reserves. It would essentially try to "fine-tune" the reserve figures in an effort to hit the overall target for growth in the money stock.

Why should the average citizen have any interest in such technical nuances? The reason was to be found in the fine print. By switching guidelines, the Fed was abandoning its previous concern for stable interest rates, and in fact acknowledging that they intended to "permit wider fluctuation."[9] In pursuing its new monetarist tack, the Fed was willing to set interest rates free, which to all seasoned observers meant sharply higher rates.

If Paul Volcker intended this announcement to catch people's attention, it worked. During the ensuing week, the business pages of the *New York Times* were peppered with endorsements of Fed policy by banking and business leaders. "I have yet to meet a single businessman who is not supportive of the move by the Federal Reserve," claimed Reginald Jones, chairman of General Electric Company.[10] "The sooner we suffer the pain, the sooner we will be through," quipped Irving S. Shapiro, chairman of Du Pont Company.[11] "Anything that will demonstrate the Fed's determination to attack the problem of inflation will be welcome," said Harry Taylor, vice chairman of the Manufacturers Hanover Trust Company.[12] Sears, Roebuck and Co. senior vice president, Jack Kincannon said, "We certainly support the action, which was a little late in coming, but still most welcome."[13] Even European bankers joined the chorus and "praised the Fed initiative as an inflation-fighting measure."[14] John Perkins, president of the Continental Illinois National Bank and Trust Company, stated that the new measures were "going to be tough and are going to pinch, but I applaud the Fed for doing it."[15] The pinch was especially sharp at Continental. Only a swift bailout by the FDIC in 1984 managed to prevent it from becoming the largest bank failure in U.S. history.

The first sign of a pinch was evident in the stock and bond markets which both proceeded to crash. During the first three days of trading following the Fed's announcement, the Dow Jones industrial average sank 3 percent to 849.3 in what was described as "tumultuous trading." Headlines in the *New York Times* business section read, "Frenzy Marks Stock, Bond Trading." A comparable collapse took place in the bond market, pushing the yield on 15-year Treasury securities to 10.2 percent, the first time any long-term government bond had passed the 10 percent threshold. President Carter's conservative appointment to the head of the Federal Reserve Board may have reassured financial markets in August, but by October he had brought them to their knees. The experiment had begun.

Although Paul Volcker was instrumental in determining the timing of the monetarist announcement, as well as its form, it would be a mistake to place the entire responsibility on his shoulders. Andrew Brimmer, a former governor of the Federal Reserve System, pointed out in 1983 that the Board had been experiencing a monetarist drift for more than a decade.[16] As early as January 1970, the Federal Open Market Committee (FOMC), including the entire Board and five of the regional Reserve bank presidents, had begun to take a serious interest in the money stock. By March of that year, the FOMC had decided to make the expansion of the money stock and bank credit an explicit target of open-market operations, exactly what the monetarists had demanded. Congress also contributed to this change with House Congressional Resolution 133 in 1975 requesting the Fed to publicly report monetary targets and the 1978 Humphrey-Hawkins Act, which changed the request to a directive. With each step, the money stock began to attain far greater status relative to all the other possible measures of economic performance. This was, according to monetarist thinking, as it should be. While these precedents still left the Fed short of a full monetarist program, they paved the way for the Fed's announcement in October 1979.

The monetarist experiment was clearly under way by the end of 1979. The discount rate that had averaged 7.5 percent in 1978, rose to 10.3 percent in 1979 and 11.8 percent in 1980. By this time it was far above its previous high of 7.8 percent, set in 1974.[17] While these annual averages provide an accurate picture of how tight monetary policy was becoming, they conceal one temporary exception. A brief recession began in February 1980, lasted six months, and brought output down 2.3 percent.[18] This recession provided the first opportunity for the Fed to demonstrate its commitment to the monetarist experiment.

When the bottom fell out of the economy, the money stock appeared to follow suit. In Volcker's opinion, the money supply "dropped precipitously."[19] Since the Fed was on record as trying to fine-tune the money supply, the appropriate response was to retreat, increase bank reserves, and cut the discount rate. This is exactly what it did. The Fed provided additional reserves in the second quarter by purchasing $9 billion worth of government bonds. Furthermore, it cut the discount rate from 13 percent in April to 10 percent by July. The recession ended the same month, and almost immediately the money supply figures rebounded.

It was becoming clear that the Fed's intention to fine-tune the money stock was no easy task. The money stock could grow slowly one month and rapidly the next, requiring an abrupt reversal in monetary policy. While clearer heads were questioning the effect this flip-flopping was having on financial markets, the Fed persisted in its pursuit of the money supply targets. The Fed followed the July reduction in the discount rate with an equivalent increase in September. The Fed had not given up the monetarist experiment.

The experiment continued through the remainder of 1980 and all of 1981. It was in this year that the contest between the Fed and the money stock reached epic proportions. Despite the Fed throwing everything it had at the money stock, it failed to respond and in fact grew even faster. The peak was reached in April 1981 when the average annual growth rate in M1 hit 11.4 percent from one year earlier. The Fed reacted swiftly, raising the discount rate to 14 percent the next month, an all-time record in the history of the Fed. This was a full 3 percentage points higher than when the monetarist experiment began and 6 percentage points higher than the previous peak reached in 1974. Open market operations were also extremely restrictive. The Fed's holdings of government bonds were down the second quarter a full $4 billion from their level a year earlier. By all indications, the Fed was starving the banks for reserves and still could not hold the money stock within its target growth rate.

The Fed held this death grip for the next six months, resisting all demands that it lower the discount rate. And finally, the rogue money stock appeared to respond. Growth of the money stock, M1, slowed about 1 percent a month for the next seven months of 1981, dipping below 5 percent in October. True to its monetarist form, the Fed eased up, lowering the discount rate from 14 to 12 percent between October and December. For all practical purposes, by March 1982, the Fed appeared to have accomplished its immediate objective. Money stock growth rates in 1982 for M1 fell within the

Fed's target range of 4 to 6 percent in March, April, May, June, July, and August.

With the money supply seemingly under control, the Fed took the opportunity to further let up on reserves, dropping the discount rate by half a percent in July and again in August to 10 percent. After selling government securities in the first quarter of 1982, the Fed began buying in the second quarter. Up to this point the monetarist experiment had remained in place, and there were at least some grounds for claiming success. Both money growth and inflation had eased. The growth of M1 (in July) was up only 5 percent from a year earlier although M2 was up 9 percent. Inflation was running as low as 3.5 percent for the first six months of 1982.

There was, however, little celebration. The economy had slipped into a profound recession in July 1981, led by a collapse in construction and automobiles, two highly interest-rate-sensitive industries. The national unemployment rate in April 1982 climbed to 9.4 percent, the highest in 40 years. Among blacks the unemployment rate was nearly double at 18.4 percent. Even this record did not last long, however, as it was soon surpassed by even higher unemployment rates in May (9.5 percent) and July (9.8 percent). Newspapers were filled with stories about the unemployed in places like Rockford, Illinois, where the jobless rate hit 19.3 percent.[20] Many thousands of unemployed migrated to the South only to find job prospects there equally thin. One such story mentioned the family of Antonio and Kay Garza who left Ohio to search for jobs in Texas. Their bodies were found in their car, along with a suicide note.[21] Johns Hopkins University Professor Harvey Brenner pointed to statistical evidence that suicides and other health problems were correlated with joblessness and national economic problems.[22] Unemployment had reached record levels and was affecting more and more families. The U.S. Department of Labor reported that unemployment in 1981 affected about one in every five workers.[23]

Although many Americans were acutely affected by the economic situation, few were probably fully cognizant of the Fed's role in it. While some analysts blamed the Fed, many discussed the role of foreign imports, the growth of technological expansion, and the influx of women and illegal aliens into the labor market. President Reagan insisted that unemployment was a temporary problem that could be largely resolved if the unemployed would only take one of the many jobs listed in the newspaper want ads.[24] When this failed to elicit much sympathy he began misrepresenting statistics in an attempt to show that monthly unemployment had declined. His advisors had to sheepishly admit that his numbers were not adjusted for normal seasonal variations and were misleading.[25]

Less benign were the president's successful efforts to reduce unemployment compensation in 13 states, at a time when joblessness was at its highest level in 42 years.[26] The Senate Agricultural Committee, led by California Senator Samuel Hayakawa, joined the chorus blaming the unemployed for their own predicament and voted to cut off their food stamps.[27] While the Fed was not exempt from the finger-pointing, the lack of a clear understanding of the monetarist experiment probably protected them from their fair share of the blame.

The reduction in M1 growth in early 1982 allowed the Fed to ease its monetary policy, but all this began to change toward the end of 1982. From a 5 percent growth rate in July, M1 growth crept up to 5.7 percent in August, 6.9 percent in September, 8.5 percent in October, and 9.2 percent in November. Growth in M2 also showed little sign of letting up. During almost three years of the monetarist experiment, the Fed's resolve had never received such a difficult test. The theory clearly mandated a renewed tightening of the monetary tools at the risk of almost certainly extending the most severe recession since the 1930s. Was the Fed's commitment to monetarism so deep that it would be willing to throw gas on a burning fire?

The first sign that the Fed was beginning to relent arose in July 1982. Volcker, in speaking before the Senate Committee on Banking, Housing, and Urban Affairs, claimed that the board was ready to "look to a variety of factors," in setting monetary policy, including "the behavior of velocity and interest rates."[28] What this meant was that the Fed's singular focus on bank reserves and money supply was coming to an end. Part of the monetarist experiment was officially repealed at the October meeting of the Federal Open Market Committee. While reiterating that the Fed was no longer exclusively concerned with the money stock, Volcker announced a half-point reduction in the discount rate, exactly the wrong move from a monetarist standpoint in the face of a rising money stock. A prominent monetarist, Karl Brunner of the University of Roch-

ester, decried the Fed's lapse in commitment to monetarist principles and predicted a "re-inflation" of the economy.[29]

Throughout the remainder of 1982, there was little doubt that
key aspects of the monetarist experiment had been dumped. The
Fed continued to lower the discount rate—to 8.5 percent by December—and to purchase government securities, further expanding
bank reserves. They did this despite the accelerating growth in the
money supply, which a monetarist would have suggested threatened renewed inflation. The recession officially ended in the fourth
quarter of 1982 although unemployment continued to rise, hitting
a postwar peak of 11.8 percent in December 1982. It would take
another five years before the unemployment rate would return to
its 1979 level.

MONETARY SQUEEZE

Not surprisingly, the extraordinary unemployment levels took a
toll on inflation. After increases of 13.3 percent in 1979 and 12.5
percent in 1980, the consumer price index only rose 8.9 percent in
1981 and 3.8 percent in 1982. It remained in this range until 1986
when it fell back to 1.1 percent.[30] The recession marked a turning
point in the battle against inflation.

Particularly visible were the smaller wage increases included in
union contracts. The U.S. Labor Department reported that pay
increases in union contracts for the first six months of 1982
averaged only 3 percent, falling to less than half what workers had
won before.[31] In fact, the acceptance of lower wages by unions,
called concessionary bargaining, became so prevalent that a growing number of union activists pleaded to stop the practice.[32]

The 1982 recession did more than temporarily weaken union
bargaining power. High unemployment had a profound impact on
union membership since several strong union sectors, like construction and manufacturing, were particularly vulnerable to high
interest rates. Employment fell almost 11 percent in manufacturing
between 1979 and 1982, and almost 13 percent in construction.
These were significant declines, especially compared to what was
happening to employment growth in less unionized sectors. Employment in finance, insurance, and real estate was up 7 percent
over the same period and the service industry was similarly up 11
percent.[33]

As a result, the monetarist experiment was particularly hard on unions. While accounting for almost 26.9 percent of the labor force in 1978, unions fell to only 20.1 percent in 1983. The rate of decline for unions during this time was two to three times faster than during all other periods between 1960 and 1990.[34] This loss might have been only temporary if union workers had been rehired during the recovery, but this did not happen. As of 1994, U.S. manufacturing employment remained approximately 14 percent below its 1979 level.[35] Any new manufacturing jobs that were created during this time were mostly filled by nonunion workers. Thus any role unions might have had in maintaining inflation was permanently impaired by the monetarist experiment.

Record unemployment and weak unions were not the only factors contributing to lower inflation. The world price for crude oil peaked at $35 a barrel in 1981 and then began to recede. The price fell to $32 a barrel in 1982 and $28 in 1983.[36] The producer price index for fuels and power hovered around 700 during 1982 before falling to 662 in December of 1983.[37] The timing for this reversal was related to the recession in the United States and the world, which depressed the demand for oil. More important were the increasing conflicts developing within OPEC. A divided OPEC could not hope to maintain world oil prices, especially in the face of collapsing demand. Just as rising oil prices contributed to both major episodes of inflation in the 1970s, falling oil prices made a great contribution to containing inflation in the 1980s.

JOBS AT RISK

Unlike most scientific experiments where the danger of failure is typically confined to the laboratory, the risk of an economic experiment can be far-reaching. In this case the risk was well known in advance, it was the danger of creating unusually high unemployment. This was apparent to all involved in the monetarist experiment, including Paul Volcker.

Prior to the experiment, Fed policy was evaluated against the backdrop of the Phillips curve, the famous trade-off between inflation and unemployment. In this world, any effort by the Fed to curtail inflation was expected to precipitate higher levels of unemployment. Consequently, the central bank was obligated to weigh the cost of unemployment against the benefits of restraining inflation.

A simple application of the Phillips curve leads to the unambiguous prediction that the Fed's monetarist experiment was going to create severe unemployment. The fact that unemployment reached a 42-year record would seem to provide strong confirmation of the theory. But this was hardly the first time that the Phillips curve had been observed in action. For decades, inflation and unemployment in the United States and Britain had generally moved in opposite directions.[38] What was unique was that it should receive such strong confirmation from an experiment intended to demonstrate the wisdom of monetarism.

Monetarists were less likely to deny the existence of the Phillips curve than to try to shift attention away from it. They pointed to a rather subtle observation made by Milton Friedman; a rapidly inflating economy was more likely to suffer a recession at some point in the future. Therefore, even if high inflation was associated with low unemployment today, it could be responsible for higher unemployment in the future. The value of a restrictive monetary policy could not be judged by the unemployment it created today, but by the unemployment it avoided in the future. This promise of a better tomorrow was used widely by the Fed to defend itself against charges that it had put millions of workers on the streets in 1982.

Volcker chose to characterize his actions as a "strong stand against inflation" and insist that the public stood willing to endure the "real pain and personal dislocation that seemed to imply."[39] In other settings, Volcker was inclined to shrug off unemployment by claiming that he "was convinced that possibility could not be allowed to dominate our decision making."[40] But he also defended himself in monetarist terms by promising a better future. Volcker claimed that "further delay in dealing with inflation would only ultimately make things worse, including the risk that any recession would be large."[41] Thus monetarism provided a rationalization for a policy that, for all practical purposes, appeared to use the unemployed to break the inflation spiral.

AFTEREFFECTS

While the procedures employed by the Fed during the monetarist experiment were abandoned in the summer of 1982, the larger goal was not. It is true that the Fed no longer attempted to fine-tune the money supply, sparing itself from a futile and sometimes meaningless task. Still, there is no question that the Fed has remained strongly committed to preserving price stability, a goal it adopted with the monetarist experiment in 1979. At that time, the Fed discarded any concern it might have had with interest rates, exchange rates, unemployment, or economic growth in order to focus exclusively on inflation. It is no small matter that this priority has also been adopted by central bankers around the world.[42]

As we shall see, the Fed has changed its operating procedure by expanding the number of targets that it employs, but one thing has not changed, each of those targets is primarily intended to provide an early warning system for inflation. In this way the Fed continues its battle against inflation that began in 1979. From the history of the monetarist experiment we know that the Fed's contribution to lowering inflation had less to do with curtailing the money supply—which it failed to do—than with increasing unemployment, which it clearly succeeded in doing.

4

A View from the Supply Side

Perhaps the most extraordinary aspect of supply-side economics was how quickly it came to dominate the discussion of economic policy in the 1980s. To many observers, it seemed that supply-side theory came out of nowhere—and in a sense it did. Before the 1970s, it had virtually no presence in the economics profession; references to supply-side economics did not exist in academic textbooks or scholarly works. Yet by the 1980s, supply-side thinking had penetrated both major political parties in the United States and captured the sympathies of the president. It became the rationale for an economic program that changed the course of the nation.

If monetarism was the first experiment of the conservative revolution, supply-side economics was the second. However, both experiments are equally important for anyone trying to make sense of the economic turmoil of the 1980s: a decade of record unemployment, breathtaking deficits, and unparalleled interest rates. Like any experiment, it is essential to understand the theory and hypotheses before one can fully appreciate the test. The origin of supply-side economics and the principles that define it are described in this chapter.

You might think that supply-side economics would be easy to explain because it was a relatively new theory in 1980. However, since supply-side economics did not originate from the work of one individual, like monetarism, a greater diversity of views exists that could be defined as supply-side economics. Many of these differences only came to a head years after the experiment. The focus here is on the main current of the theory as it existed in the late 1970s and later in the chapter, on the areas of contention.

Among the earliest proponents of supply-side thinking one finds an academic economist (Arthur Laffer), a congressman (Jack Kemp), an editorial writer for the *Wall Street Journal* (Jude Wanniski), and a congressional staffer (Paul Craig Roberts). Supply-side economics, as it is now widely understood, was primarily the work of these key individuals. There were many others of course, who made contributions along the way, but few who devoted as much time and energy to promoting this new approach to economic policy.

The minority presence of academics in this list should not be overlooked. Paul Craig Roberts, the congressional staffer in the group, explained that, "Unlike the Keynesian policy that it was displacing, supply-side economics came out of the policy process itself and not out of the universities." He attributed the modest academic base to the fact that the time had come for supply-side economics "before many professors had learned what it was."[1] There is no question that the political appeal of supply-side economics was exploited well before its technical aspects were fully investigated.

The fact that supply-siders were in short supply created additional problems for the young theory. As Roberts again noted, "The coterie of supply-siders was too small to staff a Reagan Administration."[2] This meant that a major task of the original quartet was to persuade others and win converts at the same time that they were working out the details of their economic concepts.

SUPPLY *OR* DEMAND?

The twin concepts of supply and demand are nearly synonymous with economics itself. The convention of separating those who provide goods and services from those who desire them is an old and venerable tradition in economics. On the one hand are the suppliers, motivated exclusively by profits, and on the other hand are consumers whose demand is conditioned by their tastes and expendable cash. The interaction of both sides of the market determines prices and output.

Economists may pride themselves in their ability to distinguish between supply and demand, but events in the real world can sometimes muddy the distinction. In many markets, supply and demand are both in flux, allowing output and prices to move in any direction. After any real economic event, assigning primary responsibility to either supply or demand may not be so easy, but it may be important. The treatment of any illness has a greater likelihood of success when the cause is accurately diagnosed. Such knowledge is equally useful for resolving economic problems. A supply-side recession is more likely to be alleviated by a supply-side remedy and a demand-side recession by a demand-side remedy.

Economists deploy a simple rule-of-thumb to differentiate between supply-side and demand-side recessions. If the origin is on the demand side, sales fall short of production and firms find it increasingly difficult to resist price cuts. As a result, prices typically fall. But if supply is at fault, the opposite occurs. Production falls short of desired purchases, a condition that is more likely to bid prices up, leading to inflation.

A familiar example for illustrating this rule is the Great Depression of the 1930s. By 1933, after four years of economic decline, real production had fallen by a third and prices were tumbling. The price index for Gross National Product fell approximately 20 percent, a record for the United States in the twentieth century.[3] Because of the sharp decline in prices, this was clearly a case of inadequate demand. Supply was impaired as well but it was a lack of demand that sent the economy into a tailspin.

Of the next seven recessions from 1933 to 1970, all of them appear to have originated from the demand side, although in no case was the level of deflation comparable to the 1933 experience. Prices fell slightly in 1938 and 1949, and although they continued to rise during the other recessions, the rate of inflation distinctly fell. Since postwar recessions were far less severe than the Great Depression, it was reasonable to expect the impact on inflation to be less severe as well.

In only one of these recessions did inflation actually accelerate, and this was in 1946. Prices shot up an impressive 12 percent, which is not characteristic of a demand-side recession. However, 1946 was an unusual year. With the end of World War II, wartime price controls were relaxed, allowing producers, who had been denied price hikes during the war, the opportunity to restore prices to their desired level. Because of this exception, it was possible to attribute even this recession to weak demand as the government cut back its wartime spending.

What Keynesian economics offered were government policies to moderate the severity of demand-side recessions. Government is in the unique position to make up the difference whenever consumers and businesses fail to buy enough goods and services to keep the country fully employed. It can do this in one of three ways. The first and most direct way is to simply increase public spending. In one sense, it does not really matter how the money is spent as long as it raises the income of someone who will spend it, although in reality there is always an additional benefit if the money is spent efficiently on something useful. The government can also stimulate demand by cutting taxes or increasing the money supply.

Because postwar recessions tended to be demand side, Keynesian policies were especially appropriate. Whenever demand was inadequate, government actions were available to compensate for the shortfall. While recessions were never entirely eliminated, they did appear to be less severe.

It was during this time that the concept of the Phillips curve became popular. What Phillips had uncovered was the simple fact that most recessions, up to that time, were demand-side recessions. A lack of demand would cause both rising unemployment and falling prices. As a consequence, unemployment and inflation were inversely related; as one went up, the other went down and vice versa. As long as recessions were demand side, both the Phillips curve and Keynesian fiscal policies appeared to work reasonably well.

While Keynesian policies worked best for demand-side recessions, they proved almost useless in the face of supply-side recessions. This point became eminently clear during the recessions of 1975 and 1980. These were different from earlier recessions because inflation, rather than subsiding, actually rose. Inflation accelerated to 9.6 percent in the first recession and 9.5 percent in the second. Rising prices were exactly what one would expect during a supply-side recession. In fact these were the first and perhaps the only supply-side recessions in modern history.

Keynesians were in a bind because the policies that they advocated to fight recessions—government spending, tax cuts, and money expansion—were precisely the opposite of what they advocated to fight inflation. They could not advocate solutions to one set of problems without making the other worse. The twin evils, which became known as stagflation, did not have a clear Keynesian solution. One could not apply a demand-side solution to a supply-side problem and expect any measure of success. Into this void, supply-side economics was born.

THE TAX PARADOX AND THE LAFFER CURVE

While Keynesians struggled with the problem of simultaneously subduing both inflation and unemployment, the supply-siders leapt into the debate with ready answers. If inadequate supply was the problem, they said, then a policy was needed to boost supply. And how is that done? Their answer: tax cuts, but not the traditional Keynesian tax cuts that merely leave more money in the hands of consumers. What they argued for was a reduction in tax rates for high-income tax payers to encourage them to work and save more. Supply-siders claimed that by reducing tax rates on high-income earners, supply could be rejuvenated.

This takes us to the very core of supply-side economics: the relationship between tax rates and supply. To supply-siders, taxes are much more than a vehicle for raising government revenue. They represent an adulteration of otherwise pure market incentives. If a Rolls-Royce is priced at $100,000 then that represents the proper value of the car. A 10 percent sales tax on Rolls-Royces raises the price to $110,000, overstating its value and discouraging people from buying it. Supply-siders apply much the same argument to the income tax. If income from savings and financial assets are taxed, then people will simply reduce their savings. If income from work is taxed, then people will simply work less. The disincentives to invest, save, and work, are, according to this argument, built into most tax structures, especially the federal income tax.

The antipathy of supply-siders toward taxes is especially severe when it comes to high tax rates. These, they claim, can produce perverse results. For instance, suppose the government wanted to raise additional revenue and therefore increased the Rolls-Royce tax to 20 percent. If everyone who would normally buy Rolls-Royces bought Jaguars instead, the tax base would dry up. This illustrates what I refer to as the tax paradox. Instead of producing more revenue, the higher tax rate on Rolls-Royces causes revenue to fall, in this case, to zero.

While supply-siders did not discover the tax paradox, they did attempt to elevate it from an obscure possibility to an ubiquitous peril of civilized society. Everywhere supply-siders looked, they found evidence of perverse taxes: Britain during the Great Depression, Germany during and after World War II, the Soviet Union under communism, the United States after World War I and during the 1970s. In every case, marginal tax rates were alleged to be so high that they repressed production, leading to stagnant economies or worse. The irony, it was argued, was that tax revenue could have been increased, but only by cutting tax rates. If true, countries as diverse as communist Russia and the United States were victims of the same monumental blunder.

Arthur Laffer, an economist at the University of Southern California, sketched a diagram of the tax paradox that became known as the Laffer curve. Legend has it that while pondering the effect of high tax rates during dinner, Laffer sketched out a graph on his napkin. In this figure, tax revenue rises gradually with higher tax rates until a threshold is reached, at which point the curve reverses direction and revenue falls. The tax paradox applies to all tax rates above this threshold.

At this point one may begin to wonder what the threshold tax rate is. At what point does a tax become self-defeating? Is the rate 20 percent, 50 percent, or perhaps 90 percent? Supply-siders are careful to note that the threshold tax rate is a function of particular historical and cultural conditions. The residents of Leningrad were able to endure nearly a 100 percent tax rate without a significant loss of incentives while under siege by invading Nazi forces during World War II.[4] In more normal times, the threshold is obviously lower, but how low is it? Without invoking a particular number, supply-siders believed that the threshold was low enough to produce numerous opportunities to reduce tax rates and increase revenue.

Laffer was quite aware that there were other explanations for the tax paradox that did not involve supply. Suppose people respond to high tax rates not by reducing work, savings, or investment, but by merely redirecting spending in such a way as to reduce their taxable income. When confronted with a high tax rate on capital income, some individuals are going to buy tax-free municipal bonds or invest in "growth" stocks, which pay off in capital gains rather than taxable dividends. In such cases it is possible to avoid high taxes or simply postpone them by delaying the sale of capital assets. Both corporate stocks and houses may double in value, but neither are taxable until sold. By discouraging investors from selling these assets, it is conceivable that high tax rates could produce low tax revenue.

This is an alternative explanation for the tax paradox, but not one that applies equally to all income earners. There are the self-employed who may be in a better position to evade taxes by under-reporting income. But the greatest potential for shielding income from the tax collector lies with the rich who have the resources to uncover and exploit the most obscure methods of tax avoidance. Efforts to raise taxes on the wealthy can easily be frustrated if they are given enough loopholes. To the extent that the rich successfully shelter much of their income, they may actually end up paying less when tax rates are higher.[5] In this case the tax paradox occurs not because less effort is put into production, but because more effort is put into tax avoidance.

RELIEF FOR THE POOR OR THE RICH?

There may never have been a consensus among supply-siders about the exact threshold for the tax paradox, but they were all in agreement that the top rates for the federal income tax in 1979 were excessive. Because the federal income tax is what economists define as *progressive*, wealthier individuals are assigned higher tax rates than the middle or lower classes. In the late 1970s, when supply-side economics was born, the official tax rate for the highest income class was 70 percent.[6] This rate, it was deemed, was clearly counterproductive. Not only could lower rates stimulate savings and production, but they could, as supply-siders promised, generate more tax revenue. Supply-siders Arthur Laffer and Jan Seymour may have suspected this would sound like pie-in-the-sky proselytizing, but nevertheless insisted that "correctly constituted tax rate reductions do provide the proverbial 'free lunch.'"[7]

Progressive income taxation was not the only reason supply-siders directed their attention toward relieving the tax burden on the wealthy. It is widely understood that the bulk of private savings in the United States comes from the highest income classes. After all, the rich are in a position to sink a larger share of their income into financial investments. In contrast, the lower income class and much of the middle class spend most of their income on consumption. While some families in the middle class may be prodigious savers, they are offset by other middle-class families buried in debt. Only top income earners as a group have significant net savings.

Supply-siders reasoned that an increase in savings would encourage businesses to borrow more money and increase their investments. These investments would mean new factories and equipment and a greater production of goods and services.

The problem, supply-siders argued, was that high tax rates on investment income and capital gains discouraged personal savings. Michael Boskin, chair of the Council of Economic Advisors for George Bush, concluded that "private savings is indeed strongly affected by changes in the real after-tax rate of return."[8] Therefore, supply-siders advocated a reduction in the tax rate on savings and the income generated from savings, a policy that disproportionately favors the rich.

All of this makes perfect sense if you ascribe to something called Say's Law. Jean Baptiste Say was a French economist born in 1767 and associated with the classical school of economics. Say provided the original logic behind the classical principle, "supply creates its own demand." The modern application of the law can be seen in the argument that an increase in savings, induced by tax cuts, will not only stimulate an increased supply of goods and services, but also create sufficient demand to purchase them. No wonder Say was adopted as a patron saint of the new supply-side program.

It isn't so much that Say's Law is wrong as that it isn't always right. It is certainly possible for supply and demand to expand and remain perfectly balanced, producing steady growth and stable prices. At these times, Say's Law could apply, much like the supply-siders insist. But demand is also fickle and has at times fallen woefully short of the level required to buy all the goods and services made available by a productive economy. The failure of demand to mechanically conform to supply has inspired numerous critiques of Say's Law, the most prominent among them being *The General Theory* by John Maynard Keynes.

The objections supply-siders voice against high tax rates on the rich do not extend to the middle class or even the poor. These groups already enjoy relatively lower federal income tax rates and as we have seen, they are not proficient savers. Paul Roberts must have had these ideas in mind when he criticized the progressive income tax "because it mismatches effort and reward."[9] He also attacked a proposal for more equitable tax cuts because they improve "incentives the most in the lower tax brackets (where disincentives are the least)."[10] In supply-side economics the greatest benefits of tax cuts occur only when applied to the top income earners.

Supply-side economics makes the claim that the rich respond to lower taxes by saving more, working more, earning more, and ultimately paying more taxes. One could debate this argument forever without reaching a definitive conclusion. A more productive approach is to examine the historical record. Is there any evidence that excessively high taxes have caused supply-side recessions or economic stagnation?

Along these lines, the most provocative charge was made by Jude Wanniski, who was at one time a supply-side editorial writer for the *Wall Street Journal*. He claimed that the Great Depression was a supply-side contraction. According to Wanniski, "The stock market Crash of 1929 and the Great Depression ensued because of the passage of the Smoot-Hawley Tariff Act of 1930."[11] Few scholars would dispute the argument that Smoot-Hawley, which raised tariffs by one-third, contributed to the Depression, or that misguided attempts to balance the federal budget with tax increases in 1932, 1935, and 1936 reduced the chances for an early recovery. These are all standard interpretations of the era.

Yet the argument that the Depression was a supply-side contraction initiated exclusively by Smoot-Hawley collides with a certain inconvenient fact: supply-side recessions are characterized by increases in prices and the Depression was not. If businesses responded to Smoot-Hawley by unilaterally cutting back on production, then prices should have increased. But this is not what happened; prices collapsed and the country experienced the most severe deflation of the twentieth century. The Depression was a classic example of a demand-side recession no matter how strongly one wishes otherwise.

There are other facts that do not set well with this theory. While one can talk about the loss of incentives due to tariffs, there is no denying that they also impair demand. The immediate retaliation taken by other countries to Smoot-Hawley tariffs had a decisive impact on U.S. exports.[12] As other countries moved to bar U.S.-made goods from entering their countries, U.S. businesses suffered from a lack of customers, not a shortage of the will to produce. This was a demand problem, entirely consistent with the general facts of the Great Depression.

AUTHENTIC SUPPLY-SIDE RECESSIONS

There have been only two indisputable supply-side recessions in this century, and they both occurred in the 1970s. The economic decline from late 1973 until 1975 lasted 16 months with a cumulative decline of 4.9 percent in real output.[13] During this period, inflation increased in every year, peaking at 9.6 percent in 1975. The 1980 recession was shorter (6 months) and less severe (2.3 percent decline in real output), but inflation also accelerated, this time to 9.5 percent. If the Depression was the classic demand-side recession, the 1970s provided classic supply-side recessions.

It was during this time that supply-side economics got its start. Advocates of the new theory began by blaming the Keynesians for many of the economic problems of the decade, including stagflation, the simultaneous existence of unemployment and inflation. Keynesians were blamed for allowing marginal tax rates of 70 percent as the government became increasingly involved in redistributing income and regulating the economy. According to Roberts, "The buoyant optimism of the Keynesians, which peaked with the Kennedy-Johnson tax cuts, has given way in the stagflation of the 1970s."[14] Martin Feldstein, a Harvard economist who would later play an important role in the Reagan administration, concluded in 1980 that, "The government's mismanagement of monetary and fiscal policy has contributed to the instability of aggregate output and to the rapid rise in inflation."[15] The same view was evident in the 1979 annual report of the Joint Economic Committee of Congress chaired by Democratic Senator Lloyd Bentson. "Stagflation," said the report, "is the result of policies that have stimulated demand while retarding supply."[16]

The decade of the 1970s was an ideal time for supply-siders to attack Keynesian policies because the country was being hammered by two very serious supply-side recessions. There was a problem, however; the recessions had very little to do with Keynesian policies and even less to do with supply-side solutions. At 70 percent, marginal tax rates were high in the 1970s but not as high as they had been in the 1950s, one of the most productive decades in American history. Besides, the recessions and inflations in the 1970s had nothing to do with taxes.

In retaliation against the United States for supporting the Israelis during the Arab-Israeli war of 1973, a unified OPEC slapped a major oil embargo on the United States. While U.S. consumption of oil fell only 6 percent from 1973 to 1975, real oil prices, corrected for inflation doubled from $10 to $21 per barrel (in 1987 dollars).[17] Virtually no U.S. business was left untouched. Even those who did not use petroleum directly were affected as the price of substitute forms of energy were also bid up. Initial efforts to pass on higher energy costs to consumers caused sales to falter; stagflation was off and running.

A similar drama was played out in 1979 when the government of the shah of Iran, a U.S. ally, fell to a revolution led by Muslim fundamentalists. The shah, never a candidate for the Nobel Peace Prize, was best known for the atrocities committed by Savak, his secret police. He was also fiercely loyal to the United States, perhaps in gratitude for the coup that placed him in power in 1953, or perhaps for the military assistance that the United States provided Iran in those days. Whatever the reason, the shah was instrumental in providing U.S. oil companies with access to the rich oil fields of Iran and providing a counterbalance to the militant, anti-U.S. elements in OPEC. His sudden overthrow in 1979 once again interrupted the flow of oil from the Middle East to the United States, resulting in the second major oil crisis of the decade. Oil prices began to rise and sales dropped off producing a second severe case of stagflation.

As OPEC's unity faltered in the 1980s, real oil prices came down and not surprisingly, the symptoms of the supply-side recessions also vanished. In the meantime, supply-side economics had gotten a foothold in Congress and in the business press. It was soon forgotten—that is, where it was ever understood—that the prevailing economic crisis that supply-side economics promised to resolve had nothing to do with excessive tax rates or even Keynesian tinkering.

THE GERMAN EXPERIENCE

Of all the cases cited by Jude Wanniski in *The Way the World Works* where excessively high tax rates were counterproductive, probably the best example is Germany after World War I. It was the will of the victors to impose a harsh financial settlement, requiring war reparations amounting "to 7 percent of Germany's prewar national output."[18] This was a severe burden for Germany as it attempted to regain its economic footing. By 1922 and 1923 when the economy burst into hyperinflation, it should have been clear to everyone that the postwar settlement was excessive. Price increases at this time reached the torrid pace of 322 percent a month.

But the idea that the allies leveled an excessive burden on Germany after the war did not originate with the supply-siders. It was actually a preoccupation of a young economist at the time, John Maynard Keynes. As the official representative of the British Treasury at the Paris peace conference, Keynes had a good opportunity to witness the fears and shortsightedness that produced the Treaty of Versailles.

Keynes, however, did not see the negotiations through to the end as he resigned his position and left the conference in disgust. His objection was that the terms of the Treaty, as it then stood, placed an impossible burden on Germany. In his opinion, it made no sense to require war reparations of Germany that would either starve the country or never be paid. The war was over and Keynes questioned the motives of French statesman Georges Clemenceau of allegedly attempting "to crush the economic life of his enemy."[19]

Revenge, according to Keynes, was also not in the best interests of the Allies. Europe was already sufficiently integrated in the belief that the recovery it desperately needed would only be delayed by bleeding the German economy. Keynes expressed these ideas in a powerful polemic titled *The Economic Consequences of the Peace*, which was translated into at least twelve languages.

While Keynes failed to inspire a revision of the Treaty, his foresight was vindicated by future events. War reparations were interrupted as Germany languished under the provisions of the Treaty, causing severe economic instability and opening the door for the ultimate rise of Adolf Hitler in 1933. Furthermore, the remedies called for by Keynes were closer in spirit to the more successful Marshall Plan, implemented by the United States after World War II. One has to conclude that the destructive nature of excessive taxes, in particular war reparations, was well understood by Keynes and his followers. War reparations have a uniquely harmful effect because—unlike ordinary taxes that typically reenter the economic stream through government spending—war reparations drain a country without any compensating benefit.

These subtleties were lost on supply-siders who consistently exaggerated the effect of high taxes. Only by the wildest stretch of the imagination could the Depression or the 1970s' recessions be blamed on high taxes. Still, the biggest problem with supply-side economics may be its inability to account for the impressive growth achieved by the United States when marginal tax rates were close to their peak. Tax rates on the highest income classes were 90 percent or higher from 1950 to 1963 and Gross National Product increased at a very respectable 3.4 percent average rate. Wanniski confesses that, "In spite of tax rates that kept the U.S. economy in the upper reaches of the Laffer curve throughout the 1950s, the U.S. economy continued to grow." A clearer violation of supply-side principles is difficult to imagine.

THE ROARING TWENTIES

Supply-side economics made the surprising claim that a reduction in tax rates can unleash an economic boom sufficient to replace any initial loss of tax revenue. Historical events are once again used to demonstrate this remarkable hypothesis. Supply-siders' first example is the roaring 1920s.

In many ways, the period from 1921 to 1929 is unique in American history. Following a postwar recession in 1921, the U.S. economy proceeded to expand rapidly until the summer of 1929. Economic growth surged ahead at an annual average rate of 4.8 percent with unemployment averaging less than 4 percent. In the exceptional year of 1926, unemployment even dipped to a remarkable low of 1.8 percent.[20] This was the roaring twenties in every respect except for prices. High inflation rates during World War I quickly gave way to almost constant prices throughout the decade. Although prices did not fall, the fact that they held constant suggests that supply was increasing at least as rapidly as demand.

There are other reasons to believe that supply expansion was particularly important in the 1920s. Savings climbed to over $10 billion for at least four of these years. According to one estimate, the savings rate was high, hitting 10 percent or more during most of the expansion. The government was also a net saver, running surpluses from 1922 through 1930. Little of this stimulus was provided by the money supply, which increased relatively slowly, averaging less than 3 percent growth a year through the decade.[21]

To what should we credit such an exemplary performance? Supply-siders are quick to point out that under the stewardship of Andrew Mellon, President Harding's treasury secretary, personal income tax rates were slashed from the high levels established during the war. Top rates came down from 73 percent in 1921 to 56 percent in 1922. They were cut again in 1924 to 46 percent and finally to 25 percent the following year.[22]

It is impossible to know with any certainty whether the tax cuts were indeed the cause of the economic boom in the 1920s. But if they were, it is important to remember that tax cuts also have a demand-side component since they increase the amount of money available for consumer spending. The tax cuts in the early 1920s could have had this effect, especially since rates were cut across the board from the highest income classes to the lowest. The additional spending helped pull the economy out of its postwar doldrums.

But no matter how important demand expansion was at the beginning of the decade, it cannot fully account for the exceptionally low inflation rates later in the decade. In the year 1926, for example, the economy continued to grow, unemployment fell to 1.8 percent, and prices rose less than half a percent from the previous year.[23] The coincidence of low inflation and low unemployment is an unusual occurrence, not one that you would normally expect under a Phillips curve tradeoff. At least for this period, supply appears to have led the boom, but is it fair to give full credit to lower tax rates on the rich?

The expansion in the 1920s was unique in several ways. First, finance led all sectors with the largest increase in national income.[24] A related development was the stock market boom that began in 1924 and ended abruptly with the Crash in October 1929. Beginning at 106 in May 1924, the *New York Times* average of industrial stocks climbed steadily to 245 by the end of 1927. But its trajectory took on an even steeper tilt in 1928. The market hit 331 by at the end of the year, and kept right on going to 449 by the last day of August 1929.[25]

There is more than a small chance that the sharp reduction in tax rates for the wealthy provided an initial impetus for the stock market boom. Not only did tax cuts leave wealthy investors with more money to risk in the stock market, they increased the after-tax rewards for such investments. Once stock prices got rolling, the market took on a life of its own, drawing on additional funds through the extension of credit. As personal savings and borrowed funds were increasingly dumped into the stock market, the initial effect was to enrich investors. In hindsight, given the ultimate Crash, it is hard to imagine that this activity produced much more than a fleeting exhilaration.

The real expansion was in manufacturing, which experienced a phenomenal increase in output. From the depths of the 1921 recession until 1929, manufacturing production increased at an annual rate of 8.8 percent. Even measured from its 1920 peak, production increased at the respectable average rate of 4.5 percent a year. In this important sector, the supply of manufactured goods was overflowing, causing prices to fall.

What was behind the burst in manufacturing production? One could claim that tax cuts created a greater incentive to produce, but then why didn't all sectors respond equally? Another possible explanation has to do with the opportunities for large scale production. Much of the investment spending in the 1920s was dedicated to building bigger and more efficient factories, taking advantage of what economists refer to as economies to scale. This process began with the mobilization for World War I and continued up to 1929.

Why was the desire to increase the scale of production so strong during these years? One has to go back a few more years to the period between 1899 and 1908 when the United States experienced one of the greatest merger movements of all time. Of particular importance is the fact that many of these mergers combined small manufacturing companies, all competing in the same basic industry, into giant corporations. General Motors was formed in 1908 from numerous smaller companies, as was E. I. Du Pont in 1903, General Electric in 1892, U.S. Steel in 1901 and dozens of other giant corporations near the turn of the century. The sudden growth in corporate size opened up a possibility for greatly expanding the scale of production.

Giant corporations, like U.S. Steel, found it much easier to build giant steel mills. Not only did they wield the power to finance great factories, they also found it easier to sell the output in their newly acquired national markets. World War I provided the first opportunity for these firms to take advantage of their new size by constructing larger and more efficient factories, a process that continued well into the following decade. Reinforcing this argument, iron and steel led the postwar boom with an increase in real output averaging 13.6 percent from 1921 to 1929.[26]

This provides an alternative explanation for the performance of the U.S. economy in the 1920s. One cannot prove that tax cuts for the wealthy did not stimulate them to work harder and invest more, but it seems more believable that the prosperity of the 1920s was due primarily to the growth of ever larger factories. Economies of scale have provided opportunities for expansion for many decades, but the need for such investment in the 1920s was especially keen. The rapid growth of businesses through mergers had created an unprecedented opportunity for increasing the scale of production at the factory level. The historical circumstances that coincided in the 1920s to produce economic prosperity were unique and not easily recreated. But this is precisely what the supply-siders promised to do.

Ignoring the opportunities for mass production and the wartime savings, supply-siders attributed the entire success of the 1920s to the tax cut for the rich. By cutting taxes for the rich again in the 1980s, they promised to reproduce the 1920s prosperity. In their search for easy solutions to America's economic problems, supply-siders were inclined to overlook the complexities often found in economic history.

KENNEDY TAX CUTS

In addition to the Mellon tax cuts in the 1920s, there was one other major tax reduction program prior to 1980. These were the Kennedy tax cuts in the early 1960s. In an effort to get the economy rolling after a recession in 1960, Kennedy's advisors proposed an across-the-board reduction in tax rates including a decrease from 91 percent to 65 percent for the top income class. It was their belief that there was enough savings in the economy, but not enough consumer spending. They expected to resolve the imbalance by providing consumers with an income tax reduction sufficient to revive spending.

The final tax bill was not passed until February 1964, three months after Kennedy's assassination. Tax rates were cut across the board and the top rate fell to 77 percent in 1964 and 70 percent in 1965.[27] By all conventional measures the policy was a great success. If there were any surprises, it was how quickly tax receipts recovered in such a robust economy. Revenue from the personal income tax (and nontax receipts), which had fallen by $2 billion in 1964, bounced back with an increase of $5.9 billion in 1965.[28] The greatly feared deficits were, in the end, no danger at all. Even the stock market experienced a solid advance. The Dow Jones Industrial average climbed from 800 in February 1964 to 1,000 two years later.[29]

That the Keynesians had achieved an important victory went without question. The objection raised by the supply-siders was not that Keynesian policy failed to work, but that it worked for altogether different reasons. Jack Kemp suggested that "Kennedy's economists did the right thing for the wrong reasons," and Paul Craig Roberts insisted that rather than boosting demand, the tax cut provided "a burst of saving and investment activity that spurred the economy."[30] But Walter Heller, economic advisor to President Kennedy, was unwavering in his insistence that "the record is crystal clear that it was its stimulus to demand . . . that powered the 1964–65 expansion and restored a good part of the initial revenue loss."[31] So once again it is necessary to look deeper into the issue to find evidence of whether the expansion was led by supply or demand.

Roberts presents evidence that the savings rate, as a percentage of disposable income, rose slightly in 1964 and 1965. The lower marginal tax rates, he claimed, induced households to increase their savings rate, thus stimulating a supply-side expansion. While this pattern is certainly consistent with the supply-side argument, it should be pointed out that the increase in the savings rates was neither large nor permanent. From an initial level of 6.6 percent in 1961, the savings rate rose to 7.0 percent in 1965 but fell back to 6.8 percent in 1966.[32] These are not the kind of statistics that instill great confidence in supply-side economics.

It would be entirely understandable if a noneconomist failed to appreciate the importance of this debate. Isn't it true that both Keynesians and supply-siders advocate tax cuts as a way to stimulate the economy? What does it matter if the tax cut sparks a recovery in demand or supply, as long as it works, as it clearly did in 1964? The answer has to do with inflation. If the tax cut works primarily through demand, as the Keynesians claimed, then unless the tax cut is carefully limited there is a danger of causing inflation, not immediately but after unemployment falls low enough. In contrast, if the tax cut stimulates a supply-side recovery, then there is no threat of inflation. In fact, just the opposite is likely to occur—deflation. If this is the case there is no reason to limit the size of the tax cut since more is almost always better. Therefore any debate about the effect of tax cuts turns on the question of inflation. How did prices respond to the Kennedy tax cut?

The evidence does not bode well for supply-siders. From an almost imperceptible rate of 1.1 percent in 1963, inflation steadily accelerated to 1.8 percent in 1964, 2.5 percent in 1965, and 3.5 percent in 1966. While the inflation rate was never great, at least by modern standards, it did reveal an unambiguous tendency to rise, just as the Keynesians had anticipated. The tax cuts stimulated the economy and brought unemployment rates down but at the cost of slightly higher inflation. The Phillips curve was alive and well, at least in the 1960s.

Supply-side economics is based on the belief that individuals and businesses respond to changes in tax rates by radically altering their behavior. Low rates are supposed to encourage work and thrift, while high rates encourage sloth and consumption. As plausible as this may seem, there is room for debate. For example, there is a possibility that tax cuts will stimulate exactly the opposite behavior. At least for some individuals, the higher incomes flowing from a tax cut could stimulate complacency and contentment. The result may be fewer hours of work rather than more.[33]

It is equally likely that tax rates have very little effect on behavior except at exorbitant levels. The chief executive officer of a large corporation may respond to lower tax rates by working a little more but perhaps not enough to make a noticeable difference in the company's performance. There is, therefore, no theoretical argument that can prove supply-side economics right or wrong. Only the historical record provides us with some perspective.

What stands out from the preceding survey is that at no time in U.S. history was a recession or depression clearly induced by excessive tax rates. The only supply-side recessions of the century were associated with the energy crises of the 1970s. No other economic contraction revealed the requisite symptoms of simultaneously rising prices and unemployment.

Prior to the 1980s, the United States had experienced only two significant episodes of tax reductions for the highest income classes: one beginning in 1922 and the other in 1964. In some respects, the responses were similar; both were followed by periods of solid economic growth and both marked the beginning of stock market booms. But in response to the Kennedy tax cuts, prices rose, a fact that tends to disqualify it as a genuine supply-side expansion.

Only the 1920s come close to meeting the necessary conditions for a supply-side boom because the economy expanded and prices held steady. Although taxes were cut early in the decade, the economic boom was concentrated in manufacturing where firms were clearly capturing the benefits of large scale production made possible from the preceding merger wave. Only the boom in finance could be legitimately linked to the tax cut and even this was fleeting. The stock market crash of 1929 reversed many of the financial gains of the 1920s.

THE SUPPLY-SIDE HYPOTHESES

What then are the unifying themes of supply-side economics? We can summarize these into three related hypotheses.

If marginal tax rates are cut for the highest income classes, then

1. Savings and investment rates will increase;
2. Prices and unemployment will fall; and
3. Total tax revenue will increase and deficits will tend to disappear.

SECOND THOUGHTS

Because supply-side economics represents the collective ideas of several individuals, areas of contention would be understandable. But during the formative years of the theory in the late

1970s, relatively few of these existed. It wasn't until after the theory was put to a test that the prevailing consensus began to break under the strain.

Even during the early years though, there was a curious sentiment that could only be described as a lack of conviction. It is all the more interesting because it involved the defining proposition of supply-side economics: the Laffer curve. Supply-side theorists held many beliefs in common with other, more traditional conservatives, but it was the tax issue that set them apart. They alone endorsed the idea that a reduction in tax rates would actually raise tax revenues. It was this argument, illustrated by the Laffer curve, that would be deployed to great effect in future political debates.

Among those lacking conviction was none other than Arthur Laffer himself who was quoted in *Newsweek* as saying, "There's more than a reasonable probability that I'm wrong. But . . . why not try something new?"[34] Jack Kemp, on the other hand, boxed himself in by promising something to everyone. To the country as a whole, he promised that his proposed tax cut would be "self-financing," in other words, increase total tax revenue. But in the very same statement he endorsed the results of a study that showed his proposal would "reduce the Federal income tax liability for every category of taxpayer." He stopped short of explaining how he planned to collect more taxes while collecting less from "every category of taxpayer."[35] Such are the contradictions of modern political discourse.

Statements by Irving Kristol in 1978 also demonstrated less than complete faith in the supply-side tax cut policy. He asked, "Will in fact, the Kemp-Roth tax cut generate enough economic activity, enough growth, and a sufficiently enlarged tax base, so that government's revenues actually increase to such a degree as to close the initial budgetary gap which such a tax cut will create?" His response was purely agnostic, "The only answer is that we don't know—no one knows—for certain."[36]

Why then, would Kristol, with so little confidence in the revenue impacts, emphatically endorse a tax policy, asserting that it "is exactly the right medicine for what ails us at this time"?[37] The reason is that Kristol understood, as well as anyone at the time, that the failure of supply-side tax policy could still be a success for conservatives. According to Kristol, "if government's revenue should fail to increase sufficiently, and the budgetary imbalance is not ameliorated, then (and only then) can we anticipate that our political leaders will find it possible to make sharp cuts in spending."[38]

Kristol was a sophisticated supply-sider. He joined the ranks calling for deep cuts in tax rates for the wealthy and supported the idea that tax revenues could actually rise. But he also foresaw the possibility that a failure to raise revenue would culminate in huge gaping deficits in the federal budget. It would be these deficits, or more precisely, the policies proposed to eliminate these deficits, that he believed would further the conservative cause.

How would these future deficits be eliminated? After careful consideration, Kristol concluded that future deficits would have to be eliminated by reducing the size of government expenditures. He figured that those who dared to propose raising taxes would face an uphill political battle. It is far easier to cut taxes than to restore them. With this argument, Kristol attempted to secure political support for tax cuts among traditional conservatives. As we shall see, he and other supply-siders were remarkably successful in finding that support.

5

Budget Busters

In one of the most celebrated events in American history, a band of colonists in 1773 heaved crates of imported tea into Boston Harbor in retaliation for a tax imposed by British Parliament. The enduring popularity of the Boston Tea Party can be explained in part because it symbolized the American spirit of liberty, one that would not be compromised by British law or military force. But there is a secondary explanation for the enduring popularity of this event; it symbolized a universal antipathy for the tax collector.

Proponents of supply-side economics clearly tapped into this populist theme with their call for massive tax reductions. Supply-side economics, however, was more than just another tax revolt. It included a unique argument, which if true, made the federal tax system appear utterly foolish. The claim was simple: the same amount of revenue collected by the Internal Revenue Service at prevailing tax rates could be collected at significantly lower rates. By slashing tax rates, the economy would experience such a dramatic expansion that the tax base would soar, providing more than enough funds to offset the loss from lower rates. With this argument, supply-siders raised the stakes; taxes were not just an onerous burden, they were an absurd and unnecessary burden.

The promise of supply-side economics was a free lunch, dinner, and breakfast all rolled into one enticing offer. Lower tax rates today would not force higher rates tomorrow, they would not create persistent deficits, nor would they have to be offset by spending cuts. The greater prosperity would see to it that no one suffered and that everyone gained. There was, however, one small catch. The initial tax cuts could not be given to the middle class or even the poor. In order to be successful, tax cuts had to be directed primarily toward the wealthy because of their larger role in saving and investing. If wealthy individuals were to be enticed to set aside a larger share of their income to finance the supply-side renaissance, they would require a tax cut to raise their after-tax income. Tax cuts for everyone else might stimulate additional consumption, but that was not what supply-side economics was all about.

FIRST STRIKE

Supply-side economics preceded Ronald Reagan, but not by much. One of the first major pieces of supply-side legislation was the Kemp-Roth Bill that would have reduced personal income taxes 10 percent each year for three years. While proponents emphasized the "across-the-board" nature of the bill, the actual effect was intentionally slanted to favor the upper-income class. A 30 percent reduction would, for example, drop someone in the 70 percent tax bracket into the 49 percent bracket. Someone in the 10 percent bracket would slide back to only a 7 percent bracket. The intent of Kemp-Roth was to reduce tax rates as well as the total tax burden for those in the higher brackets without the perception of bias.

The leading sponsor of this bill, Representative Jack Kemp from New York, had worked for years to lay the groundwork for the supply-side approach. In a surprisingly close vote in the U.S. House of Representatives, Kemp-Roth tax cuts were narrowly defeated as an amendment to the Humphrey-Hawkins full-employment bill in March 1978.[1] The final tally, 194 to 216, suggested that supply-side tax cuts were no longer the fantasy of a small fringe group but had penetrated the highest levels of American politics. The House again rejected a Kemp-Roth tax cut in August 1978, this one combined with spending limits. The vote was even closer this time, 201 to 206.[2]

In October 1978, the initiative moved to the Senate, which soundly defeated a supply-side tax cut 36 to 60. Yet when across-the-board tax cuts were tied with spending limits in an amendment sponsored by Senator Sam Nunn, a Democrat from Georgia, the Senate reacted favorably, passing the legislation 65 to 20.[3] This historic victory for supply-side economics was reinforced by a House vote to support the Nunn amendment in the follow-up conference between the House and Senate. Supply-side economics would have become law in 1978 if not for the Carter administration, which threatened to veto any tax bill that contained the Nunn amendment. The Democratic House and Senate conferees dutifully purged this language, postponing the supply-side revolution to the election of a new president.

THE SUPPLY-SIDE CANDIDATE

The supply-side cause achieved a significant victory even before the 1980 Republican presidential campaign was fully under way. In 1979, Jack Kemp cut a deal with the Reagan campaign in which he offered to forgo competing for the nomination in exchange for being "in on the ground floor on policy."[4] Kemp had by this time become the field marshal for the supply-side movement. According to David Stockman, Jack Kemp's office in the late 1970s provided the setting for something "of a postgraduate seminar in supply-side economics."[5] Regular participants included prominent supply-siders: Jude Wanniski, Arthur Laffer, Paul Craig Roberts, Steve Entin, John Mueller, and freshman representative from Michigan, David Stockman.

It was in the heat of the Republican contest to see who would get to oppose Jimmy Carter that someone in George Bush's campaign decided to add up the promises of their opponent, Ronald Reagan. Across-the-board tax cuts, major increases in defense spending, and a balanced budget all had wide appeal with some part of the electorate but did not add up in terms of dollars. Although it was technically possible to reconcile all of these promises, a huge chunk of the federal government would have to have been eliminated. This included a significant part of the social security system, which was widely viewed then, as now, to be the equivalent of political suicide. It was this simple accounting exercise that prompted George Bush to characterize Ronald Reagan's economic program as "voodoo" economics.

George Bush apparently used the expression "voodoo economics" in April 1980 while he was still battling Reagan for the nomination and on February 9, 1982, denied ever having made the statement. Unfortunately for him, NBC chose to follow the broadcast of his denial with a tape of his actual statement in 1980.[6] There was no question that he used the expression "voodoo economics." Even if George Bush came to regret this indiscretion after becoming Ronald Reagan's vice president, the comment successfully highlighted a weakness of the Reagan plan that would become more conspicuous over time.

Not long after Kemp had negotiated his pact with the Reagan camp, he was provided the opportunity to work his supply-side magic on the candidate. In early 1980, Jude Wanniski joined Arthur Laffer and Kemp for an informal seminar with Reagan in California, instructing him about the fundamentals of supply-side economics. Kemp left the session convinced that the candidate was on board, or at least 90 percent on board. Even if Reagan failed to fully comprehend the details of supply-side reasoning, Kemp could claim he at least had an intuitive understanding of the issues.[7]

Ronald Reagan's intuition about the Laffer curve was evidently rooted in his own personal experience. During World War II the federal government incurred great expenses that it funded by means of higher taxes and extraordinary borrowing. Individual tax rates hit 90 percent for the top tax brackets, which Ronald Reagan was able to attain after making only four motion pictures. Reagan was easily convinced by Laffer that a reduction in tax rates would spur more effort and consequently more tax revenue. In his own experience during World War II, Reagan chose to stop working after he made enough income to hit the top tax bracket. He bragged that he could have made more movies during World War II, but he was not about to in a 90 percent tax bracket! According to David Stockman's version of the story, Reagan told his advisors, "So we all quit working after four pictures and went off to the country."[8]

Certainly requiring someone to pay 90 percent of their earnings in taxes is asking a lot but this was a temporary surcharge in effect during World War II. Also, to hit this high tax rate one had to have sufficiently high income and a seriously incompetent accountant, one with little understanding of deductions, credits, and assorted loopholes. Yet people were expected to pay these high taxes during World War II because others were making far greater sacrifices on the battlefield. On the other extreme was Ronald Reagan who extended his country vacations rather than pay more war taxes. Here was a true supply-sider!

Ronald Reagan's presidential campaign received a significant boost from one of the most peculiar economic performances in American history. Even with unemployment levels attaining a relatively high level of 7.1 percent, inflation raced along at a disturbing rate of 12.5 percent in 1980. Carter's reelection bid languished even though he was hardly responsible for the deteriorating economic conditions. The coincidence of high unemployment and high inflation was nothing more than a textbook case of a supply-side oil crisis. The 1979 oil crisis left in its wake almost exactly the same damage as that left by the previous crisis in 1973. In truth, the origin of 1980 stagflation was to be found closer to the Middle East than Washington D.C. None of this helped Carter, however, as the electorate was easily swayed by the promises of Ronald Reagan.

After winning the election, Reagan's transition team came through on their agreement to place some of Kemp's supply-siders in on the ground floor. David Stockman was granted his wish to head up the Office of Management and Budget, a position he would wield to great effect in designing budgets and setting spending priorities. Other supply-siders went to the U.S. Department of Treasury where they would have more direct influence on Reagan's tax policies. Paul Craig Roberts was appointed assistant secretary of the Treasury for economic policy and Norman Ture became Treasury under-secretary. Paul Craig Roberts brought along fellow supply-sider Steven Entin as his deputy.[9] In addition, the appointment of Don Regan as Treasury secretary cinched the new administration's commitment to supply-side tax cuts. With these key players in position, the Reagan administration took the field ready to begin the process of translating their supply-side magic into national policy. The game plan was to pass an across-the-board multiyear tax cut based on the Kemp-Roth Bill, 10 percent a year for three years. The trick was to get it through Congress.

A LATE CHRISTMAS

After the 1980 elections, Republicans constituted a slim majority in the Senate but a minority in the House. Despite the split, the prognosis for a major tax reduction looked quite good in early 1981.

Party affiliations alone tended to exaggerate the Democrats' power in the House since Southern Democrats, the so-called Boll Weevils, stood ready to deal with the new Republican administration. It is also worth remembering that supply-side tax cuts had passed both houses of Congress in 1978 when Democrats held a majority in each.

Timing is important in any legislation, and the tax cuts were no exception. Under the convention of Keynesian economics, tax reductions were supposed to be reserved for periods of recession as a way to bolster a sagging economy. But in early 1981, there was some indication that the economy was already pulling out of the mild 1980 recession. The bigger problem appeared to be inflation, which had closed out the year at 12.5 percent. The last thing a Keynesian would advocate would be a major tax cut during inflation, the economic equivalent of throwing gas on a fire. This was but one obstacle facing supply-side revolutionaries as they began to sell their program on the hill. There were others.

Across-the-board tax cuts were popular with wealthy constituents, but there was little in it for particular corporations and other important congressional constituents. The new Republican administration and its congressional supporters were committed to changing business-as-usual, but they were not about to deny their financial patrons a share in the spoils of victory. Even before the Reagan officials had settled into their new offices, supply-side tax cuts for the wealthy were amended to include another major tax cut, this one for corporations. Its name, 10–5–3, featured accelerated depreciation and promised to reduce business taxes by billions of dollars. This addition also set an important precedent for negotiations between the administration and Congress: supply-siders would get their tax cuts as long as everyone else got theirs.

The compromise tax cut produced by these negotiations contained supply-side cuts: 5 percent in July 1981 followed by 10 percent in both 1982 and 1983. It was also larded with so many extras that they became known to insiders as "ornaments." One ornament, with important consequences, was a reduction in the maximum capital gains tax. A capital gain occurs when an asset, such as a stock or a house, appreciates in value. The official maximum tax rate on this "unearned" income of 70 percent was more than a little deceptive since most of that was exempted leaving an effective capital gains tax of only 28 percent. While supply-siders were railing against the 70 percent tax on capital gains, the actual tax was much lower. By slashing the top rate on income from 70 percent to 50 percent, the new effective rate for "unearned" capital gains fell from 28 to 20 percent. The benefits of this provision were consistent with supply-side theory since they were confined to those in the highest tax brackets.

The 1981 Economic Recovery Act also included an ornament for wealthy families who planned to leave a substantial inheritance. The exemption in the estate tax was scheduled to increase gradually from $175,000 to $600,000 by 1987 and inheritances of spouses were excluded altogether. While this would help farm families it also benefited those with vast accumulations of savings. In supply-side reasoning, this provided the wealthy with yet another reason to save, they could be assured that a much larger part of their estate would fall into the hands of their children rather than the IRS.

Several more ornaments were designed to beef up the savings incentive. One allowed 15 percent of net interest income to be exempted from income tax by 1985. This exemption was limited to $450 for a single taxpayer, $900 for a joint return. Americans were encouraged to save more by a second ornament that granted generous income deductions for individual retirement accounts. Many more employees, even those covered by company pension plans, were now eligible to participate in this tax concession. Another special tax benefit was directed at investors in public utilities. Rather than tax their dividend earnings at the conventional rates for ordinary income, it was to be taxed at the lower capital gains rates. The stated purpose of reducing each of these taxes was to encourage more savings, the backbone of the promised supply-side boom.

Businesses also stood to benefit significantly from the tax cuts. The key feature was accelerated depreciation, which allowed companies to increase their reported costs and decrease their calculated taxable profits. Businesses also benefited from a 25 percent tax credit for R&D and more liberal tax treatment of executive stock options. For those companies that had more credits than they could legally use, the new tax law allowed them to sell tax breaks to other corporations, a practice that became known as *safe-harbor leasing*.

This was not tax reform that attempted to simplify and eliminate unnecessary tax provisions. It was a Christmas tree decked out with enough ornaments to ensure economic expansion for at least one sector in the economy: tax lawyers and consultants. According to the *New York Times*, "People who have never before relied on financial or tax advice could now seek help to navigate the newly created opportunities. And lawyers, accountants and other tax advisers are gearing up to help these people, anticipating a field day."[10]

The administration's tax package ran into a small pocket of resistance in the Senate. The administration's original tax proposal had not included any special tax cuts for the oil industry. However, the final package, representing the work of a Senate and House conference committee, included a generous rollback in windfall profits tax on crude production. Since the major oil companies are involved in all aspects of the petroleum industry, including crude oil production at the well-head, Senator Edward Kennedy, Democrat from Massachusetts, was prompted to characterize the bill as tax relief for "big oil."[11] Kennedy estimated the oil provisions to cost $33 billion over the ten years left in the profits tax, compared to $11.7 billion estimated by Senator Bob Dole, Republican from Kansas. Kennedy's effort to send the bill back to conference in order to reduce the tax relief for the oil companies was rejected, 55 to 20. The actual vote was notable only because voting with Kennedy was Senator William Roth, Jr., Republican from Delaware and one of the coauthors of the original Kemp-Roth supply-side tax cut bill.

The administration went to great lengths to ensure enough votes to pass the tax cut. They arranged for five air force transport planes to ferry senators back to Washington D.C. from their vacations to cast their ballots. In the final Senate vote, many Democrats joined the Republican majority to pass the historic tax cut, 67 to 8.

A small insurrection in the House also focused on the same tax break for the oil industry, but it also was swept aside. Despite the Democratic majority in the House, the tax cut bill passed 282 to 95. In the final tally, 113 Democrats had joined 169 Republicans in voting for the bill. With the support of a majority of House Democrats, supply-side economics was christened as a bipartisan experiment. Dan Rostenkowski, Democrat from Illinois and powerful leader of the Ways and Means Committee, came to symbolize the position many Democrats had taken with regard to the bill. While he insisted on characterizing the supply-side tax cuts as the work of President Reagan, not the Democratic majority, he still congratulated the president on his accomplishment and voted for the bill. If this seemed a little disingenuous it was not out of character for Rostenkowski. In 1996 he was sentenced to 17 months in prison and fined $100,000 for two federal corruption charges related to mail fraud.

All that remained was for President Reagan to sign the bill. This was done on August 13, 1981, with the traditional photo-ops and showmanship pioneered by the Reagan administration. Here was a president who not only knew how to talk about rugged individualism, he knew how to dress the part. Adopting a western motif, the president appeared in front of his stucco ranch in the Santa Ynez Mountains in California dressed in faded jeans, denim jacket, and cowboy boots. Armed with 24 pens, the president signed the tax bills and ushered in the supply-side revolution, an estimated $130 billion in tax cuts for the first three years, accumulating to $750 billion by the end of the fifth. The first part of the tax cut, the 5 percent reduction in rates was scheduled to take effect October 1, 1981. Not only was this the largest tax cut in history, it was the first one designed by supply-side economists. By the end of the fifth year, the tax burden on high income earners and savings would be drastically reduced.

There is quite a contrast between this tax-cutting exercise and the one engineered under Kennedy in the 1960s. Kennedy's economists carefully calculated the optimum size of their tax cuts for 1962 and 1964. These economists believed that a tax cut could be too large as well as too small. Working backward from the economic growth they wanted to achieve, Kennedy's advisors calculated the desired reduction in taxes.

No such deliberations characterized the supply-side approach: they wanted as much as they could get. If a small tax cut would create economic growth and higher revenue, then a larger tax cut would produce even greater growth and even more revenue. The only limit on the size of the tax cut was expected to come from Congress. Yet since many in Congress were more interested in securing their own tax cuts than limiting those of the administration, the final figure was by all accounts monumental. It required the optimism of a true supply-sider to suggest that this only meant more tax revenue.

THE BUDGET BATTLE

The centerpiece of the Reagan revolution was now in place: massive supply-side tax reductions that would be phased in over a period of several years. Other aspects of the Reagan revolution— reductions in social spending and increases in defense spending— were passed in the administration's budget package that same summer. A picture was beginning to take shape. Since massive increases in defense spending easily offset the cuts in social programs, the smaller government promised by Ronald Reagan never came to pass. Corrected for inflation, government spending rose 3.5 percent in fiscal year 1982, the first full year of a Reagan budget, and 4.2 percent the following year. Not only was the first budget larger, so was the second, and the third. For the most part, real increases in government spending kept pace with growth of the overall economy. As a percentage of gross domestic product, federal spending changed little during the Reagan years, rising from 21.8 percent to 22.6 percent during the first term and sliding back slightly to 21.7 percent during the second. The Reagan revolution had little impact on the overall level of government spending.

Supply-siders as a group were not overly concerned with the size of government spending. Perhaps because of their generally conservative outlook they would have preferred a smaller government, but it was not critical to their plan. In fact, they had argued just the opposite. Where traditional fiscal conservatives had insisted that tax cuts be balanced with spending cuts, the supply-siders demurred. They had ridiculed this view as the old austerity solution, as archaic as the Keynesian ideas they reviled. It was not necessary to match tax rate reductions with spending cuts, they insisted, since lower tax rates would raise revenue!

As it became clear that federal spending as a whole was not going to be roped in, the success of supply-side economics became imperative. It was one thing to speculate on a napkin about the powerful impact of tax cuts on the economy, it was quite another to cut $750 billion in taxes and wait for a $3 trillion economy to respond. If supply-side economics failed, it would be difficult to hide. Without the prospect of lower federal spending, any loss of revenue would result in a conspicuous deficit. One did not need a napkin to prove that even a small error in the theory could produce a flood of red ink. If these deficits materialized they would present both an economic and a political problem for the president, who had dedicated much of his campaign to promoting balanced budgets.

MISGIVINGS

Before the luster had worn off the supply-side legislative victory, one of their inner circle got cold feet. Responsible for preparing the president's annual budget projections, David Stockman was perhaps more than anyone in the administration aware of the risk behind the tax cut. Stockman recognized the problem as early as February 1981. At the time, a group of administration analysts was attempting to prepare an economic forecast. Their original scenario was optimistic, including strong economic growth and low inflation. Real production in the economy was expected to expand at least 5 percent for the next four years. Given that the postwar average was 3 percent, the economists had added in 2 percent growth for the Reagan revolution and its tax incentives. However, even this was not enough. For a smaller tax cut, 5 percent growth could have brought in enough revenue to eventually balance the budget, but this was no small tax cut. To recover $750 billion would require much, much more.

Economists of all persuasions are prepared to disagree on many issues especially forecasts about future growth rates. But still there is generally much more agreement about what distinguishes a reasonable forecast from an unbelievable one. Certain forecasts are so far out of line with historical experience and general economic principles that they are universally considered incredible.

For real growth rates that threshold is crossed at 6 percent. For the three years following the Kennedy tax cut in 1963, real growth rates in GDP had averaged 5.7 percent but not since World War II had they exceeded 6 percent. The problem for the analysts from the Treasury, Office of Management and the Budget, and the Council of Economic Advisors sitting around that table in February was that they needed to cross that line in order to balance the projected budget by 1985. According to Stockman's estimate, with only 5 percent real growth they were facing a $150 billion deficit in 1985, more than twice the size of any deficit under Jimmy Carter. But no one was willing to make the move to raise projected growth beyond the 6 percent threshold. Of all the supply-siders in the room, none was willing to promise that their unprecedented tax cut would provide unprecedented growth.

Was voodoo economics catching up to the Reaganites? Was it impossible to slash tax rates at the top, accelerate defense spending, and still balance the budget by 1985? Certain facts were clear. Ronald Reagan had committed himself to tax cuts and military expansion, and on these two issues he was not willing to retreat. But how could his administration issue a report showing that these policies would create the largest peacetime deficits in the history of the nation?

The solution to the problem was submitted by Murray Weidenbaum, the new chair of the Council of Economic Advisors.[12] Murray's answer was to raise the forecasted inflation rates because higher inflation also brought in more tax revenue. It typically does not matter whether family income grows because of high purchasing power (real growth) or because of high inflation; in either case, tax revenue increases. By raising the projected inflation rate to 7.7 percent, the deficit projection was reduced to a politically acceptable size. When asked where he got this inflation projection, the chief economic advisor reportedly slapped his stomach and claimed it came from his "visceral computer."[13]

Inflation at the time was running over 12 percent but no one in the room believed that the Federal Reserve was going to relent until it had driven inflation much lower than 7.7 percent. In case anyone had forgotten this fact, Beryl Sprinkel, a monetarist from the Treasury, was there to remind them. However the forecast was not intended to be realistic; it was intended to make things add up. The higher inflation rates served that purpose for the time being.

Stockman was perceptive enough to realize that the funny inflation numbers would not last forever. Equally clear was that the president stubbornly refused to reconsider the tax cuts or defense spending. Steady economic growth over 6 percent could prevent exploding deficits, but no one believed such rapid growth was possible for more than a year, including the supply-siders. The only hope from Stockman's view was to slash government spending, and it was to this end that he redirected his energies. From the start, Stockman set out to cut spending for black lung programs, veteran pensions, nutritional programs for pregnant mothers, education, handicapped programs, social security, and a host of programs directed at low-income families.[14] He was easily dissuaded from pursuing cuts in defense and other programs that benefited corporations including the oil-depletion allowance, tax-exempt industrial-development bonds, and user fees for the owners of airplanes and barges.[15]

In the final accounting, total spending cuts fell far short of what Stockman figured was necessary to balance the budget. Adding to Stockman's frustration was his impatience with other administration officials who failed to share his concern with the deficit. Some, like Ed Meese, failed to understand that the additional revenue from the tax cuts was already figured into the projections in the form of high growth rates.[16] Whatever figure Stockman showed them, Meese would claim that they just needed to wait for the supply-side mechanism to kick into gear and produce more tax revenue. Meese did not appreciate the fact that 5 percent growth rates were the best that even a supply-side economist would venture, and these were already part of the revenue forecast.

Stockman continued to hammer away inside the administration for the remainder of 1981 through the beginning of 1982 before he was able to convince key members of the administration, including James Baker and Michael Deaver, that a large tax increase was necessary to offset impending deficits. The more difficult task was to convince the president. The president took the opportunity during his State of the Union Message on January 26, 1982, to reiterate his opposition to taxes by claiming that, "Raising taxes won't balance the budget."[17] Only a few days later, however, Reagan submitted his 1983 budget to Congress that included $22 billion in higher taxes.[18] This was enough to weaken the resistance to tax increases in Congress and widen the scope for budget negotiations with Congress.

After months of negotiations between the administration and Congress, the total tax enhancement had gotten larger, not smaller. By August 1982 Congress found itself facing a vote to raise taxes by $98 billion over three years and by some estimates, $228 billion over five years.[19] Where the administration had campaigned for a $750 billion tax cut one year earlier, they were now twisting some of the same arms in Congress to pass a tax increase. The political price tag for raising taxes is higher than cutting them, and this was reflected in the final vote. The bill squeaked by the House 226 to 207 with an equally close vote in the Senate, 52 to 47. Once again a majority of House Democrats joined a majority of House Republicans to pass the bill.

While the *New York Times* called the final vote "a crucial victory" for President Reagan, that was not obvious by the way it was handled.[20] It was clear that the president was reticent about the new direction, explaining, "Personally, I had to swallow very hard. I believe in 'supply-side,' and that tax increases slow the recovery."[21] Having fought for supply-side tax cuts in 1981 with the promise of closing the deficit, he then signed a tax increase in 1982 to finish the job. At the last moment, the signing was moved from Washington to the president's California ranch where photographers were banned. According to an administration spokesperson, the signing was witnessed privately by two aides.

The resulting legislation was proclaimed the largest tax increase in history, expected to raise $228 billion over five years. Whether this was really the largest tax increase required a few qualifications that will be discussed in Chapter 8.[22] The 1982 tax increase was viewed as a defeat by the remaining supply-siders, although it hardly began to undo the supply-side experiment. First the tax increases were considerably smaller than the tax cuts that preceded them, and second, the new taxes did not rescind the Kemp-Roth tax cuts for the wealthy, which was the flagship of the supply-side agenda. In fact, many of the increased taxes were inconsequential to the supply-side program. Of the total tax increase, 28 percent was dedicated to increasing compliance of already existing tax measures through additional withholding and IRS enforcement. Another 12 percent was obtained from raising the federal excise tax on cigarettes and telephone services. Only one important part of the generous business tax cuts of 1981 was rescinded in 1982. This was the "safe harbor leasing" provision that allowed businesses to sell tax benefits to each other, ensuring that none would go to waste. The remainder of the tax increases affected unemployment insurance, pensions, medical care, health insurance, and life insurance.[23]

Looking back at the radical changes in tax rates in 1981 and 1982 it becomes apparent just how far economic thinking had strayed from Keynesian principles. During the fourth quarter of 1980 and the first quarter of 1981 the economy was showing signs of a robust expansion with real GDP rising 4.3 percent and 7.9 percent, respectively. Under these conditions, the last thing a Keynesian would have supported would have been a tax cut, but this is exactly what Congress enacted in the summer of 1981. In fact it was the largest tax cut in history. By early 1982 it had become apparent that the economy had changed directions and that the United States was slipping into a profound recession. Real GDP tumbled 5.3 percent in the fourth quarter of 1981 followed by an equally devastating fall of 5.1 percent in the first quarter of 1982. This time Keynesians would have advocated a tax cut and yet Congress passed one of the largest tax increases in history.

By now, the Keynesians were being routinely ignored. The timing, magnitude, and composition of the tax cuts were all determined by supply-side doctrine. Timing, for supply-siders, was irrelevant since tax cuts are always good for the economy. Magnitude was equally irrelevant since bigger tax cuts only meant higher growth and more tax revenue. Bigger was better. And as far as composition, it only mattered that tax breaks be directed toward businesses and the wealthy, the most visible savers and investors.

The 1982 tax correction was merely an effort to scale back the original experiment when the magnitude of possible future deficits became clear. But even this retreat was influenced by supply-side thinking because it preserved lower tax rates at the top along with many of the tax breaks for corporations. In all of this, Keynesians and their ideas were nowhere to be found. They were out of the loop.

In some respects it is incredible that the supply-side experiment was ever implemented. Beginning with no more than a room full of conspirators—politicians, business writers, congressional staffers, and economists—a supply-side tax cut passed both houses of Congress and was signed into law by the president of the United States. Along the way there had been ample opportunity for failure. There were the dissenting economists and editorialists, the Boll Weevils, the lobbyists, and vested interests, but over all of these obstacles, supply-side policy prevailed.

The only question was whether or not it would succeed. Would the tax cuts pay for themselves in a relatively short period of time? Would they spark record levels of economic growth and usher in another golden decade like the 1920s and 1960s? Would they inspire a flood of new savings sufficient to finance the "temporary" budget shortfall? The time for theorizing and strategizing had passed. It was time for the new incentives to work their magic.

6

The Free Float

The fact that America was preparing to embark on two risky economic experiments in the 1980s inspired by conservative theories did not go entirely unnoticed by the general public. Any reader, if willing, could have found debates over the wisdom of supply-side economics and perhaps even monetarism somewhere in the popular media. At least one did not have to resort to inscrutable economics texts in order to find out what supply-side economics and monetarism were all about.

The third experiment of the 1980s was different. It was largely ignored before, during, and after its execution. If there is a reason for this omission it probably rests with the arcane nature of international finance, an area of public policy once reserved for aristocrats and their bankers. Currency crises, devaluations, and balance of payments problems all conjure up images of distinguished gentlemen rushing off to New York, Paris, or London for secret talks with their international counterparts. The actual substance of such talks would seldom seep much further than the pages of the *Wall Street Journal* or the *Economist*.

Consequently, when the U.S. Treasury announced that it was embarking on an experiment of "free floating" in 1981, it was met with a loud yawn. But three years later, with the dollar grossly overvalued relative to other currencies and the trade deficit at the highest level in U.S. history, the question came up as to why the U.S. Treasury was not doing anything about it. The fact that the Treasury was practicing "free floating" meant very little to anyone except international bankers and economists. However, this relatively obscure policy was precisely the reason that the Treasury permitted the U.S. trade situation to deteriorate until it attained the status of a full-fledged currency crisis. As events gradually made clear, the practice of free floating may have been poorly understood, but it was not unimportant.

Free floating can easily be defined as allowing currency markets—comprised of bankers, traders, investors, and speculators—to determine exchange rates, the price of any one currency in terms of another. Exchange rates in this setting respond to the balance or imbalance between sellers and buyers. If, for instance, there are more sellers than buyers, the exchange rate for that currency is likely to decrease. The market in this case is characterized by an excess supply and a decrease in the exchange rate means that the currency weakens or depreciates. Alternatively, currencies are more likely to get stronger or appreciate under conditions of excess demand, when there is more interest in buying the currency than selling it.

In any monetary system, there is always the possibility of having either an excess demand or excess supply of currency. The only difference between monetary systems is how this imbalance is dealt with. In free floating, conditions of excess supply or demand are resolved exclusively by the market and changes in exchange rates.

But the true significance of a free float is not what the market does but what public agencies do not do. In a free float, central banks and national treasuries do nothing to alter the value of a currency. In the modern world, this means that central banks and treasuries will not buy or sell their own currency, a practice described as *official reserve intervention*. It also means that they will not regulate or control the exchange of foreign currency, called exchange controls. Additionally they will not attempt to discourage imports or encourage exports merely to change or protect their currency. While one may be for or against free floating on purely philosophical grounds, it is the practical issues that make all the difference.

In order to appreciate the significance of free floating it is essential to understand exchange markets as well as the historical development of exchange rate policy. The policies that we live under today are very different from what existed thirty, fifty, or one hundred years ago. Each system, however, holds in common the fact that the government has always taken some amount of responsibility for regulating or stabilizing currency markets, that is, until the free floating experiment of 1981.

There is an important feature of currency markets that needs to be explained before tracing the evolution of government intervention. Every currency market is in fact two distinct markets. Currency transactions fall into one of these two markets depending on how traders use their foreign exchange. In one market, currencies are exchanged exclusively to conduct international trade in goods and services and carry out transfers. The export of automobiles from Japan to the United States or the sale of U.S. wheat to Russia requires an exchange of currency. All these transactions are recorded in the United States on an annual basis in what is called the *current account*. The purchase of American goods by foreigners counts as a positive value (credit) in the current account and the purchase of foreign goods by Americans counts as a negative value (debit). Adding up all of these transactions yields the balance in the current account with a negative value associated with a trade deficit.

Not all currency exchanges are for the purposes of trade. Some are conducted by investors and speculators whose goal is to earn capital income in the form of profits, interest, dividends, or capital gains. Foreign investors buy dollars (credit) to invest in the United States and American investors exchange dollars for foreign currency (debit) to invest abroad. The sum of these transactions is represented in the *capital account*.

Together the current and capital accounts constitute the market for international currency. In practice the two markets are not so distinct. It hardly matters to international bankers whether someone is selling dollars to buy imported French wine or a German bond. Although one is recorded in the current account and the other in the capital account, both are dollar sales. On the other hand, dollars may be bought either to invest in the United States or to buy U.S. products.

This raises a key point: while neither the current account nor the capital account needs to balance, when taken together they must. The reason is that every dollar sold in a currency market must be matched by a dollar purchased. Sometimes economics can sound complicated even when it is not. This is one of those cases. If the current account (including the trade deficit) is in the red by $100 billion, then the capital account must be in surplus by $100 billion. This is always true except when dollar exchanges slip past the watchful eye of government auditors, an understandable omission given the magnitude of the market. The sum of these oversights is reported as an error term, which ensures that the accounts will always balance.

At any moment, there is always a possibility that the desire for a currency and its availability will be out of balance. Excess supply or excess demand for any currency is unavoidable. Free floating is one way to deal with these imbalances while historically other methods have been used, including the gold standard.

THE GOLDEN AGE

There was a period in world history when most of the economically advanced nations voluntarily adopted gold as their uniform standard of monetary value. The period from 1879 to 1914 is known as the era of the classic gold standard. Every so often, when the world seems to be on the edge of chaos, a small group will inevitably call for a return to the gold standard, much like what existed during that time. But the significance of what it means to be on a gold standard is likely to escape most people, even those calling for its return.

As a U.S. citizen during the gold era, it was entirely your choice of whether you conducted your business in gold coins or paper money. The additional convenience of folding money—a little lighter and perhaps less conspicuous—ensured it a primary role in daily commerce. Any superstitious preference for gold was balanced by the Treasury's pledge to provide as much gold as demanded at $20.65 per ounce. Anyone doubting the claim could test the U.S. Treasury's resolve by cashing in their paper money for gold. The need to conduct such a test gradually subsided as the Treasury consistently made good on its promise.

Under the gold standard from 1879 to 1914, the world came as close as it ever has to having a single currency. The reason is because as long as all (or most) countries subscribe to the gold standard, each national currency is in effect a proxy for gold. Ultimately, if all currencies can be converted into a specified amount of gold, then the world is operating on a single currency. Such a system would so greatly simplify economic relationships that I suspect it would put a number of economists out of business.

Furthermore, if each currency exchanges for a fixed amount of gold, then it must also exchange for a fixed amount of other currencies. In the previous example where an ounce of gold exchanged for $20.65 or 4.25 British pounds, then the pound must exchange for $4.86. If not, someone could make a lot of money trading in dollars, pounds, and gold. The term for such profiteering is *arbitrage*, and there is never a shortage of such traders. The important point, however, is that a universal gold standard also locks in exchange rates.

From 1879 to 1914, anyone with $20.65 or 4.25 pounds was assured of being able to buy one ounce of gold, and at these rates the pound was also worth $4.86. However, it would be a mistake to assume that an official declaration of a gold standard was sufficient to ensure its existence. If not for government intervention, this rate would probably not have lasted more than a month, much less the 35 years that it did.

The key to the gold standard was the government's willingness to exchange currency for gold, what is known as *convertibility*. The U.S. government guaranteed convertibility between dollars and gold from 1879 until 1914 when such a practice was temporarily interrupted by World War I.[1] Without convertibility, the gold value of a currency is little more than an empty promise. If the government claims that the dollar is worth $20.65 per ounce of gold, but is unwilling to exchange it at that rate, then it is unlikely that anyone else will either. Suspension of convertibility marks the end of a gold standard.

How were excesses in supply or demand addressed under the gold standard? In this regard, the operation of the gold standard was rather ingenious. For example, when an excess supply of dollars appeared, the value of the dollar would drop slightly relative to the pound or other currencies. Only a small decrease in its value would need to occur before arbitrageurs found it profitable to use the cheap dollars to buy gold in the United States and ship it abroad. The United States would lose gold while Britain or the rest of the world would gain.

Before all the gold could flow out of the United States, however, certain mechanisms would kick into gear, eventually stemming the gold outflow. First, with less gold in the United States, money would become more scarce and interest rates would rise, thus attracting more demand for dollars from abroad. Foreigners who would like to invest at the higher interest rates would have to buy dollars to do so. This alone could reduce the excess supply of dollars, but there were other possibilities.

With less gold, the money supply was likely to drop, which can have the effect of reducing inflation. Less inflation in the United States would encourage foreign demand for U.S. goods and further increase the demand for dollars. There was also the possibility that less money and higher interest rates would retard economic growth. This usually meant less demand for imports and a reduction in the supply of dollars for this purpose. In every one of these examples, the macroeconomy adjusts in some way, which tends to eliminate the excess supply of dollars that originally caused the problem. An excess demand for dollars would start up many of the same mechanisms, but in reverse.

Balance under the gold standard was provided by a more or less automatic adjustment in key measures of economic performance: interest rates, inflation, and national income. During the early gold period, these macroeconomic adjustments were the primary method of addressing imbalances in currency markets. The fact that the adjustments were made more or less automatically in response to gold flows was, to some observers, a desirable feature of the system.

Although the classic gold standard is long gone, the possibility of using macroeconomic policies to alter an exchange rate is not. Modern societies seem most willing to resort to such policies when the exchange rate has become a national priority. A good example of this took place in Britain in September 1992. At the time, an excess supply of pounds developed and created strong pressure for depreciation. Given that Britain's leaders were dead set against depreciation, they were willing to go to great lengths to resist it. Since there was no automatic gold outflow, Britain attempted to directly raise interest rates for the sole purpose of increasing the desirability and value of the pound. The details of this event are presented in a later chapter, but it illustrates here that macro-economic adjustment remains an alternative in a modern economy, although a rare one.

FROM FLOATING TO EXCHANGE CONTROLS

The collapse of the world gold standard in 1914 ushered in one of the earliest experiments in floating exchange rates. The burden of World War I drained gold from many countries causing them to terminate or at least restrict gold convertibility. As nations left the gold standard, the world's system of fixed exchange rates went with it. Imbalances created by the war were severe, creating pressure on the dollar to appreciate relative to currencies in most other countries. These tendencies were resisted by central banks and authorities who wished to avoid or at least minimize the amount of exchange rate adjustment.

In the aftermath of the war, countries struggled to return to the gold standard; the United States and Britain both returned in 1925. But the new gold standard was never as solid as it had once been. Under the severe strain of having to pay war reparations, Germany left the gold standard again in the summer of 1931, but rather than permit the mark to float, that is, be determined by the market, they instituted a tightly controlled system of exchange control. In September 1931 Britain also left gold and permitted the pound to float, culminating in a devaluation. The United States followed in April 1933, three years ahead of France, Belgium, Holland, and Switzerland.[2]

None of these experiences constitute a valid test of free floating. In most cases individual countries continued to intervene in mar-kets in some manner, involving exchange controls, official reserves, or trade policy. To the extent that currencies were permitted to float, it was hardly "free." Besides, the economic conditions present during the Depression and the two world wars would have dis-torted almost any kind of exchange rate experiment.

When Germany opted to end gold convertibility in 1931, it did so under pressure of an excess supply of currency.[3] Since they did not want to see the currency devalued, they chose instead to introduce a system of tightly regulated exchange controls. Under exchange controls, a government limits the ability of traders or investors to exchange currencies. In its most extreme form a country could prohibit or regulate the sale of foreign currencies in order to limit imports or capital outflows. This constitutes yet another method for addressing imbalances in currency markets.

A key element in German controls was the power of the Reichsbank to commandeer all foreign exchange at the official rate and then distribute it according to national priorities, to purchase key imports for example. Under the government of Adolf Hitler, the import priorities would take on a conspicuous turn toward the rearmament of Germany.

The biggest challenge for those implementing exchange controls was to prevent foreign exchange from being hoarded or sold in black markets. These were natural responses since foreign currency at the official rate exchanged for relatively few marks. Businesses and individuals with foreign exchange figured they could do better in black markets than the official bank price. In order to enforce the law, the German government had to monitor exports since traders had an incentive to hide their foreign exchange. As an additional measure the government monitored the mail for illegal currency transactions.

By the time of World War II, many other countries adopted exchange controls, each with their own unique methods of enforcement. Under these policies, scarce foreign exchange was essentially rationed, thus postponing the day that they would have to depreciate their own national currency. In every case, successful enforcement required a strict crackdown on black market operations.

Government intervention during the war years included another method—trade policy. In this case, countries attempted to control the value of their currency by discouraging imports or encouraging exports. If the United States, for example, could discourage imports by invoking a tariff, quota, or regulation, the supply of dollars in the markets would diminish and the price of dollars would rise. These efforts are not always successful, especially if they ignite a round of retaliation from other countries.

These examples illustrate some of the different ways that a government can intervene in markets to correct currency imbalances and alter exchange rates. Another possibility, official reserve intervention, was used widely by Bretton Woods, the world financial system after World War II.

BRETTON WOODS

The post–World War II system for international economic relations was organized by the United States and Britain before the war ended in Europe. By the time the final agreement was formally approved in 1944, participation in the new monetary system was broadened to include forty-four nations. In an uncharacteristic departure from past precedence, the international meeting was held outside the centers of world finance, in a small town called Bretton Woods, New Hampshire. This was the origin of what is simply referred to as Bretton Woods, a system of international commerce and finance.

Bretton Woods brought back fixed exchange rates and a gold standard with the value of an ounce set equal to $35. Once again, the fact that exchange rates were fixed meant that currencies could experience excess demand or excess supply. The real innovation of the Bretton Woods system was the set of rules it proposed for addressing these imbalances.

Stability in the new system depended on the ability of governments to buy and sell their currencies to compensate for immediate imbalances. If an excess supply was the problem, the government would buy the excess using its stock of foreign reserves to pay for it. If an excess demand was the problem, the country could sell its currency and build up its foreign reserves. In this way a government could enforce the fixed exchange rates without resorting to automatic gold flows that characterized the earlier period.

Bretton Woods enhanced the options for government intervention. First, the International Monetary Fund was created and authorized to make loans to countries that found themselves short of foreign reserves. In addition, the dollar joined gold as a widely accepted reserve currency. Together these developments greatly expanded the capacity of countries to buy and sell currencies with the purpose of controlling the international value of their own money.

The use of official reserves was only one method for enforcing fixed exchange rates under Bretton Woods, but it was an important one. The other forms of currency intervention were becoming less popular. Bretton Woods discouraged the use of trade policy and instead supported the opposite, an expansion of free trade. Even exchange controls gradually fell out of favor, contrary to the wishes of John Maynard Keynes who led the British delegation at Bretton

Woods. Keynes believed that trade could be free, but currency exchanges for investment should be controlled. As early as 1933 Keynes suggested that: "Ideas, knowledge, science, hospitality, travel—these are the things which should be international. But . . . above all, let finance be primarily national."[4] However, exchange controls were gradually lost as one country after another dismantled them during the twenty years after the war.

The reduction in exchange controls was the goal of the other powerful delegation at Bretton Woods—the United States. If the United States was to expand its role in world trade it would be necessary to reduce tariffs, quotas, and exchange controls throughout the world. The fact that this principle was expressed in the Articles of Agreement establishing the International Monetary Fund constituted a small victory for the U.S. position.[5] The task of dismantling controls was resisted by some countries, but the message was certainly clear; exchange controls would not play a major role in the future.

Another option for addressing imbalances was the explicit possibility for countries to depreciate or appreciate their currency. While such actions appear to violate the spirit of fixed exchange rates, it was more widely perceived as a stop-gap measure, essential to ensure the viability of fixed rates at all other times. These "revaluations" were explicitly recognized in the IMF articles of agreement under conditions of "fundamental disequilibrium." Any change in currency value less than 10 percent did not require IMF approval; those over 10 percent did, although even in this case the request was little more than a formality. Bretton Woods brought back fixed exchange rates with more flexibility and new options for enforcement.

During Bretton Woods, floating rates were generally shunned with one significant exception—Canada from 1950 to 1962. Canada was more willing to allow its dollar to fluctuate in the market, but it continued to stabilize the currency when necessary by using official reserves.[6] The vast majority of other countries adhered more closely to the spirit of fixed exchange rates.

THE FIRST FREE FLOATER

An alternative to Bretton Woods is free floating, which requires governments to resist buying or selling foreign reserves, to refrain from using exchange controls, and to forgo any form of trade policy. In other words, the government takes a back seat in international exchange markets leaving private bankers, traders, investors, and speculators in the driver's seat. Currency traders are free to seek currency prices that clear the market, that is, provide some semblance of balance between supply and demand.

One of the most prominent, if not earliest, appeals for free floating was made by Milton Friedman in 1953. In his essay, "The Case for Flexible Exchange Rates," Friedman outlined the classic arguments for free floating that influenced a generation of free market economists.[7]

His objections to exchange controls and trade policy were entirely consistent with his general philosophy of favoring the market over any form of government intervention. On this account, Friedman met little resistance within the economics profession. At best, exchange controls were viewed as an unfortunate necessity, precipitated by extraordinary times. Germany had pioneered controls during the Depression era while most other countries adopted them during World War II. In most cases they just got in the way of U.S. corporate interests attempting to secure foreign markets and establish financial ties.

Friedman's criticisms of exchange controls in 1953 were therefore directed less toward the United States than toward its allies, where the practice still continued. He blamed these policies for aggravating the very problems they were intended to solve. It was well known that countries normally resorted to exchange controls when there was a shortage of foreign exchange. But the controls themselves, said Friedman, caused a further reduction in foreign exchange because investors naturally avoided a currency whose uses were limited by the government. Rather than conserve scarce foreign exchange, Friedman argued, controls only made them more scarce.

Of all the problems with exchange controls, the most difficult was perhaps the problem of enforcement. Unless one was prepared to inspect all exports and international mail as the Nazis did, exchange controls would, Friedman argued, be largely evaded through black market exchanges.

The option of applying direct controls on trade flows was also rapidly falling out of favor at that time. The United States was not above exploiting its position as chief financier of Europe's reconstruction to attack excessive trade barriers. The adoption of multi-lateral trade agreements in the postwar period, such as the first General Agreement on Tariffs and Trade (GATT), signaled the initial attack on all trade barriers. Friedman enthusiastically embraced this trend as it eliminated yet another form of government intervention.

Friedman's objections to using exchange controls and trade policy were entirely consistent with his fundamental distrust of government intervention. His objections to using macroeconomic policies to maintain fixed exchange rates, however, were more practical than ideological. While raising interest rates could conceivably rescue a currency experiencing a free fall, it did so at considerable cost, including increasing unemployment. Friedman figured that the days were gone when a country would willingly accept higher unemployment merely to maintain the value of its currency.

Between 1971 and 1973, the Bretton Woods system collapsed, ushering in a new era of floating exchange rates. However, the demise of the system had much less to do with Milton Friedman's vision of a free market than the unwillingness of countries to adjust exchange rates to correspond with shifts in economic power. The pound was widely understood to be overvalued and the mark and yen undervalued. The coup de grace, however, was the unavoidable dollar devaluation and the closing of the U.S. gold window in 1971. By 1973, the dollar and most of the major currencies were floating. As the stable anchor provided by the dollar was withdrawn, the world currencies were set adrift, marking the end of fixed exchange rates for most of the industrialized world.

One widely used argument in favor of fixed exchange rates is that they provide a certain level of security for international traders and investors. The exporter who counts on a foreign sale six months in the future has less to worry about if future exchange rates are stable and predictable. The same is true for U.S. investors buying foreign stocks or bonds. When it comes time to cash-in foreign securities and bring dollars home, investors may appreciate not losing money on the exchange. The fixed exchange rates were intended to reduce these potential losses or so-called "exchange rate risks," and thus encourage more international trade and investment.

With the end of fixed exchange rates, the world's traders and investors were exposed to this new danger. How did exchange rate risk affect international trade and finance? Did occasional adverse revaluations wipe out profits? As it turned out, the concern about exchange rate risk was quickly forgotten. One reason was because the revaluations leading up to floating rates had prepared the world for some degree of uncertainty. Along with this was the other important fact that businesses and bankers quickly developed new ways to avoid these risks involving the development of futures markets.

If, for instance, a business is worried that a future devaluation of the pound will reduce the value of a million pound payment due to be received six months from now, they can sell those pounds now in a futures market at a known exchange rate, thus avoiding much of the risk. Futures markets do not eliminate potential losses from exchange rate movements, but they do provide a vehicle for traders to buy their way out. There is always someone who will accept the risk, that is, for a fee. The fear that floating rates would discourage international commerce was greatly exaggerated.

From 1973 to 1981 it would appear that many of Milton Friedman's policy prescriptions outlined in 1953 had come to pass. Exchange rates were no longer fixed in terms of gold or each other, but were allowed to float in international markets. The use of exchange controls had been widely eliminated, and national trade policies were steadily yielding to the powerful influence of multilateral trade agreements like GATT.

Regardless of the wisdom of such developments, it is truly remarkable how many of Friedman's ideas had become part of the economic landscape by 1980. In most cases, the evolution of these changes had less to do with Friedman and his arguments than with the general drift of economic history. Floating exchange rates were introduced in 1973 because there was no agreement on a new set of fixed rates and the old rates were no longer enforceable. Under the new floating exchange rates countries were relieved of most of their responsibility for intervening in foreign markets. Exchange controls and independent national trade policies peaked during World War II and have been in decline ever since. Their demise was accelerated by the United States's expansionary interests, IMF principles, multilateral agreements, and finally, floating rates. Macroeconomic policy remained a practical tool for exchange rate stabilization, but this was hardly a problem for Friedman, who encouraged this approach, especially when it involved restrictive monetary policies. In summary, Friedman's vision of floating exchange rates was nearly complete by 1980.

There was, however, one element that had not fallen into place and continued to prevent floating from becoming free floating. Countries continued to intervene in markets by buying or selling their currencies in order to manipulate its values. Free floating would never actually take place until the central banks and treasuries curtailed the use of official reserves for stabilization efforts. As scholars have observed, countries continued to use official reserves for intervention as frequently after the introduction of floating rates in March 1973 as before.[8] Rather than free floating, the world had adopted managed exchange rates, what became known as *dirty floating*.

FEAR OF FLOATING

While countries may intervene in currency markets for any number of reasons, there are two that are warranted by economic principles. Both reasons are due to flaws in currency markets, one in the current account and one in the capital account. To illustrate the first flaw, consider what happens when there is an excess demand for dollars. In the market for anything else, an excess demand creates pressure for prices to rise. This market is no exception and one could reliably anticipate an increase in the value of the dollar relative to other currencies.

This is where the similarities end. A rising price for apples is expected to eliminate the excess demand as it encourages sellers to sell more and at the same time discourages buyers from buying as much. The immediate response in currency markets can be quite different, in fact, even the opposite. *The rising price of the dollar means that in order to buy the same mix of imports as before, Americans can spend even fewer dollars.* Rather than increasing the supply of dollars, the rising exchange rate (stronger dollar) actually causes the supply to decrease, making the problem even worse. Rather than a small excess demand for dollars, there is now a large excess demand. As a result, the dollar will continue to rise higher than it should creating a problem known as *overshooting*.

There is a solution to the problem but it is generally late in coming. The solution starts when Americans realize that the strong dollar has lowered the effective price of imports. As they gradually switch to foreign-made alternatives, the supply of dollars in currency markets increases. At the same time foreigners, recognizing that U.S. exports are relatively expensive, gradually buy fewer U.S. goods, thus decreasing their demand for dollars. As these responses gradually take effect, the value of the dollar will eventually fall, but all of this can take an additional year or two. In this market there is a clear danger that the dollar will initially overshoot its long-term rate, bouncing back later like a bad shock absorber.

One way to avoid this problem is with government intervention. By carefully timing its sale and purchases of dollars, the Treasury can manipulate the dollar's trajectory and prevent overshooting. A successful intervention would cause the dollar to go up like an elevator rather than a roller coaster. This is one of the reasons why many economists believe that government intervention in currency markets is essential.

The other reason for intervention has to do with speculators in the capital market. A temporary excess demand in the capital market is likely to lead to an increase in the value of the dollar. Again, this is to be expected in any market. The problem occurs when investors speculate that the rising trend will continue. They will then buy even more dollars which, by its very act, pushes the value of the dollar up. In any speculative market a simple expectation that a price will rise is often sufficient to make it rise. What investors merely expect to happen then becomes reality. In this market, it does not take long for a small appreciation to snowball into a full-scale speculative bubble. What should have been a small increase in the dollar can turn into a major appreciation. This phenomenon has been called the *snowball effect*. Once again, astute government intervention can nip this problem in the bud with correctly timed intervention.

The fact that prices change rather quickly on currency exchanges acts like an immense magnet, attracting investors from around the world. The sums of money are sufficiently formidable to dwarf all other forms of gambling, legal and otherwise. Estimates are that up to a trillion dollars worth of currency are exchanged in modern currency markets on a daily basis. At this rate, the amount traded in only two weeks exceeds the value of all goods and services produced in the United States in a year! The scale of speculation that occurs in this market is overwhelming.

By itself either overshooting or the snowball effect is quite capable of creating chaos, but because the two markets are intertwined, the potential for chaos is magnified. For example, a small appreciation in the dollar may be exaggerated by overshooting and then exaggerated even more by speculators through the snowball effect. These flaws in currency markets are the major reasons for government intervention and the reluctance to experiment with free floating.

Even Friedman clearly understood and appreciated the dangers of these problems. In regard to exchange rate changes, he observed that "the actual path of adjustment may involve repeated overshooting and undershooting of the final position, giving rise to a series of cycles around it or to a variety of other patterns."[9] Friedman was also well aware of the opposing view that "the foreign-exchange market is not nearly so perfect," nor is "the foresight of speculators so good."[10] It might be expected that such clear deficiencies in foreign exchange markets would warrant some form of government intervention. However, Friedman did not earn a reputation as a champion of free markets by conceding so easily.

Instead, Friedman invented a scenario of how currency markets operated. He began by acknowledging that overshooting is a real phenomenon that tends to exaggerate exchange rate changes. However, he insisted that the problem could be offset, not by government intervention but by speculators. The catch was that this worked only if speculators were blessed with perfect foresight and understanding. It is true that if speculators had perfect foresight and understanding both overshooting and the snowball effect would be avoided, but it is also true that speculators would never lose money. The problem with preposterous assumptions is that they often lead to preposterous conclusions. One of these conclusions is that speculators never lose money; the other is that overshooting and the snowball effect are not real problems. Friedman seemed to have realized how far he had strayed from reality and attemped to excuse himself by claiming that, "We are here entering into an area of economics about which we know very little."[11]

It may seem unbelievable that his argument could constitute the theoretical rationale for a major international experiment. Nevertheless, it did. It was on the basis of this scenario that Friedman was able to conclude, "it seems to me undesirable for a country to engage in transactions on the exchange market for the purpose of affecting the rate of exchange."[12] It was his support that opened the door for free floating.

THE FREE-FLOATING HYPOTHESIS

What precisely do free-floaters claim? In the absence of government intervention, world financial markets should be more stable. The incidence of speculative bubbles or currency crises should diminish with the free and unimpeded movement of exchange rates. Many of the problems Friedman discussed in currency markets were related to governments attempting to preserve an exchange rate against the will of the market. Free floating would make these kinds of crises impossible. Furthermore, without the interference of national governments, speculators should be free to work their magic and impart additional stability on the markets. While exchange rates would still respond to underlying economic forces, wasteful and unnecessary changes in exchange rates would be avoided.

These hypotheses can be summarized as follows:

1. Free floating should eliminate any unnecessary movement in the exchange rate, resulting in a more stable currency; and

2. Under free floating, the chances of a speculative bubble (or the opposite: a run on a currency) should diminish.

Opponents of course would expect just the opposite. They would expect that overshooting in the current account and snowball effects in the capital account would tend to magnify any small movement in the exchange rate. Consequently, under free floating it should be even more likely that the currency will explode into a speculative bubble or degenerate into panic selling.

Up until 1981 no real experiments in free floating had been conducted since governments had never relinquished their right to intervene. Free floating, up to that point, was little more than a theory outlined in Friedman's 1953 essay. This is approximately where the debate stood prior to the great experiment in free floating, which commenced in 1981.

7

Global Shock Waves

By themselves, the monetarist and supply-side experiments of the 1980s were destined to affect U.S. economic relations with the rest of the world. Interest rates and budget deficits cannot be detonated without expecting some fallout on foreign investment and trade. Any hope that these international effects would be small and inconsequential was lost on May 5, 1981, when the U.S. Treasury announced a new policy with regard to the dollar. The Treasury decided to limit its intervention in currency markets to only rare "disorderly conditions," a policy that they claimed had been in place since February. Thus began the free-floating experiment of the 1980s. The value of the dollar would no longer be determined by civil servants in central banks and national treasuries, but by the free and unfettered market!

One of the more remarkable aspects of this experiment was its uncelebrated beginning, attributable no doubt to the widespread ignorance of foreign currency markets. The Treasury's announcement of its new commitment to nonintervention was buried on page 13 of the *New York Times* Business Section. The editors apparently gained a greater appreciation for the significance of Treasury intervention during the four years that the policy was in place because the end of the experiment was reported on the front page with several accompanying stories. A recklessly overvalued dollar and record trade deficits had forced many people, including *New York Times* editors, to come to grips with the uninviting world of foreign exchange.

The experiment was formally launched in a statement delivered to the Joint Economic Committee of Congress by Beryl Sprinkel, then under secretary of the Treasury for Monetary Affairs. When asked what the new policy meant, Sprinkel answered, "it means that when I work in the office, the markets will take care of the exchange rate and not the Treasury and the Federal Reserve." Why the change? Sprinkel claimed that "significant and frequent intervention by governments assumes that a relatively few officials know better where exchange rates should be than a large number of decision-makers in the market."[1]

Even Sprinkel recognized that government intervention would be required during extraordinary circumstances. One had already occurred prior to his announcement. On March 30, 1981, a gunman shot and wounded President Reagan and scared investors into selling dollars. At the time the United States spent $80 million buying back dollars to reassure jittery investors. This was offered as one of those few extraordinary events that warranted intervention.

Demand for the dollar was climbing at the beginning of 1981 because relatively higher U.S. interest rates were attracting funds from around the world. Furthermore, the recession in the United States meant that Americans were buying fewer imports so that the supply of dollars was shrinking. The combination of these events caused an excess demand for dollars. As soon as the Reagan administration came into office, however, the U.S. Treasury effectively terminated any effort to counteract this imbalance. The free-floating experiment had begun.

FREE FLOATERS IN THE U.S. TREASURY

All of this might have been different if Donald Regan had not been appointed U.S. Treasury secretary. Within the U.S. government, the Treasury determines the extent of government intervention in currency markets, although it is the New York Fed that actually conducts the business of buying and selling dollars. Therefore, as Treasury secretary, Regan was in an ideal position to alter the exchange rate policy of the U.S. government.

Still, there was no prior indication that the new secretary had any desire to experiment with international exchange rates. Donald Regan's career as a Wall Street banker began when he joined Merrill Lynch at the end of World War II and continued until 1980 when he became chairman of the company. During his tenure he had established himself as an adept manager and capable administrator, credited with transforming Merrill Lynch into a widely diversified financial business. Where it had once concentrated on its brokerage business, by 1980 Merrill Lynch was involved in investments, commercial banking, real estate, consumer lending, and credit cards.

Donald Regan's banking accomplishments were far more familiar than his economic ideas. After all, he had a degree in English, not economics, from Harvard. The *New York Times* noted that he was perceived by fellow bankers "more as a manager and administrator than as a policy analyst. Indeed . . . he has not been outspoken on economic policy issues."[2] Certainly Regan had been exposed to international financial markets through subsidiaries, Merrill Lynch International Bank, Ltd. and Merrill Lynch International Inc. This exposure was not from the perspective of a government official attempting to stabilize the currency, but from the perspective of an international banker attempting to profit on fluctuations in exchange rates. While no one predicted the change in policy at the Treasury, it could hardly have been a surprise that a Wall Street banker would be open to the idea of turning responsibility for the dollar over to private bankers and currency traders.

There was no such uncertainty surrounding the economic views of another Treasury official, Beryl Sprinkel, under secretary for Monetary Affairs. Sprinkel, who came to be identified with the policy of nonintervention, was a product of Milton Friedman's monetarist school. In fact, before becoming chief economist for Harris Trust and Savings Bank in Chicago, Sprinkel had earned a Ph.D. in economics and finance from the University of Chicago, where he also taught for a brief time. While some may say that the Economics Department at the University of Chicago was closely associated with the theories of its most famous professor, Milton Friedman, a less generous observer could describe it as a doctrinaire program that demanded strict adherence to monetarist dogma. In either case, Sprinkel's monetarism was not difficult to trace, nor was his commitment to another Friedman principle, free-floating exchange rates. The Treasury's interest in free floating had essentially developed overnight with the appointment of Don Regan as Secretary and Beryl Sprinkel as his high-ranking assistant.

Conditions in currency markets can change rapidly, requiring particularly astute civil servants if intervention is to proceed smoothly. Between 1976 and 1979 there was downward pressure on the dollar because the U.S. economy was temporarily growing faster than economies in the rest of the world. This meant that the United States would be demanding relatively more imports, in effect, supplying more dollars.[3] An excess supply of dollars like this tends to push its value lower relative to other currencies. While the U.S. Treasury stepped aside to let this happen, foreign banks prevented a speculative rout by buying more than $30 billion a year in 1977 and 1978. This effort by central banks allowed the dollar to drift gently downward rather than follow a steep descent.

By 1980, conditions had almost entirely reversed. Growth had declined in the United States, which now lagged well behind the rest of the world, especially our European trading partners. With relatively strong demand for U.S. exports the dollar was poised to rise. Furthermore, the monetarist experiment was beginning to take effect in the United States and U.S. interest rates were rising rapidly. At first, foreign countries responded by increasing their own rates. Eventually though, it became apparent that the Federal Reserve's resolve to eradicate all signs of inflation far exceeded that of its foreign counterparts. As a consequence, U.S. interest rates surged ahead of foreign rates. Foreign investors, always attuned to a higher return, redirected their investments to the United States, giving the dollar an additional boost.

In order to offset this upward pressure on the dollar, the Carter administration intervened with the largest sale of dollars since exchange rates had been permitted to float. In this case, intervention successfully withstood the upward pressure on the dollar. According to the official, inflation-corrected index, the dollar increased a mere 2 percent. The actual index is based on the value of the dollar in terms of all major currencies with the value in 1973 arbitrarily set at 100. This index rose from 83.2 in 1979 to 84.9 in 1980. In January of the following year, 1981, control of the U.S. Treasury was passed to President Reagan's appointees.

SET ADRIFT

In May 1981, Beryl Sprinkel of the Treasury made his fateful announcement about the new policy of nonintervention. While the Fed had stepped in immediately following the shooting of President Reagan in March, the action was quickly overshadowed by the general absence of active trading by the United States during the remainder of the year.

Also in 1981, interest rates in the United States reached record levels—far higher than the rest of the world—fostering an influx of foreign investment and raising the demand for dollars. At the same time, the U.S. economy experienced a weak recovery and economic growth fell below that of the rest of the world. This depressed the demand for imports and reduced the supply of dollars. Markets were rapidly acquiring a large excess demand for dollars. If the Treasury had wished to intervene, this was their opportunity. They could have attempted to stabilize the dollar by continuing the dollar sales started by the Carter administration, but they did not. As a consequence, the index representing the value of the dollar relative to other currencies shot up from 84.9 in 1980 to 100.9 in 1981, a large enough increase to capture the attention of all money dealers.

Currency markets are uniquely comprised of many diverse traders. Some buy and sell currency to conduct international trade, but in fact the amount necessary for these transactions is probably not much more than 5 percent of the total currency being traded. Another group are the multinational corporations that exchange currency to conduct their foreign operations and purchase foreign resources and capital. A third group are the financial investors who move their money in search of the best return for a given risk. And finally there are the speculators, the ones who buy currencies they expect to appreciate and sell those that they expect to depreciate. This final class of investors are not finely distinguished from those with legitimate trade or investment objectives since any regular participant in foreign exchange markets is likely to speculate to some extent.

The fact that speculators can profit on even a brief change in exchange encourages them to act swiftly. It is a fact that speculators can quickly overwhelm a foreign exchange market, and that they are rewarded when a majority of them act on the same hunch. If most speculators expect the dollar to increase, their purchases alone may be sufficient to convert this expectation into a reality. Speculators are unfortunately rewarded for what amounts to nothing more than reckless behavior that threatens to destabilize the international economy.

Currency markets in 1981 were attractive to speculators. Relatively higher interest rates and slower growth in the United States created pressure for dollar appreciation. In the past, speculators had to weigh the implications of these strong predictors against the likelihood of government intervention. With government intervention temporarily sidelined, the smart money began betting on a rising dollar, thus augmenting the demand for the dollar and amplifying its appreciation.

The following year, 1982, brought some relief as the monetarist experiment was terminated late in the year. However, as U.S. interest rates came down, so did those in the rest of the world. Furthermore, the U.S. economy sank back into a serious recession. Once again, relatively higher interest rates in the United States and stronger economic activity abroad combined to create ideal conditions for further dollar appreciation.

Twice during 1982 a question was raised as to whether or not the Treasury was reconsidering its noninterventionist position. First in June, Secretary Regan announced that the Treasury had intervened to smooth out what it considered to be "erratic markets."[4] This was in the aftermath of a devaluation of the French and Italian currency relative to the German mark. While some suspected that the Treasury may have begun to abandon its commitment to nonintervention, Regan insisted that its behavior was entirely consistent with the policy of intervening only in the occasionally disorderly market.

A second lapse was reported in December 1982 by the Treasury that claimed to have intervened four times between August and October.[5] This time, analysts were much more confident that a fundamental change had taken place at the Treasury. The actions were considered a "political defeat" for Beryl Sprinkel whose influence was thought to have all but disappeared.[6] Such pronouncements were premature. The Treasury continued to insist that no policy change had occurred, and it reiterated that "market forces must determine foreign-exchange rates."

As it turned out, each of these interventions was rather insignificant; the sale of dollars that year was not particularly different from the year before, and on both occasions sales were less than those during Carter's final year. The Treasury seemed to be doing very little to arrest the increase in the dollar whose index continued to rise from 100.9 in 1981 to 111.8 in 1982. The dollar gains in 1981 and 1982 were the two largest since the dollar began to float in 1973. The upward trend became firmly established in 1983 when it jumped to 117.3.

Nonintervention began to spread. Not only did the United States fail to increase the sale of dollars, but other countries held back as well. They were apparently unwilling to intervene without support from the United States, which steadfastly refused to budge. The U.S. exchange rate experiment had spread to the rest of the world.

In addition to cooling speculation, another feature of government intervention was probably not fully appreciated by the Reagan Treasury. As mentioned earlier, every currency market is comprised of two very different types of exchanges. There are those who are purchasing currency to conduct the business of international trade, and those who are using it to finance some form of investment or speculation. When the government acts to stabilize a currency it has the effect of insulating these two types of dealers from each other.

Take 1982 as an example. In that year, there was considerable excess demand for dollars on the investment side of the market (capital account) because of the relatively higher interest rates in the United States. The trade side of the market (current account) was hardly prepared to provide additional dollars. In fact with the severe recession, U.S. import demand was depressed and accordingly, so was the supply of dollars. If the government had stepped in and provided dollars to meet the excess demand on the investment side, the value of the dollar in all likelihood would have experienced much less change. Yet without this emergency supply, the dollar was rapidly bid up, a phenomenon that unavoidably spilled over into the trade side of the market.

The fact that foreigners must buy dollars before they can buy U.S. products is often underappreciated. Foreigners can be deterred if the price of U.S. exports is high or if the value of the dollar is high. What took place at this time was that investors bid up the price of the dollar which, as a side-effect, made U.S. exports more expensive to foreigners. Responding as consumers anywhere would, foreigners gradually scaled back their consumption of products made in the United States, creating severe problems for many U.S. businesses, especially manufacturers and farmers.

The neutrality pledge taken by the U.S. Treasury made all this possible. Since it no longer bought and sold dollars to stabilize the exchange rate, the wall between the trade side and investment side of the currency market was effectively broken. It was now possible for investors to effectively outbid traders for dollars, allowing more foreign investment in the United States at the expense of reduced exports.

The trade effects of the high dollar were first evident in 1982. Following a sharp increase in the dollar, U.S. merchandise exports to the rest of the world fell 11 percent in 1982. Much of this could be blamed on the increase in the dollar, although economic growth did slow down for U.S. trading partners. The same could not be said of 1983 when growth abroad rebounded, but U.S. exports fell an additional 4 percent.[7] It became increasingly apparent that the strong dollar was choking off the sale of U.S. exports. This was happening despite an economic expansion abroad, which would normally benefit U.S. exporters. The exchange rate experiment was starting to do more than pinch, it was squeezing U.S. foreign sales and jobs.

While the rising dollar made U.S. exports more expensive, it also made foreign imports cheaper to U.S. consumers. A strong dollar can buy relatively more foreign currency, which tends to make all imports cheaper. This was not immediately evident in 1982 because the deep recession in the United States depressed demand for everything, including imports. But by 1983, merchandise imports rebounded a strong 8.5 percent and an additional 24 percent in 1984.[8] Americans would have bought more imports in any case due to the economic recovery, but the strong dollar made imports even more attractive.

The combination of weak exports and strong imports caused the trade deficit to expand and contributed to a significant loss of jobs in the United States. Not only were foreigners buying fewer products made in the United States, but U.S. consumers were increasingly passing over U.S. products for foreign ones.

By 1984, the U.S. trade deficit for goods and services had soared to a record $109 billion. A careful study released early in 1985 by Data Resources Inc., a prominent economic forecaster, claimed that appreciation of the dollar and associated trade deficits had cost the nation 2 million jobs, 75 percent of which were in manufacturing. The trade imbalance therefore accounted for approximately a fourth of all unemployment existing in 1984. Particularly hard hit were those who manufactured leather products, textiles, apparel, chemicals, rubber, and plastic. Jobs were lost as export markets dried up for some U.S. firms and others lost markets to burgeoning imports. Some companies, like E. I. Du Pont, found they were better off shutting down U.S. facilities—which the overvalued dollar had made uncompetitive—and shifting production to existing or even new facilities abroad.[9]

The upward trend in the dollar continued and the index hit 128.8 in 1984. By then the dollar was a phenomenal 44 percentage points higher than it had been in 1980. What had begun as a simple experiment, led by a monetarist zealot in the Treasury, was beginning to have profound impacts on the United States and world economies. Things were rapidly getting out of hand.

Throughout all of this, the Treasury secretary remained remarkably unperturbed. In 1982 he reiterated his opposition to intervention except during times of crisis. He maintained, "Intervention can never prevent the long-range course of the relationships among international currencies."[10] In an interview in 1983, he conceded that while a cheaper dollar would help U.S. exports, it "doesn't mean we're going to do anything about it."[11]

WARNING SIGNS

Criticism of the Treasury was beginning to mount, and the belief that the dollar was fundamentally overvalued gained wider and wider credence. In response, the Secretary struck back with an argument that he would use repeatedly in 1983 and 1984: the dollar was strong simply because foreign investors had immense confidence in the U.S. economy. According to this view, the strong dollar was little more than a vote of confidence by the international business community. The American economy, he insisted, had become an "exceptionally attractive investment" opportunity under President Reagan's leadership.[12] The dollar was not overvalued in his view because in an era of floating exchange rates, it made little sense to talk about the "true" value as distinct from market rates. Currency had only one value, and that was what it could command on the open market.

In a different time under different circumstances, these arguments may have appeared far less ludicrous than they did in 1985. After all, the dollar was on an upward trajectory unparalleled in modern history. On its way up, it was pulling U.S. imports to record heights and simultaneously sinking U.S. exports. Even staunch conservative allies in the Reagan administration were having difficulty swallowing the Treasury's reassurances. Paul Volcker, at the helm of the Federal Reserve Board, politely pointed out that "responsible officials do have an obligation to ask to what extent we can work more effectively to dampen extreme exchange rate swings that, by common agreement, seem far out of keeping with underlying needs and trends." He claimed to personally favor limited intervention when "exchange rates seem clearly wrong."[13]

The Council of Economic Advisors, under the direction of Martin Feldstein, was equally concerned about "wrong" rates. In the Council's 1984 *Economic Report of the President,* the dollar was estimated to be "about 32 percent above its long-run real value" based on the prevailing interest rate differentials then existing between the United States and its trading partners.[14]

The alarm was also sounding in corporate boardrooms and editorial offices. A spokesperson for Caterpillar Tractor Company complained, "Over the last few years we have lost close to $1 billion, and partly that has been because of the strong dollar."[15] A *New York Times* editorial lamented, "The strong dollar registers the failure of the industrial nations to coordinate their economic policies. The longer the dollar flies high, the greater the risk of an international economic collapse."[16] On the one hand the greatly inflated dollar was clearly depressing the foreign sales of "farmers and other efficient American producers" and at the same time fostering a veritable import explosion.

In all of this discussion there was more than a little confusion over where to place the blame. Relatively high interest rates in the United States were undoubtedly part of the problem. In some circles, it became popular to attribute this phenomenon to the large federal budget deficit. The Council of Economic Advisors suggested that reducing the size of the deficit would lower real interest rates and thereby lower "the real value of the dollar."[17] Paul Volcker at the Fed was much more adamant, "The plain logic of the situation to me and most economists was to reduce the budget deficit."[18] According to Volcker, Reagan's tax cuts had created a "built-in deficit" that kept "interest rates higher than they would otherwise be, a point that seemed self-evident to most of us, although it was denied by some enthusiastic Treasury supply-siders."[19]

It should be pointed out that Volcker's attack on the budget deficit at this time could easily be interpreted as self-serving. If the budget deficit could be blamed for relatively high interest rates, then perhaps the Fed's own culpability could be overlooked. Tight money and high interest rates were essential ingredients in the Fed's resolute crusade against inflation. The fact that the Fed's chairman would blame high interest rates on the budget deficit—or anything else for that matter—was better politics than it was economics.

It was seldom suggested during this time that the dollar could have been careening off the map simply because the Treasury was experimenting by sitting on its hands. The Treasury seemed to successfully avoid criticism through its insistence that it was incapable of controlling the dollar. Political critics are more accustomed to challenging political leaders on their undeliverable promises than on their confessions of helplessness. If the Treasury claimed to be incapable of deflating the dollar, then who was to say otherwise.

Insiders, however, with a sound grasp of the fundamentals of international finance, were not fooled by the Treasury's excuses. According to Paul Volcker, overtures by Japanese and European officials requesting the United States to join them in selling dollars and ending the speculative bubble were "rejected by the Treasury as a matter of principle." The administration "simply didn't seem to care."[20]

For all the pain created by the dollar boom, no one believed that it could go on indefinitely. Real anxiety was reserved for the dollar bust, which was almost certain to follow the boom. Paul Volcker, in reflecting on those times, claimed that "Sooner or later . . . there would be a sickening fall in the dollar, undermining confidence." The fear was perfectly rational; if the appreciation of the dollar was based on little more than a small disparity in interest rates and speculation, then what was to hold it up? According to a *New York Times* editorial, the "press of a few telex buttons" is all it would take to send the dollar crashing, causing tens of billions of dollars to "desert the American economy."

The higher the dollar climbed, the more concern grew about its eventual collapse. There was the equally disturbing possibility that the Treasury, which had stubbornly refused to do anything about the dollar's advance, would do nothing about its decline, almost guaranteeing a free fall of epic proportions. It was probably this fear more than the plight of American farmers and industrial workers that brought an end to the Treasury's experiment in free floating.

THE RESCUE OPERATION

The official explanation for the end of the experiment, dutifully conveyed by the press, was that the Reagan administration felt compelled to do something to forestall protectionist measures reported to be gaining momentum in Congress. There may be some truth in this. It is worth remembering, however, that standing between Congress and the application of protectionist policies was President Reagan's veto which, in all likelihood, would have torpedoed such legislation. What is certain is that it was easier for a Treasury official to attribute the policy reversal to a concern for protectionist Democrats than a fear that the dollar would eventually collapse, culminating in an unprecedented and possibly perilous free fall.

The beginning of the end of the experiment was marked by the removal of Donald Regan from the Treasury on January 8, 1985, shortly after President Reagan began his second term. The action was carried out by a mysterious job swap between Regan and James Baker III, who was then chief of staff at the White House. According to the press releases, James Baker had always been itching for a cabinet level position and Regan was attracted by the power of the White House. Other than these pedestrian motives, commentators were at a loss to account for such a curious substitution. In addition to reporting the official rationale, the press suggested that Baker was needed to assist the president's tax reform and negotiate budget reductions with Congress while Regan would in all probability exert discipline and order on the White House staff.[21] Absent was the simple observation that Donald Regan's experiment in free-floating exchange rates had profoundly distorted international finance to the point where many observers foresaw economic catastrophe.

On February 21, 1985, the purge of Treasury experimenters was completed when Beryl Sprinkel was offered the chairmanship of the Council of Economic Advisors. His appointment was sponsored by his one-time boss and loyal supporter, Don Regan.[22] Volcker had described Sprinkel as the man who "had stonewalled exchange market intervention and was cool toward most other forms of active international coordination."[23]

Changing personnel was an important first step toward dismantling the experiment but significant challenges remained. In early 1985, the dollar index was hovering near 144. Could the new Treasury pop the speculative bubble and still catch the dollar before it fell through the floor? If they had as little control over the dollar as Donald Regan had insisted, their efforts would fail.

Shortly after he was sworn in at the Treasury, Baker began to put plans into place to reverse the policies of the previous four years. His first step was to reopen discussion with the other Group of Five countries (G-5)—Germany, Japan, France, and Britain—about bringing the dollar down.[24] With a green light for intervention, foreign central banks began a massive sell-off of dollars in early 1985. After increasing their dollar reserves by almost $7 billion during the fourth quarter of 1984—Donald Regan's final quarter as Treasury chief—the world's central banks turned around and sold $11 billion during the first quarter of 1985. Not surprisingly, the dollar responded and began to fall. Between the first and second quarters of 1985 the dollar fell from 144 to 137.

Up to this point the U.S. Treasury was careful not to disclose, at least publicly, that it had revoked its predecessor's policy of nonintervention. Furthermore, it would have been impossible to discern the policy reversal from Treasury records since most of the intervention that took place during these initial months was by foreign central banks. Apparently unwilling to publicize its break with past policy, the Treasury instead offered quiet encouragement to foreign finance ministers to intervene on behalf of the United States. This was essentially Volcker's impression, claiming that "Upon taking office, they [Baker, and his new deputy secretary, Richard Darman] readily joined efforts already begun at the initiative of the other G-5 countries to restrain the appreciation of the dollar. A substantial slide down the exchange rate roller coaster began."[25]

Before concluding that government intervention shot down the dollar in 1985, two other important developments should be noted: the U.S. economy began to slow relative to the rest of the world and U.S. interest rates slipped, falling relative to other countries. A slower U.S. economy normally corresponds with fewer imports and a smaller supply of dollars, resulting in a tendency for the dollar to rise. Since the dollar actually decreased in this year, something else was evidently driving exchange markets.

By far the most common explanation for the dollar's decline in 1985 is the reduction in U.S. interest rates. While the interest rate is seldom unimportant, its significance in this instance is probably exaggerated. A proper accounting for the falling dollar in 1985 would give interest rates much less credit and give government intervention much more. Why is this? First, U.S. interest rates did come down relative to the rest of the world in 1985, but this was from a historic record set in 1984. Even after its decline, U.S. interest rates on government bonds in 1985 remained a solid 2.3 percentage points above the rest of the world. This margin was actually higher than those in 1981 and 1983 when relatively high interest rates were blamed for the *appreciating* dollar.[26] It may be worth asking how the same interest rate gap could have been too high in 1981, causing a dollar appreciation, but too low in 1985, causing a depreciation. The interest rate gap did not really close until 1986, and by then the dollar was well along on its descent.

Furthermore, the interest rate story presumes that relatively lower interest rates in the United States reduced the demand for dollars by foreign investors. However, statistics show that foreign private investment in the United States continued to grow in 1985 as did net portfolio investment, the one most sensitive to interest rate differentials. These facts do not fit particularly well with the conventional explanation and consequently have not received much attention.

Foreign government intervention in early 1985—with the quiet support of the U.S. Treasury—was instrumental in reversing the upward trajectory of the dollar. Yet by summer its descent began to falter. While the dollar continued to fall, the movement was described as "tentative." Most observers considered this plateau premature since the dollar had not fallen enough to offset the four-year boom. It was only 14 points lower than the peak in early 1985, but 30 points higher than it had been in 1980. Insiders began to question whether quiet support for intervention by the U.S. Treasury was enough. When it was decided that it was not, Baker organized a top level meeting of finance ministers from Japan, Germany, Britain, and France as a platform to publicly launch the new interventionist policies of the U.S. Treasury. The "Plaza Agreement," named after the New York hotel where it was held, marked the official end of the exchange rate experiment, although it had informally ended in January with the departure of Donald Regan from the Treasury.

The relatively short meeting at the Plaza Hotel on September 22, 1985, of the G-5 countries concerned little more than the wording of a nine-page statement, the content of which had been worked out well in advance. In the cautious rhetoric of financial diplomacy, the ministers signaled their collective interest in a cheaper dollar, one that would "better reflect fundamental economic conditions than has been the case." Still, the statement that caught the most attention was the claim that the participants "stand ready to cooperate more closely to encourage [a lower value of the dollar]."[27] Not only had the United States abandoned its noninterventionist policy of the previous four years, but it stood ready to coordinate its actions with other nations.

For four years the administration had insisted that government intervention was ineffective, but the market was not convinced. The day after the announcement, the dollar fell more than 4 percent, an event that one observer called "unbelievable." A dealer in New York for the Banco di Sicilia said, "When the markets opened, there was only one thing to do: Sell dollars." Understandably "people are very nervous about holding dollars," said a New York dealer for Barclays Bank.[28]

Although the Fed did not immediately disclose its foreign exchange transactions, they did report in December that in preceding months they had sold large quantities of dollars in "a visible manner." Total sales for August, September, and October for the United were $3.2 billion and $7 billion by other central banks, with most of that occurring after the September 22 meeting.[29] Many of these sales were carefully timed to stamp out any anomalies that threatened to interrupt the steady depreciation of the dollar.

The dollar slide was back on track, falling to 128.5 in the third quarter of 1985 and 118.4 in the fourth. It continued to fall through 1986 and slipped below 100 in the middle of that year. U.S. interest rates assisted its descent, returning to the world level. Well before this threshold was reached, however, central banks had switched over and were buying large amounts of dollars to break its fall. By 1988 the dollar index slipped below 90 where it remained for most of the next five years. The great dollar binge was over.

ASSESSING THE DAMAGE

While the dollar eventually returned to the same level as it began in 1980, other aspects of the U.S. economy were not so quick to recover. Many U.S. manufacturing firms discovered that it was easier to be squeezed out of a foreign market by a costly dollar than to reenter with a cheap one. Strong efforts were necessary to recover foreign distributors, customers, and market shares lost during the previous four years, and even these efforts were not always successful. Some of the U.S. firms that lost sales to imports were no longer in business.

The cheap dollar also failed to automatically reduce imports. It is commonly understood that consumers develop strong buying habits and are inclined to simply pay higher import prices at first and only later seek alternatives from domestic producers. As a consequence, the initial effect of a falling dollar can make the trade deficit even worse, which is exactly what happened in 1985 and 1986.

The slow turnaround on imports was made even slower by many foreign producers who, rather than raise their dollar prices to reflect the relatively higher cost of their own currency, held dollar prices steady. They were, in essence, offsetting the depreciation of the dollar with a reduction in their own prices. The extent and duration of this phenomenon, what economists refer to as "limited pass-through," caught most analysts by surprise. It was clearly much more difficult to extricate foreign producers from U.S. markets with a cheap dollar after they had gotten a foothold in the market.

The wisdom of free floating or nonintervention was dealt a decisive blow by this experiment. By itself, the unsustainable appreciation of the dollar from 1981 to 1985 should have been enough to silence even the most stubborn believers. If this lesson was insufficient, however, the success of massive government intervention in 1985 should have sealed the case. As John Kenneth

Galbraith is fond of saying, only someone inclined to place belief above facts could disagree.

Not surprisingly, there was one notable voice of dissent. In an article in the *New York Times*, December 26, 1985, the father of free floating came to its defense. "Let Floating Rates Continue to Float" was the title of the essay in which Friedman defended the Treasury's experiment. In his opinion, "The finance ministers of the Group of Five major trading countries are behaving very unwisely by intervening in the market." What was surprising about this essay is that it lacked the usual superlatives that Friedman typically used to describe all private market functions. For example, he claimed that the "system of floating exchange rates was working" but conceded, "not perfectly." In another passage he confessed, "As someone who has always strongly favored floating exchange rates, I must admit that I did not anticipate the volatility in the foreign exchange markets that we've had." All mention of the wonderful benefits that floating exchange rates were supposed to offer was noticeably absent from the article. In their place was the bitter observation that "floating rates are the only game in town and will remain so for as long as anyone can see."[30]

The ultimate intervention by central banks was useful in discrediting another particularly specious belief—the one that insisted that the overvalued dollar was the exclusive fault of the large federal budget deficit. A year and a half after intervention and a year after U.S. interest rates returned to the world level, the dollar returned to its previous level of 1981. The large government deficit, on the other hand, showed little sign of abating, and in fact reached even greater heights in the 1990s without affecting exchange rates in the slightest. The causal relationship that ran from budget deficits to an overvalued dollar was, despite Paul Volcker's insistence, quietly and conveniently forgotten.

8

The Reckoning: A Decade of Economic Records

The purpose of all three major experiments being conducted during the 1980s was to improve the economic performance of the U.S. economy. Certain policy levers were pulled and certain consequences were predicted. Continuing to apply the scientific method to these historic experiments, the next step is to determine whether the predicted results actually occurred. There is probably little doubt by now that the experimenters' hypotheses were consistently wide of the mark. How far off, though, is the focus of the first part of this chapter.

It is true in science as well as economics that the more interesting aspects of experiments are often the unintentional side effects. It is the unusual or unexpected outcomes of an experiment that pique the imagination in search of better theories. During the economic experiments of the 1980s there was no shortage of side effects. In fact it is probably safe to say that the United States experienced more unusual economic events during this decade than at any other time except for the world wars and the Depression. In the 1980s interest rates, unemployment, the savings rate, government deficits, the value of the dollar, trade balances, foreign debt, mergers and acquisitions, the stock market and income distribution all careened wildly off course. To the average observer watching the economy set one record after another, it must have appeared as though we had sailed off into uncharted waters. In a sense, we had.

While there is no guarantee that all of these events were related to the three experiments, there is a good possibility that many of them were genuine side effects. After all, the experiments created major distortions in some parts of the economy, which could conceivably show up as distortions elsewhere. The second half of this chapter reviews some of these curious events that coincided with the three experiments.

Lurking behind the statistics in this chapter is the question of how all these events are related to the experiments. With this question, however, we risk getting ahead of ourselves. The careful accounting in this chapter of actual events is essential preparation for the question of why all this happened.

EXPERIMENTAL ERROR

Taxes in the supply-side world are more than unpopular, they are destructive. The massive tax reduction in 1981 was specifically designed to alleviate this burden, especially as it impacted high income taxpayers. Did this policy—estimated to cost $750 billion over 5 years—produce the economic magic it promised? Did it stimulate savings and investment? Did national output and income boom? Was there a delayed, but observable increase in tax revenue despite lower tax rates? An affirmative answer could be given to any one of these questions, but not without sacrificing a considerable amount of intellectual integrity.

Let's start with the least controvertible evidence. Economists calculate an annual savings rate as a fraction of personal income; all other income is spent on some form of consumption. This measure, the *personal savings rate*, serves as the best indicator of the average degree of thrift being practiced by American families. In 1981, the year the supply-side tax bill was passed, the personal savings rate was a robust 8.8 percent. This may not have been as high as the rate in Japan, but by U.S. standards it was relatively high. It was certainly higher than the 1970s average of 7.8 percent and even higher than the 1960s average rate of 6.7 percent. Despite a legacy of a high capital gains taxes and allegedly "excessive" tax rates on the wealthy, U.S. families were saving at nearly record rates in 1981; they saved almost 9 cents out of every dollar earned!

The fact that the savings rate was clearly not "broken" did nothing to deter supply-siders from attempting to "fix" it. They were not going to let a relatively high savings deter them from their crusade. In 1981 they pushed through their reduction in capital gains taxes and tax relief for the rich to be phased in over the next three years. To ensure success, they introduced additional incentives to save through beneficial tax breaks on "individual retirement accounts."

The savings rate did change after 1981, but it did not increase, it fell. It slid to 8.6 percent in 1982, 6.8 percent in 1983, and rebounded to 8 percent in 1984 before collapsing to 6.4 percent in 1985. Four years and hundreds of billions of dollars later, Americans were saving less than 7 cents out of every dollar earned. While this did not look good for supply-siders, it looked even worse by the end of the decade when the savings rate slid into the 4 to 6 percent range where it remained from 1987 to 1994. In this range the savings rate was so low that, by itself, it qualified as a minor crisis.

Supply-siders could not have picked a worse time to promise an increase in the savings rate. The savings rate in 1981 was, by historical standards, quite high and more likely to go down than up. In its dramatic slide, the savings rate fell to the lowest level since 1947, a year in which Americans went on a consumption binge following World War II. Rationing and shortages during the war forced people to save more than they probably wanted to, but when the war was over, families compensated for excessive saving during the war with a little excessive spending after it was over. Nothing even remotely similar took place in the United States during the late 1980s, and yet the savings rate fell to its lowest level since 1947.

Savings plays a crucial role in supply-side theory. Without an increase in savings, there is unlikely to be an increase in investment; and without more investment, the new surge of economic growth is equally unlikely. Therefore, the failure of supply-side policies to increase savings essentially sealed the fate of supply-side theory. Without higher savings the chain reaction was broken, there would be no supply-side miracle.

The relationship between savings and investment qualifies as perhaps one of the ten great lessons of economics, which has earned it a place in every macroeconomic textbook of any repute. In the stripped down simplistic model of an economy without a government, international trade, or business savings, the only money left to fund investment is personal savings. In this small, hypothetical world, investment and savings are always equal. If this model accurately represented reality, then investment would be doomed to follow the same dismal course as personal savings. In the real world, however, there are more possibilities since investors can borrow from businesses or foreign investors when personal savings are insufficient. Business investors could actually increase investments even if personal savings fell by borrowing from foreign investors or the government. All things considered, business investment may not have been predestined to follow the same track as personal savings in the 1980s, and yet it did.

Once again supply-siders would have been hard pressed to have picked a less opportune moment to experiment. Rather than appearing to be a problem, business investment by historical standards was extraordinarily high. A particularly useful measure, called the investment rate, is equal to the share of the nation's total output, gross domestic product or GDP, dedicated to business investment, including equipment and buildings. In 1981, the investment rate of 13.5 percent was at a record level, much higher than the 11.2 percent average of the 1970s or even the 10.0 percent average of the 1960s. Out of every dollar of value produced, the nation was setting aside 13½ cents for investment—more than it had for at least 35 years! Supply-siders were not about to concede that President Carter—their political and philosophical nemesis—had left the nation with one of the highest investment rates since the last world war. Instead, supply-siders pushed ahead with their agenda, slashing corporate and individual income taxes for the wealthy.

Like savings, investment responded, but in the wrong direction. The investment rate slipped to 13.1 percent in 1982 and 11.7 percent in 1983 before rising slightly to 12.4 percent in 1984 and 1985. Thereafter, the investment rate continued to fall and never again rose above 12 percent. By 1992 the rate finally bottomed out at 9.4 percent, the lowest rate since 1963. It is difficult to imagine a supply-side revolution with declining savings and investment, but this is exactly what took place following the Reagan tax cuts beginning in 1981.

Why did savings and investment recede at this particular time? Was it because of the tax cuts? Was it related to some other reason or was it just another economic mystery? Discussion of these questions will have to wait until later chapters, but it is quite clear at this point the real world was not kind to supply-side economics.

Economic growth was another key feature in the supply-side promise, but what happened to it? Economic growth is commonly represented by changes in real GDP, that is, the total annual production of goods and services with appropriate account being taken for inflation. One way to gauge the effect of the Reagan tax cuts is to compare real economic growth for the years immediately following the tax cuts with those immediately preceding it. The only question is how many years to include. Three years would be a minimum since much of the tax cut was phased in over a three-year period, and one could expect at least two to three years before the full impact of the tax cut would be realized. It therefore seems reasonable to compare growth rates for five or six years before and after the 1981 tax cut.

The average growth in real GDP for the five years immediately following the 1981 tax cuts was 2.8 percent compared to 2.6 percent for the five years immediately preceding the cuts. The difference of .2 percent suggests that GDP did grow faster after the tax cut, but only a little faster. In fact it appears that real GDP grew only about $7 billion or $8 billion faster per year because of a $750 billion tax cut. If the time period is extended to 6 years, the effect of the tax cuts looks even worse since economic growth was higher *before* the tax cut than after. I suppose it is possible to argue that even 6 years is too short a time period to capture the full impact of the tax cuts. But if one extends the comparison to a full ten years, average growth rates were still higher before the tax cuts. It is difficult to find evidence of faster growth following the 1981 tax cut, much less the kind of growth required to actually raise tax revenue. On this score, supply-side economics failed again.

Recall that in early 1981 Stockman faced a dilemma. In order to project a balanced budget by the mid-1980s—a promise Ronald Reagan had made on the campaign trail—Stockman figured it was necessary to forecast average economic growth significantly higher than the 4 percent average attained during the 1950s and 1960s. By his calculations, even 5 percent growth appeared to fall short of the growth required to balance the federal budget. Yet to forecast average economic growth in excess of 5 percent, for example 6 or 7 percent, would risk public humiliation. As a dodge, Stockman and the other advisors instead chose to fudge the inflation numbers.

When actual average growth came in under 3 percent, the fate of the budget was sealed. Government revenue would not increase anywhere near enough to offset the huge tax cut. The result was a record expansion, or more accurately, an explosion in the budget deficit that soared from $79 billion in 1981, Reagan's first full year as president, to $128 billion in 1982 and $207 billion in 1983.[1] Not only were these the first 12 digit deficits in the history of the country, they were also an embarrassment for supply-side economists who had promised to close the deficit. This was a problem that time would not heal. During the next ten years, the deficits shrank during economic expansion and grew during economic contraction, but still averaged about $200 billion a year. Despite endless debate and negotiations, the budget deficit created during the first three years of Reagan's first term in office has outlasted the reign of many of the politicians and economists who were responsible for it.

The central feature of monetarism is the relationship between changes in the money supply and inflation. The two variables, money and inflation, have historically demonstrated a certain tendency to rise together, especially during episodes of hyperinflation. From this correlation, Milton Friedman worked out his famous monetarist slogan, "inflation is everywhere a monetary problem." That is, if there is inflation it must be caused by an excessive increase in the money supply, and if there is an excessive increase in the money supply, then there must be inflation.

The monetarist experiment from October 1979 to October 1982 was based on this simple principle. In an effort to smother the raging inflation of the time, Paul Volcker embarked on a radical experiment to limit growth in the money supply. Between 1979 and 1981 increases in M1, the narrow definition of money, grew at a steady average rate of 6.8 percent, down from 7.6 percent during the previous three years. Over the same time, M2, the broader definition of money, was growing at 8.9 percent compared to 10.7 percent in the previous three years.

These results during the first two years of the experiment were not especially promising. Despite a clear reduction in the money supply, the average inflation rate for all goods and services in the economy continued to ratchet up from 8.6 percent in 1979, to 9.5 percent in 1980, and finally 10.0 percent in 1981.[2] The results up to this point were unambiguous, lower growth in the money supply was associated with higher inflation. This was precisely the opposite of the monetarist hypothesis. The year 1982 was pivotal in that during this year, the economy collapsed into a major recession, putting more people out of work than at any time since the Great Depression. The inflation rate finally did come down, easing to 6.2 percent in 1982 before reaching the comfortable level of 4.1 percent in 1983. Slow monetary growth, advocated by the monetarists, failed to make any headway against inflation until 1982, at which point the economy imploded, bringing inflation down with it.

Although monetarism had performed poorly during the experiment, it was not bad enough for monetarists to concede defeat. They stubbornly insisted that their policies had been responsible for reducing inflation, even if it took three years and a major recession for their policies to actually work. Such ex post facto reasoning may be distasteful, but it is not uncommon among economists. The effectiveness of monetarism would no doubt have been the topic of another decade of academic debate if not for what happened next. Ensuing events demonstrated quite clearly that the money supply was not the exclusive source of inflation as monetarists had claimed.

It was in the fall of 1982 that the Fed officially abandoned the monetarist experiment. Torn between a morose economy with record unemployment and a rising money supply, the Fed chose to worry about unemployment. They permitted the money supply to increase for the rest of the year, and in fact, for the next four years. From 1983 to 1986, M1 rose rapidly at an average annual rate of 11.3 percent followed closely by M2, which experienced a 9.6 percent annual increase over the same period. The money supply was growing considerably faster than it had been during the monetarist experiment from 1979 to 1981. Based on this, monetarist theory predicted that the inflation rate should accelerate.

Monetarists objected as much to unstable increases in the money supply as to rapid increases. Either, they insisted, could cause inflation and economic instability. From 1983 to 1986 the money supply not only grew rapidly, it grew erratically. M1 increased only 6 percent in 1984 but screamed ahead at 16.8 percent in 1986. M2 growth was almost as volatile.[3] With the money supply growing rapidly and erratically, monetarists saw two flashing lights. The economy in their view was headed for certain inflation. The only problem was that there was none. In fact, between 1983 and 1986 the inflation rate fell from 4.1 percent to 2.6 percent, precisely the opposite of what monetarists had predicted.

It was this experience that created serious credibility problems for monetarists. The unique relationship between the money supply and inflation on which they had based their theory was not reliable. This simple historical event demonstrated that. If the money supply could increase rapidly without causing higher inflation, then money was not the unique source of inflation that monetarists had insisted it was for some thirty years. There are relatively few instances where an economic theory was as soundly defeated as monetarism was in the mid-1980s. Monetarists did not disappear of course, but monetarism languished.

Proponents of free floating offered one major justification for their policy—stability. International currency markets would be more stable, they argued, if governments would simply leave them alone. Every act of government intervention was, by definition, an attempt to alter the outcome of the market. Despite the known problems of overshooting and the snowball effect, free floaters insisted that the market was far better than the government at regulating and stabilizing international currency markets.

There should be no question that free floaters put a lot of faith in speculators. In fact, Friedman's theory, which validated free floating, included the extraordinary assumption that speculators are unerring and omniscient. As preposterous as this assumption may sound, it is no more so than assumptions underlying many contemporary economic theories where reality takes a back seat to simplicity. At any rate, speculators with perfect foresight would indeed provide great stability to the market. It is when their foresight fails that markets can erupt into chaos.

Was the value of the dollar more stable during the exchange rate experiment, which lasted from 1981 until 1985? A simple measure commonly employed to measure stability is a *standard deviation*. While it helps to know how a standard deviation is calculated in order to understand what it means, it is not absolutely necessary. At a minimum, you must know that the standard deviation represents something like the average movement in a series. The higher the standard deviation, the more it moves around and therefore, the less stable it is. If you compare the prices of various stocks over a period of time, the one with the highest standard deviation is the least stable. In order to compare the stability of the dollar at different times, the best, most direct method is to compare standard deviations.

The dollar began to float officially in 1973 and has continued to do so up to the present. Throughout this time, the U.S. Treasury, often with the cooperation of foreign treasuries or national banks, has intervened with the intention of stabilizing the value of the dollar. The only exception was the period from 1981 to 1985 when the exchange rate experiment temporarily introduced free floating. Official U.S. intervention in currency markets came to an abrupt halt during the experiment, a practice that was largely emulated abroad.

Between 1973 and 1980, the international value of the dollar, corrected for inflation, gradually receded from 99 to 85. During this period the standard deviation was 6.8, indicating a relatively stable currency. During the next seven-year period, from 1981 to 1988, the dollar rose rapidly from 101 to 132 before falling again to 88. These sharp movements produced a significantly higher standard deviation of 16.3. In this case it does not really matter how you divide up the time periods. The standard deviations are always larger when they cover the years of the exchange rate experiment between 1981 and 1985. Based on this simple comparison, it appears that free floating coincided with greater instability. This conclusion is backed up by looking at a comparable seven-year period from 1986 to 1993 when free floating was abandoned. At this time, the standard deviation fell to 6.2, about where it had been during the earlier period. There is no question that the dollar was far more volatile during the experiment with free floating than it has been at any other time since 1973. Critics of free floating never believed that it would result in a more stable currency, and based on this experiment, they were right. As they feared, the dollar was highly unstable during free floating.

A CONTRAST

There is quite a contrast between the 1980s experiments and the Keynesian experiments. Keynesian theory was tested twice, once during World War II and again during the Kennedy tax cuts in the early 1960s. In both cases budget deficits were increased, and although conventional economists feared economic collapse, Keynesians predicted economic expansion. Their theory predicted that larger deficits would increase economic growth. They were not disappointed. Economic growth during World War II was spectacular and unprecedented, even to the point of spilling over into inflation, another fully expected outcome. Economic growth during the early 1960s was less spectacular than during World War II, but it was perhaps even better for Keynesians because it was based on a calculated economic experiment.

If economic growth had been less than stellar during either of these two periods, Keynesian economists would have been forced to account for their failure. The fact that economic growth was so strong during both periods spared them this fate. Instead they could point to two remarkable successes. They won converts and credibility.

The fate for monetarists, supply-siders, and free-floaters was just the opposite. Having failed to produce the promised results, they were all forced to resort to excuses and rationalizations. Monetarists could still insist that their experiment had been abandoned prematurely. Supply-siders could blame the lack of economic growth on monetarists. And free-floaters could still insist that their experiment was foiled by external events. The mere fact that it was even necessary for them to resort to such rationalizations, however, meant that they started at a disadvantage. It is always more difficult to win a following for your theory when you spend most of your time explaining failures rather than recounting successes.

The economic performance of the economy during the 1980s may not have been good for monetarists, supply-siders, and free-floaters, but for others the effects were far more devastating. Small business owners, unskilled workers, farmers, exporters, and many others lost businesses and jobs during the course of these experiments.

Much of this trauma would have been avoided if the experiments had succeeded or at least not produced so many pernicious side effects. In a sense, it was the side effects that made the 1980s so devastating.

INTEREST RATES

Interest rates appeared to climb to their highest level in American history at the beginning of the 1980s; but which interest rate?

There are many different interest rates applying to everything from credit cards to passbook savings accounts. Each interest rate depends on many conditions but the two most obvious are the amount of risk and the amount of time the money is committed. This makes it difficult to talk about one rate except for the fact that all of these different interest rates tend to move in parallel over time. When interest rates drop on high risk loans they also tend to drop on low risk loans, and although long-term and short-term interest rates have been known to move in opposite directions, this tends to be the exception rather than the rule. This uniformity makes it possible to use one rate to illustrate historical trends for all interest rates.

A rate often used for this purpose is called the *prime interest rate*, the one charged by banks to their best corporate customers. For anyone else less credit worthy than the nation's largest corporations, the interest charge will generally exceed the prime rate. One advantage of using the prime rate to illustrate interest rate levels is that it can be traced back many decades, at least to 1929.

Prime interest rates started at 5.75 in 1929 and declined precipitately during the Depression. They hit a low of 1.5 percent in 1939 where they remained as a matter of public policy throughout World War II. In the postwar years the prime rate drifted up to 3 percent in the 1950s, 5 percent in the 1960s, and reached 8 percent in the 1970s. Up until then much of the upward drift was related to the generally rising inflation rates. Yet after 1979 the prime interest rate began to surge far more than could be explained by inflation. For three consecutive years, from 1979 to 1981, the prime interest rate set historical records. It hit 12.7 percent in 1979, followed by 15.3 in 1980 and 18.9 in 1981. Nothing like this had ever happened before. The previous record for the prime rate was set in 1974 when it was 10.8 percent. After 1981 the prime rate again began to drift down reaching 7 percent in 1994.

This record is the same whether you look at interest rates for long-term debt, short-term debt, government debt or private debt, The interest rate for 30-year U.S. Treasury securities peaked in 1981 at 13.5 percent as did three-month U.S. Treasury bills at 14.0 percent. Short-term private interest rates for commercial paper also peaked in 1981 at 14.8 percent. In the economics hall of fame, 1981 will be remembered as the year with the highest recorded interest rates.

TAX RECORDS

The Reagan tax cut of 1981 was billed as the largest tax cut in history, which in fact, it was. The initial estimate of $750 billion in forgone tax revenue over a five-year period was far greater than any in history. The Kennedy tax cuts of 1962 and 1964 only totaled $9.9 billion (or $30 billion measured in 1982 dollars). Even the famous Mellon tax cuts of the 1920s were only a few billion dollars.

It has also been said that the Reagan tax increase of 1982 was the largest tax increase in history. Although this tax hike pulled in more revenue than either the Vietnam surcharge of 1968 or the "windfall profits" tax of 1977, it was comparable in size to the social security tax increase of 1977. Estimates that the social security tax increase would increase revenue by $227 billion were remarkably close to the Reagan hike of $228 billion over five years. Measured in inflation-corrected dollars, the social security tax raised more money but over a longer period of time. Whether the Reagan tax increase was the largest in history depends on how it is measured. But no matter how it is measured, it will always be many times smaller than the Reagan tax cut that preceded it.[4]

UNEMPLOYMENT RATES

Measuring unemployment is not as easy as one might think. One problem is how to count people who are partially unemployed, that is, working less than they would like to or working at a level far below their capacity. Our national unemployment rate ignores these fine distinctions and counts every single underemployed person as fully employed. The old Soviet Union took advantage of a similar convention to make its unemployment rate look better than it actually was. They were able to report full employment only by conveniently ignoring rampant underemployment, which appears to have been no small problem in the Soviet economy. The unemployment statistics in the United States are similarly improved by ignoring underemployment.

There is also a question of how to exclude the voluntarily unemployed—those who could work, but have chosen not to. The deciding factor in the U.S. unemployment statistic is whether a person actively sought employment during the past four weeks. It is expected that a voluntarily unemployed person would not look for work and therefore would not be counted as unemployed. While a person could lie about this, the larger problem appears to be individuals who are available for work but do not look because they have at least temporarily given up. In many cases, these discouraged workers are no less unemployed just because they may have lost hope of finding work.

Despite all these weaknesses in the official unemployment rate, it has one redeeming factor: the method for collecting the data has hardly changed since 1940 when the Bureau of the Census conducted its first unemployment survey. The Reagan administration made a bold attempt to alter the statistic in 1982 by including the military, a fully employed group. As a result, the unemployment rate dropped slightly, maybe .2 percent. Economists frequently ignore even this modification by continuing to use the old civilian unemployment rate which remained consistent over time. The only other major change in the unemployment statistic took place in the 1990s when some of the survey questions were reworded, a change that did more to improve the quality of the measurement than to alter its meaning. Because the unemployment statistic has changed so little over the years, it is still useful for historical comparison.

The all-time unemployment record for the United States still lies with the Great Depression. At no time—at least since unemployment rates have been reliably calculated—have we even approached the 24.9 percent rate prevailing in 1933. After 1941, the economic devastation of the Depression was soon left behind. Unemployment averaged only 4.5 percent in the 1950s and 4.8 percent in the 1960s. The 1970s was a setback with the rate averaging 6.2 percent. As bad as the 1970s were, they could not compete with the 1980s. The unemployment rate averaged 7.3 percent during the 1980s and in 1982 hit a postwar record of 9.7 percent, exceeding the previous record set in 1975 of 8.5 percent. This meant that in 1982, nearly 11 million were out of work. It was a staggering waste of human talent and economic productivity.

In this century, unemployment has not risen higher than this very many times. In 1921, as the country demobilized from World War I, the economy sank into a deep recession and unemployment rates shot up to 11.7 percent, but fell rapidly over the next two years.[5] In contrast, unemployment rates after 1982 did not recede nearly as fast. Unemployment in 1983 was still 9.6 percent and in 1984, 7.5 percent. The year 1982 should be recognized for having the highest unemployment rate of the century except for the Depression and 1921.

FEDERAL BUDGET DEFICIT

There are many different ways to represent the actual size of the federal deficit, but for historical comparison only some of them make any sense. One could, for example, point out that the federal deficit in 1992 was the largest in the history of the United States at $291 billion. But for the sake of historical comparisons this is not quite fair since the dollar was worth less in 1992 than in any previous year in American history.

Recalculating deficits in 1987 dollars, called *real* deficits, allows for a more sensible comparison. Based on a comparison of real 1987 dollars, deficits reached record levels during three years of World War II—1943 through 1945. In 1987 dollars these deficits never fell below $350 billion. These deficits are impressive by this measure but even more impressive when we consider how much smaller the economy was in 1945 than it is today. One way to take this difference into account is to compare the deficit to gross domestic product. From 1943 to 1945, the deficit never fell below 22 percent of gross domestic product and hit an all-time record of 28 percent in 1943.

World War II was of course an extraordinary event as was World War I when the deficit hit 18 percent of gross national product and the Civil War when it was approximately 14 percent.[6] At most other times in American history the federal deficit has been relatively small with the exception of the 1980s. Between 1946 and 1994, the deficit exceeded 3 percent of GDP in only 15 years, 12 of them following the Reagan tax cut of 1981. The highest relative deficit of the postwar period occurred in 1983 when the deficit hit 6.1 percent of gross domestic product. In fact the four highest relative deficits during this period were recorded in the 1980s. The deficits then spilled over into the 1990s where the next highest budget shortfalls were recorded.

The deficits may have been larger during World War II, but they did not last as long. For the five years between 1941 and 1945 the government accumulated a total debt of $1.4 trillion (1987 dollars) by running large annual deficits. In just a few more years, the federal deficit generated a comparable amount of debt between

1982 and 1989. Since the deficits continued after 1989, the total amount of real debt accumulated during this period actually surpassed that of World War II. The actual deficits of the 1980s were not as great in individual years as those of World War II but over time they managed to accumulate more debt than at any other time in our nation's history.

VALUE OF THE DOLLAR

The dollar is one of the few economic topics that can signal a crisis when its value is exceptionally high or exceptionally low. In the 1980s the dollar was exceptionally high. What exactly does that mean? The value of anything is usually determined by the number of dollars it sells for. Similarly, the value of the dollar is determined by the amount of foreign money it exchanges for. The difficulty here is that there are as many different values of the dollar as there are foreign currencies. A dollar may be worth 100 Japanese yen or 1.5 German marks, but the only way to compare the value of the dollar over time is to take an average of all currencies, weighted by their importance in total trade with the United States. The resulting index is called the *trade-weighted nominal exchange rate*. By this convention, the value of the U.S. dollar measured in Canadian dollars is more important, as it should be, than say, in Salvadoran colones.

The value of a currency is also affected by inflation rates. When a country experiences a relatively high inflation rate, the purchasing power of its currency is adversely impacted leading to a loss of value in international currency markets. Because of this, it is often useful to adjust exchange rates for inflation. The measure that does this is called the *real exchange rate*.

Exchange rates have been accurately calculated since 1973. Going back any further is difficult because it includes years of fixed exchange rates and very different ways of handling money. Consequently the starting point for many of these comparisons is 1973.

Since 1973 the lowest value of the dollar was reached in 1980 in nominal value and in 1979 for the real value. In 1979 the real value of the dollar was 17 percent below its 1973 level. Much of this had to do with a second major run-up in oil prices and a strong expectation of rising inflation.

In the other direction, there was a clear explosion in the value of the dollar in the early 1980s, culminating in its highest value ever in 1985. Again, allowing for inflation, the value of the dollar was 32 percent higher in 1985 than in 1973. This is even more remarkable since the dollar had been drifting down since 1973 as the competitive advantage of the United States slipped.

It is safe to say that the dollar reached its highest value during the great exchange rate experiment. The remarkable strength of the dollar is even better represented by the exchange rate between the dollar and the British pound. Although the dollar had been gradually gaining ground against the pound for over a hundred years, its relative value peaked in 1985. In that year it cost as much as .77 pounds to buy a dollar, the highest price ever paid, or at least since 1879.

TRADE DEFICIT

It is easy to forget after more than a decade of trade deficits that they are a relatively recent problem. In fact, between 1896 and 1970 the United States consistently ran trade surpluses, exporting more than we imported. The largest trade surpluses were achieved during World War I and World War II.

In an even earlier period, from 1881 to 1895, the United States did run trade deficits. The largest one occurred in 1888 when the deficit rose as high as 1.9 percent of gross product. This, however, pales in comparison to modern deficits that peaked in 1987 at 3.1 percent of gross domestic product. In this year the United States imported $152 billion more in goods and services than it exported. This trade deficit, established in the wake of the 1980s economic experiments, is undeniably the largest for the entire period of reliable data from 1881 to the present.

FOREIGN DEBT

The concept of personal debt is not unfamiliar to many Americans who owe more money every year to banks and credit card companies. In these cases, individuals calculate their debt by adding up all the money they owe. As far as a measure of net indebtedness, however, this is not very useful. The problem is that it does not take into account an individual's ability to pay the debt.

It is quite possible, even likely, that a wealthy individual will owe more money than a poor one because it is so much easier for a rich person to establish a line of credit or borrow money from a bank. What makes a rich person rich is not the absence of debt but the accumulation of assets. A person who owes $50 million may still be rich if he or she has $500 million in savings deposited in a bank or owns $500 million in corporate stock. Wealth is more appropriately measured by net worth, which is the difference between assets and liabilities, what you own minus what you owe.

International debts for countries are calculated in much the same way as net worth only it is called net international investment or more simply, *foreign debt*. We begin by adding up the value of total foreign assets, ranging from property to government bonds, owned by Americans. This is the total share of the rest of the world owned by Americans. From this number is subtracted the total value of U.S. assets owned by foreigners to arrive at net international investment. The significance of this number, when it is calculated correctly, is that it indicates how dependent the United States is on foreign capital. When net international investment is positive, as it was most of the time prior to 1987, then the United States is essentially a net creditor or lender to the rest of the world. When it is negative, as it was after 1987, the United States is a net debtor.

The fact that the United States switched from being the world's largest net creditor prior to 1987 to the world's largest net debtor afterward made a brief splash in the media even though its precise meaning may never have been very clear. It was, in fact, true that the United States did become the world's largest debtor during the late 1980s. Foreigners, especially the Japanese, greatly expanded their ownership of U.S. economic assets between 1985 and 1992. By 1992, foreigners owned nearly $600 billion more of the United States than vice versa. The foreign debt was truly immense. It was also another dubious record for the United States in the 1980s.

STOCK MARKET BOOM

In its essential form, the stock market is nothing more than a venue for investors to buy and sell pieces of paper transferring legal ownership of corporations. Such an institution would scarcely attract the attention it now receives if not for the spectacle of billions of dollars changing hands at lightning speed. The fascination this creates is only enhanced by its nearly perfectly random nature. Scores of scholars, with the assistance of sophisticated computer programs, have reached the conclusion that the stock market is about as predictable as a pair of dice. The similarities between the stock market and the average gambling casino are not exaggerated.

Some economists pride themselves in seeing order in all this chaos. They insist that stock prices provide immediate and accurate information about the underlying profitability of corporations. However, even devotees of this point of view are regularly baffled by every turn in the market. Theorizing about the collective wisdom of the stock market is easy, but trying to prove it is another matter. The market seems to be driven more by what John Maynard Keynes referred to as "animal spirits" than by collective wisdom.

Since 1871 there have been only three great expansions in the stock market and perhaps four smaller ones. One way to measure these expansions is to use Standard and Poors' prices for 500 common stocks, corrected for inflation. By this measure, the largest expansion lasted 16 years and saw stock prices rise 338 percent. This was during the postwar years from 1949 to 1965. In another great expansion, the stock market soared 203 percent over seven years from 1922 to 1929.

This brings us to the next great expansion. During the 11 years from 1982 to 1993 the stock market expanded 152 percent. Real stock prices rose at an average rate of 8.8 percent a year throughout this period. Although the stock market expansion during the 1980s was not the largest on record, it was the second longest and the third largest. The stock market explosion that began in 1982 followed on the heels of the three economic experiments. That stock prices were somehow affected by the experiments is a possibility that is considered in a later chapter.

It is still a little early to conclude that the recent expansion is over. The torrid pace of stock price increases let up after 1993 and then surged again in 1995 and 1996. But what will happen when it is over? Following the big postwar expansion, real stock prices proceeded to fall steadily for ten years until they hit 42 percent of their 1965 level. The decline following 1929 was of course far more precipitous. Including the crash of 1929, the market fell 67 percent in only three years. While it would be irresponsible to predict that the market is facing imminent collapse merely because it happened before, it is also true that the stock market cannot go up at 8.8 percent a year for very long before it overshoots its appropriate long-run level. The most we can be sure of is that the current stock market trend cannot continue indefinitely.

MERGERS AND ACQUISITIONS

There is another event that would qualify as an economic record in the 1980s, the merger boom from 1984 to 1990. This seven-year period qualifies as the second most active period of merger activity in the United States. For seven years American corporations bought each other and foreign entities at breakneck speed. The amount spent on such activity averaged 4 percent of gross national product, a phenomenal expenditure if you consider that it merely transferred ownership without directly producing a single useful commodity.

A number of these mergers involved industrial titans. In 1984, the first year of the boom, Chevron bought Gulf Corporation for a record $13.3 billion. During the next four years Mobil bought Superior Oil Company for $5.7 billion, General Electric bought its longtime rival RCA for $6.1 billion, and Philip Morris bought Kraft Inc. for $12.6 billion. The merger wave swept through virtually every American industry as firms scrambled to find the best buy and capitalize on easy growth.

The only other comparable period of mergers took place at the turn of the century between 1898 and 1904. In this seven-year period, outlays on mergers and acquisitions averaged 5 percent of gross national product, the highest rate ever recorded in modern American history. In fact in 1899, merger expenditures reached 13 percent of gross national product, a level that has never been surpassed.

Except for these two merger booms, merger expenditures rarely topped 1 percent of gross national product for even a single year. The merger frenzies that took place during the turn of the century and during the 1980s stand out as truly exceptional events in American economic history.

DISTRIBUTION OF INCOME

The average or median income provides some information about the average well-being of citizens, but it says nothing about how that income is distributed. For that information it is necessary to look specifically at income distribution statistics. What you will find is that over the past 50 years there has been a general trend for income to be distributed more equally. In 1935 the wealthiest 20 percent of the population collected approximately 52 percent of the nation's income (before taxes and transfers). This share fell in 1950 to 43 percent where it remained, give or take a couple percentage points, until 1980 when it was 42 percent.

The 1980s were different. After little change for more than three decades, the income share of the wealthy rebounded to 45 percent by the end of the decade and continued to rise to 46 percent by 1993. The relative gains made by the rich during the 1980s were matched by relative income losses by all other income groups farther down the scale. This included the very poorest 20 percent whose income share fell from 5.3 percent in 1985 to only 4.2 in 1993. This was a record shift in the income distribution.

Only one other time in this century does it appear that the rich gained so much at the expense of the rest of the country. This occurred in the 1920s. The income share of the top 5 percent rose from 22 percent in 1920 to 27 percent in 1928. During the 1980s the gain for the same income class rose from 15 percent in 1980 to 18 percent in 1989. In both the 1920s and 1980s the evidence shows that the relative economic condition of the rich improved dramatically.

SUMMING UP

Actual economic events were not kind to monetarists, supply-siders, or free-floaters. In every case, promises were not kept, or in experimental terminology, hypotheses were not validated. Federal deficits careened off the map, the link between the money supply and inflation evaporated, and international financial markets bordered on chaos.

Even when experiments fail we should be able to learn something from the experience, otherwise we have paid a tremendous cost for nothing. Why did the experiments fail? Why were so many other records set during the 1980s? Is there a consistent, plausible explanation that accounts for all of these events? Are there gaps in our knowledge that require future experiments? We will return to these questions, but first we turn to the experimenter's explanations. The next chapter looks at how the experimenters viewed these dismal results.

9

A Falling Out

It is one thing to make promises that fail to come true. It is far worse to make promises in which the opposite occurs. Supply-side economics, monetarism, and free floating had the unfortunate fate of promising the opposite of what actually happened. In every case, there was little doubt that the experimenters failed to deliver on their key promises. A scientific theory, suffering a comparable failure, would not have much of a future. Economic theories, however, have much more resilience.

The results of a laboratory experiment can be just as important when they confirm a hypothesis as when they refute it. In either case something is learned. The same principle does not necessarily apply to macroeconomic experiments. In these experiments there are no laboratory controls to eliminate extraneous factors. Results can always be contaminated, which raises the question of how important these other things are. The failures of these experiments ignited a desperate search for confounding factors. The failure of the three experiments to fulfill their promises led to a variety of explanations and excuses. At stake was the reputtion of more than a few professional economists.

COMMON ROOTS

Although their proponents did not end up on good terms, supply-side economics and monetarism shared similar classical roots. Both theories openly assume the superiority of the private market when left unregulated by government. In fact in the theoretical world, monetarists and supply-siders had a lot in common. It was in the political world, where choices have to be made, that they disagreed. If a reduction in both government spending *and* taxes were impossible, which one of the two should take priority? For supply-siders the choice was clear: reduce tax rates. Milton Friedman, however, had a strong preference for cutting spending. He had said, more than once, that the total burden on the tax payer was the amount the government spent, not the amount that it taxed. He reasoned that government spending would be paid for one way or another, either from current taxes or government debt. Both monetarists and supply-siders would have been content if the government had spent less and taxed less. However, if forced to choose only one policy, they would have chosen different options.

Supply-siders and monetarists also disagreed about the appropriate policies governing money and exchange rates. Supply-siders were among the small group in the United States advocating a return to the gold standard. They would have put the federal government back in the business of guaranteeing the dollar with gold at some fixed rate of exchange. Friedman preferred strict rules regulating the Fed's control of the money supply. The two also disagreed over the cause of the Great Depression. Supply-siders blamed the Smoot-Hawley tariffs for the Great Depression and Friedman blamed the Federal Reserve. Both were inclined to place the blame on government action rather than the private sector and stock market speculation.

Disagreements between supply-sider theory and monetarism were more over a means rather than the ends. Both dreamed of a world where governments played a much smaller role and had little influence over the money supply or exchange rates. Their differences were over the best way to accomplish these goals in the practical world of economic policy.

REAGANOMICS

In the first few days of the Reagan administration there were relatively few disputes between the monetarists and supply-siders. Monetarists were preoccupied with controlling the money supply and reducing inflation, and supply-siders were busy planning tax cuts that would generate a great economic expansion. It was for all practical purposes a convenient division of labor. Monetarists would solve the inflation problem while supply-siders would eliminate unemployment and generate economic growth. It was not long before the simultaneous application of monetarism and supply-side theory became known by the simpler term, Reaganomics. By working in unison, the two approaches were designed to beat back the stagflation of the Carter years.

Stockman described this division of labor as a "push-pull" dynamic. Within the supply-side circle it was believed that the strict discipline of monetarist policies would pull down inflation while the supply-side tax reductions would push up the rate of economic expansion. The simultaneous application of both theories presented no real problem that anyone in the administration could foresee.

These sentiments were echoed by Paul Craig Roberts in the Treasury. According to Roberts, "Monetarists and supply-siders continued to read about how they were at each other's throats, while in truth we were jointly fighting to fend off policy traditionalists and political manipulators."[1] For Roberts, the traditionalists were the Keynesians, mutual adversaries of both monetarists and supply-siders. In the November 16, 1981, issue of *Fortune*, Roberts insisted that the policies advocated by supply-siders and monetarists were entirely compatible.[2]

The economy inherited by the incoming Reagan administration was bad enough that almost anyone would figure they could do better. Economic growth during 1980, the last full year of the Carter administration, was a negative .5 percent and inflation was 12.5 percent. Even the dollar was in trouble, slipping 15 percent below its original value in 1973. The economic team that took charge in 1981 was exceptionally confident of its ability to straighten things out. Here was an opportunity to put into practice the theories that they had come to believe in with almost a religious fervor. Stockman, perhaps because of his divinity school training, characterized his own conversion to supply-side economics as his "quest for the Grand Doctrine."[3] The beliefs of other supply-siders and monetarists were no less inspired.

Back in his days as a freshman representative from Michigan, David Stockman had produced his first budget forecast based on the fiscal priorities of the Reagan camp. On the strength of this forecast, showing a $60 billion surplus by 1985, he became known as a budget expert, a reputation that no doubt helped him get appointed director of the Office of Management and the Budget. The fact that Stockman himself would later characterize the forecast as "neither logical, careful, nor accurate within a country mile" hardly damaged its popularity among Republicans, especially among members of Reagan's transition team.

Stockman's preparation for this position included a degree from Harvard Divinity School, a highly respected program, but not one known for turning out great budget directors. In fact Stockman was the first to concede that he "didn't know much about budgets," a shortcoming that he was able to rationalize because he still "knew more than the rest of them."[4] In light of Stockman's own unusual academic preparation, it is perhaps a little surprising that he would refer to one of Carter's energy officials as an "obnoxious troll" and a "self-important appointee possessed of a degree in English."[5] It did not bode well for the future that Stockman's new colleague heading up the U.S. Treasury, Don Regan, also possessed a degree in English.

The trouble started when Stockman plugged the new budget parameters into the Office of Management and Budget (OMB) computer and printed out projected deficits for the next few years. It seems that even with optimistic assumptions, including real economic growth averaging 5 percent a year, the computer could not reconcile a major military expansion and a supply-side tax cut without producing a sea of red ink. The budget deficits not only rose every year, they attained levels far beyond the scope of any previous administration, Democratic or Republican.

Rather than rock the boat, Stockman desperately searched for a way to improve the budget projections. First, he accepted an unrealistically high inflation figure from Murray Weidenbaum, the chair of the Council of Economic Advisors. Higher inflation generated higher income and higher tax revenue, something the budget needed quite badly. Later he resorted to a "magic asterisk," a spending reduction of unspecified programs. Other deceptions were more reckless. As Stockman describes the process of budget-making, "Jones, Panetta, Gramm, and I—spent the entire month of April rigging the numbers to the point that even we couldn't understand them."[6] Ultimately, even these contrivances could not hide 12-digit deficits!

On January 7, 1981, Stockman forecast a 1984 deficit of $75 billion. By the first week of February he raised his forecast to $130 billion.[7] Much later, Stockman began to distribute these budget projections, partly to impart an urgency to his agenda of spending cuts, and partly to scale down the gargantuan size of the pending tax cuts. On August 3, Stockman forecast deficits of $60 to $100 billion every year for the next four years. The deficit was expected to rise to $81 billion by 1983 and $112 billion by 1984.[8] Finally, by November 1981, OMB was forecasting a deficit of $97 billion in 1982, $146 billion in 1984, and $170 billion by 1986. This was at a time when the largest deficit in history had been Carter's $74 billion in 1980. These were disturbing figures for many in the Reagan administration.

The projections were disturbing to supply-sider Paul Craig Roberts, who was convinced that Stockman was promulgating unrealistic deficit estimates just so he could sandbag the supply-side tax cuts. Roberts took great pride in the Treasury's resistance to Stockman's efforts "to project larger deficits."[9] Stockman's August 1981 deficit projection was described by Roberts as a monstrous figure. In retaliation, the Treasury submitted a more modest, understated figure.[10] Roberts figured that Stockman was using his high deficit forecasts to "terrify" House Republican leadership into considering a correction in the original tax cut.[11] Much of Roberts's book, *The Supply-Side Revolution,* is dedicated to attacking fellow supply-sider Stockman, and faulting the Reagan administration for not firing him when the opportunity arose.

Over in the Senate, Stockman's budget projections met resistance of another sort. Pete Domenici, Republican senator from New Mexico, was nervous about the funny numbers he was asked to sign off on as chair of the Senate Budget Committee. He was tempted to throw out Stockman's magic asterisk and release deficit numbers that were more realistic.[12] According to Stockman, Domenici initially took the high ground, "Gentleman, I'm tempted to designate this $44 billion with a magic asterisk. But I won't," only to concede, "But, come to think of it, that's our only choice. And so I will."[13] In the end, Domenici actually rejected Stockman's figures and released his own, higher deficit projections.

A similar objection was voiced by Stockman's one-time mentor, Rep. John Anderson from Illinois. While considering the problem of cutting taxes, raising defense, and still balancing the budget, Anderson speculated that it could be done, but only with smoke and mirrors. Stockman's response was to call it a "silly charge."[14]

In the end, even Stockman's November deficit forecasts turned out to be too "conservative." Actual deficits were $128 billion in 1982, $185 billion in 1984, and $221 billion in 1986. If Stockman's estimates were too low, then where does that put Paul Craig Roberts who demanded even lower projections? One conclusion, perhaps the most generous, is that Roberts suffered from a personal deficit of forecasting talent. The other possibility is that Roberts wanted Stockman to shave his deficit forecasts simply to mislead Congress and prevent the tax rate correction in the 1982 tax bill. Distinguishing between incompetence and deceit is seldom easy in matters involving economic judgment. It is even more difficult in Roberts's case, which most likely involves some of both.

The dispute between supply-siders Stockman and Roberts hit a low point in September 1981. According to Stockman, Roberts lit into him at a dinner at Jack Kemp's house. "You better get back on the team or get out. You're panicking everyone on the deficit! You've objectively joined the enemy camp."[15] For his part, Stockman referred to Roberts and Wanniski as intellectual hooligans and suggested that they had their "heads buried in sand, living an economic fantasy."[16]

Stockman's pragmatism was nothing less than blasphemy as viewed from the high altar of supply-side economics. The feud went public in December 1981 when the *Atlantic Monthly* published an extensive interview with Stockman conducted by his friend and confidant, *Washington Post* editor, William Greider. In this famous exposé, Stockman conceded that in his view, supply-side economics was a "Trojan horse to bring down the top [tax] rate." Stockman went on to claim, "Supply-side is 'trickle-down' theory," meaning that tax breaks for the rich would provide some benefits, however small, for everyone else.[17] It would be a mistake to presume that Stockman had abandoned his conservative principles merely because he resorted to the unflattering rhetoric, "trickle-down." He never lost his enthusiasm for slashing government social programs and taxes, believing that the benefits for the rich would ultimately help everyone else.

What Stockman had lost faith in was the idea that immense tax cuts could close an immense deficit. The 1981 article revealed Stockman's lack of confidence in the Laffer curve, a fact that he reiterated in his 1986 book. "I never bought that literally and didn't think they did, either. I put it down to salesmanship."[18] Without the Laffer curve, however, supply-side economics loses its identity as a truly unique economic theory.

Perhaps the most amazing aspect of Stockman's indiscreet confession in the the *Atlantic Monthly* is that he was not fired. Instead, Reagan's publicity team orchestrated a meeting between Stockman and the president which carried the folksy imprimatur of a "trip to the woodshed." Roberts was irate that Stockman was not summarily dismissed. The decision to retain Stockman, he claimed, cast doubts on the president's judgment and demoralized the true supply-siders in the administration, including himself. He even went so far as to suggest that James Baker, the chief of staff, was protecting Stockman in a ploy to sabotage Reaganomics and improve the presidential prospects of his mentor, George Bush.[19]

The *Atlantic Monthly* flap, which infuriated Roberts, involved Stockman's public defection from supply-side economics and its fetish, the Laffer curve. However, only three years later Roberts himself claimed that the Laffer curve "obscured the issue," and that he himself was "careful never to base any of [his] work on the Republican budget resolutions on the Laffer curve."[20] Although Roberts's confession was similar to Stockman's, it failed to make headlines. He was not quite the insider that Stockman was, but more important, he was a little late. By 1984 it was all too clear that the supply-side tax cuts were not going to pay for themselves, and it was no longer newsworthy to say so. When it would have been newsworthy, Roberts was still too much of a team player to criticize Arthur Laffer and Jude Wanniski. It was not until after things began to unravel that Roberts accused Laffer and Wanniski of "hyperbole" and "exaggeration."[21]

Prior to the supply-side experiment, Roberts had been more sympathetic to the Laffer curve. Writing in 1979, Roberts suggested that the Kemp-Roth Bill would help to reduce high deficits. He lashed out at Walter Heller, chair of the Council of Economic

Advisors under Kennedy, for denying that the Kennedy tax cuts had paid for themselves.[22] Even then, however, Roberts, was less rigid than some of the other supply-siders. He allowed for the possibility that supply-side tax cuts could be self-financing in two ways—one by increasing tax revenue and the other by increasing the amount of savings. It would be relatively easy for the government to finance deficits by tapping into this projected flood of new savings. By 1984, when Roberts's book was published, it had become obvious that the tax cuts would not be self-financed through higher tax revenue. Quite pragmatically, Roberts retreated to the position that the tax cuts would at least be self-financing through additional savings.

By 1988 it became clear that the tax cuts were not self-financing through either higher taxes or higher savings. Households in 1988 were saving a much smaller percentage of their income than at anytime since at least 1959.[23] On average, households were saving 4.4 percent of their income compared to 7.9 percent in 1980, Carter's last full year as president. Roberts had some more explaining to do. He claimed that the supply-side incentives were overwhelmed by the young workers from the baby-boom generation who were not saving much. The term "young" might have been stretching the facts since the top end of the baby-boom generation was already well into their forties by then.

There is an adage that says when you find you have dug yourself into a hole, stop digging. But Roberts would not stop digging. He defended himself with another prediction, "As the demographic trend reverses in the 1990s, the personal savings rate will rise." Recent statistics show the savings rate did not rise but instead dropped to 4.1 percent in 1994.[24] It is difficult to blame the decline in savings on demographics when the baby boomers are the ideal age for saving.

Roberts's one-time colleagues at the Treasury, Norman Ture and Stephen Entin, had a slightly different take on the savings problem. Writing in 1990, they claimed that Americans did not save because "Our present tax laws are biased against savings."[25] They then proceeded to describe how savings are discouraged by taxation. What they forgot to explain is why a reduction in these tax rates during the 1980s resulted in lower, not higher savings. The capacity of economists to stick to their beliefs in the face of all manner of contradictory facts should never be underestimated.

The split within the supply-side camp expanded. Stockman placed the blame for exploding deficits on overzealous supply-siders, a club to which he once belonged. He complained, "What the Treasury supply-siders were doing, I feared, was fleeing the misery of politics by turning economics into magic."[26] As the deficits began to inflate, Wanniski and Laffer went "completely around the bend," Stockman stated, "telling fairy tales to anyone who would listen that all the nation's fiscal and political problems would vanish overnight if the gold standard were restored."[27] Stockman was not above criticizing his "friend," Jack Kemp, for "giving goofy lectures about the gold standard."[28] Perhaps Stockman's ultimate disillusionment was when he lost faith in Irving Kristol, whom he had once described as the "secular incarnation of the Lord Himself."[29]

Kristol was doing nothing more than sticking to his original plan. Cut taxes for the wealthy and if the supply-side magic does not eliminate the deficit, wait patiently until spending cuts become the only way out. Stockman understood this strategy, but he was too impatient. In his view this was "the worst kind of intellectual sophistry there is" because "to rationalize such destructive policies and urge the conservative political party to adhere to them is unpardonable."[30]

Stockman's ability to forecast impending deficits turned out to be one of his few economic talents. When it came to forecasting the future effects of these deficits, he was way off the mark. In his book, written in 1986, he predicted that an excessive tightening by the Federal Reserve would initiate a recession. Equally likely in his view was the prospect of renewed inflation, but not just any inflation. "If we stay the course we are now on," Stockman predicted, "the decade will end with a worse hyperinflation than the one with which it began." In fact "increased fragility and instability" would make this "inflationary cycle even more violent and destructive."[31] Stockman's old comrades in the Treasury had no monopoly on erroneous economic forecasts. There was no inflationary cycle, violent or otherwise.

WHO CAUSED THE RECESSION OF 1981–82?

Almost simultaneous with the first supply-side tax cuts in 1981 was the beginning of the 1981–82 recession, the worst, in many respects, since the Great Depression. Recessions are, to this date, an inevitable part of our economic condition, although there is much debate over the government's ability to postpone, moderate, and in some cases aggravate them. By most accounts the high interest rates prevailing in 1981 and 1982 contributed to making the recession unusually severe. Most explanations of this recession involved some discussion about the link between government policy and interest rates.

Paul Craig Roberts should be given credit for proposing the most original cause of the recession. In 1982 the *New York Times* reported that Roberts held David Stockman personally responsible for the recession. Political bickering is likely to lead to exaggerated claims, but seldom does name-calling achieve this level. Nevertheless, according to the *Times*, Roberts insisted that Stockman had "triggered the recession by insisting on delaying the start of the first round of 1981 income tax cuts to Oct. 1 from Jan. 1 and reducing the first installment of the tax cut to 5 percent from the 10 percent earlier proposed."[32] I believe it safe to say that this view was not widely shared.

Roberts himself appeared to have forgotten this accusation by 1984 when he redirected the blame for the recession toward the Federal Reserve and its chair, Paul Volcker. It is a reasonable view that the Federal Reserve was largely responsible for high interest rates, contributing to a far worse recession than would otherwise have occurred. For Roberts, the Fed not only caused the recession, but they may have done so intentionally to sabotage the administration's supply-side economic policy.[33] His primary objection was that the money supply had been too tight between May and November 1981. There is at least one consistent theme in Roberts's many accusations. Whoever caused the recession, David Stockman or Paul Volcker, Roberts was sure that their intentions were nothing less than to guarantee the failure of the supply-side program.

Volcker was indeed skeptical of the supply-siders' promises. According to his 1992 book, "The more starry-eyed Reaganauts argued that reducing taxes would provide a kind of magic elixir for the economy that would make the deficits go away, or at least not matter."[34] If high interest rates had aggravated the recession, Volcker was not taking credit for it. The high interest rates, according to Volcker, resulted from the "built-in deficit," a product of the "extreme tax reductions in 1981."[35] The recession of 1981–82 created a big problem for both supply-siders and monetarists. It is not surprising that they chose to blame each other for its occurrence.

A BAD FORECAST

According to an old expression, if all you have is a hammer, everything starts to look like a nail. Milton Friedman's hammer was his historical study of the money supply in the United States. From this work he concluded that especially rapid increases in money led inexorably to a period of heightened inflation, typically followed by a recession. Consequently, when the Federal Reserve abandoned the monetarist experiment in the fall of 1981 and initiated a rapid increase in the money supply, Milton saw a nail and raised his hammer.

At first he had hopes that the rapid increase in the money supply would be short-lived. He noted in February 1983 that the money supply (M1) had been racing ahead with an annual average growth rate of 15 percent since July 1982. This would help the economy pull out of the recession, he noted, but not without the risk that "it will also produce a renewed acceleration of inflation and a sharp rise in interest rates."[36] By May 1983, Friedman still had some hope that inflation could be avoided but less hope than before. Even if the Fed abruptly switched to an ideal course, the outcome would likely include "a rise in short-term [interest] rates, a slowdown in the expansion and a moderate increase in inflation." In fact, Friedman thought the Fed largely incapable of hitting the ideal course. "Past experience," said Friedman, "gives little reason to put much confidence in the judgment of the 'senior Federal Reserve Board official [Paul Volcker].'" He concluded with a question, "How is it that an institution that has so poor a record of performance nonetheless has so high a public reputation?"[37]

Public reputation is quite appropriately a subjective concept. The Fed's reputation was probably no higher than Milton Friedman's own at the time. Friedman's book, *Free to Choose*, coauthored with his wife, Rose, was quickly becoming a best-seller. He had won the Nobel Prize for Economic Science in 1976 and had gained a wide audience for his ideas through his regular column in *Newsweek*. Given this forum and the Fed's allegedly misguided increase in the money supply, he saw an opportunity to promote his favorite economic policies. He had seen examples of excessive money growth in his study of the past 100 years of monetary history, and he thought he knew what was coming. The hammer began pounding. In July 1983, Friedman reported that the Fed had in fact done "additional damage" and that we "shall be fortunate indeed if we escape either a return to double-digit inflation rates or renewed recession in 1984."[38] By September 1983, the economic fate of the United States was evidently sealed. As a consequence of Fed policy, Friedman proclaimed, there was "bound to be renewed stagflation—recession accompanied by rising inflation and high interest rates."[39] According to his calculations, inflation was still due in 1984. The business press began to take heed. A commentary in *Business Week* in December 1983 noted that Friedman was forecasting "stagflation" for 1984. The commentator noted at the time that "virtually no one is forecasting a recession," much less a recession and inflation.[40]

Following a rapid increase in the money supply from July 1982 to July 1983 (13.4 percent), the Fed switched gears and money growth slipped to only 2 percent between July and December 1983. The Fed was surely in trouble, swinging from one extreme to the next, claimed Friedman in January 1984. Again, he claimed that this was a familiar pattern, with the likely outcome being "that the economy will relapse into recession."[41] The signs were already pointing toward "a decided slowdown in GNP growth," to which Friedman added the ominous warning that "the worst is yet to come." In addition to the recession, Friedman forecast that "inflation is likely to be headed up rather than down." The day of reckoning still appeared to be sometime in 1984.

Economic forecasters, as a rule, tend to exude immense confidence on general statements that cannot be refuted while hedging their bets on predictions that could prove wrong. If they are wrong, they can point to their caveats; if they are right then that is all that matters. On the question of impending recession and inflation, however, Friedman had few, if any doubts. In fact, having barely made the prediction, he went right ahead and criticized the Federal Reserve for causing it. "How," he questioned, "can our sophisticated managers of money at the Fed have allowed this to happen?" The answer, which he also provided, was that the Fed suffered from a combination of slow reactions, slow learning, and myopia. The problem, he claimed, was that "we have been paying, and shall continue to pay, a heavy price for their continued myopia."[42]

No forecaster can claim to have a perfect record, but few are granted a regular column in *Newsweek* to launch their predictions. Fewer still have the confidence to forecast a major economic crisis and then, without waiting for the outcome, blame the government for causing it. As it turned out there was neither high inflation nor a recession in 1984. In fact, just the opposite took place. Inflation rates for consumer prices in 1984 remained a remarkable low and steady 3.9 percent and the economy expanded at a very impressive 6.2 percent.[43] If there was a word for the opposite of "stagflation" then that is exactly what occurred in 1984! Mercifully, Milton Friedman's regular column in *Newsweek* ended in 1984.

A couple of years later Friedman made a return appearance in *Newsweek* and revisited the topic. Nowhere in this article was there an explanation of how his monetary theories had failed him. Nor was there even an admission of his mistake. Instead, he stuck to his guns and reiterated, "The recent high rates of monetary growth are bound to produce higher inflation—but just when that will occur and how far it will go are far more difficult to judge."[44] Friedman could not admit that his forecast was wrong, only that it was premature. Yet inflation rates continued to ease in 1985 and fell even lower in 1986 without any sign of recession. If there was a statute of limitations on economic forecasts it would have expired by then.

There was a reason why Friedman did not just drop the forecasts or at least revise them. He could not admit the failure of the forecast without admitting the failure of the theory it was based on, monetarism. What this meant to Friedman should not be underestimated. He had been the principal advocate and defender of monetarism throughout the great debates with Keynesians in the 1950s, 1960s, and 1970s. Monetarism was the intellectual fox hole from which he assailed Keynesian fiscal policy and Federal Reserve policy. Monetarism had provided the economic framework for his research in monetary history, which constituted the basis for his 1976 Nobel Prize in economics. For decades he had been blaming inflations and recessions on the incompetent application of government fiscal and monetary policy. To admit that his forecast was wrong would have been tantamount to acknowledging the failure of a lifetime of work. This he could not do. Neither could he find any solace in the data, which was unambiguous: stagflation had not occurred.

In January 1996 I had the opportunity to ask Milton Friedman at an economics conference why large increases in the money supply in the early 1980s failed to ignite inflation. He assured me that I was mistaken because every large increase in the money supply is followed by inflation two years later. When I repeated my question about why this failed in the 1980s, he directed me to go back and check my data. Still, the phantom inflation of the 1980s exists only in the theories of Milton Friedman.

VOLCKER ON FREE FLOATERS

In addition to supply-side economics and monetarism, free floating suffered an equally debilitating setback in the 1980s. By 1984, and at least by 1985, just how far things had gotten out of hand was quite clear. The extraordinary appreciation of the dollar in 1985 was shaking the foundation of U.S. import and export industries and creating doubts about the future stability of international exchange markets.

All of this appeared to be a problem, said Paul Volcker, "except to some dedicated members of the administration team who interpreted it all as a vote of confidence in U.S. policy."[45] They were inclined to believe that the strong demand for the dollar was due to new incentives and the pro-business environment created by tax cuts and deregulation. Any overtures by foreign banks to bring the dollar down "were rejected by the Treasury as a matter of principle. Instead, the strength of the dollar came to be cited by some officials as a kind of Good Housekeeping Seal of Approval provided by the market, honoring sound Reagan economic policies."[46]

At first, Volcker was receptive to the rising dollar; it was a relief from the falling dollar of the 1970s. As the dollar continued to strengthen, however, he claimed to realize that "The competitive position of our industry was being undermined in a way that might do lasting damage." In addition he feared that the ascent would be followed by a "sickening fall in the dollar, undermining confidence, as had happened so often in the 1970s."[47] Volcker's views on this subject were reflected in a memo written for him by his staff. "I am increasingly concerned about the continued rise of the dollar and the implications of the dollar's appreciation for our domestic and international economy."[48] Although Volcker's preferred solution was always to reduce the budget deficits, he also thought that "we ought to be intervening."[49] Intervention would require the Treasury to authorize the sale of dollars, thus reducing its value.

Volcker was relieved to see James Baker III and Richard Darman move into the Treasury, commenting that they were a "pragmatic political team." A doctorate in economics was not required, according to Volcker, to see what needed to be done. Baker and Darman of course almost immediately terminated the experiment in free floating. Volcker suspected that Don Regan was too busy in his new post as chief of staff to pay much attention to the end of his experiment.[50] Besides, Volcker never believed that Regan ever had a very deep stake in the experiment. The same could not be said of Beryl Sprinkel.

When the administration's game of musical chairs ended in early 1985, Beryl Sprinkel was found sitting as chair of the Council of Economic Advisors. In the Council's annual economic report, he took the opportunity to criticize the end of the free-floating experiment. "Intervention in foreign exchange markets to force down the value of the dollar," the report argued, "is not an appropriate long-term strategy to resolve external imbalances."[51] This intervention, it went on to say, will either be ineffective or will perhaps cause inflation. The fact is that the intervention initiated in 1985 appeared to be neither ineffective nor inflationary. The dollar's value went down and stayed down and inflation did not occur. From his new position, Sprinkel had a small opportunity to register objections, but his power to direct economic policy had been effectively terminated.

ROSY SCENARIO

Many of the original economic forecasts developed by the Reagan administration were based on what became known as the "rosy scenario." In this forecast, every economic policy was expected to achieve its goals. Supply-side economics was supposed to reduce tax rates and stimulate sufficient economic growth to recoup the lost tax revenue. Monetarism was supposed to bring money growth down to the targets, thus suppressing inflation, and free floating was supposed to provide stability in international exchange markets.

As things began to fall apart, schisms developed between and even within the various economic camps. Supply-siders attacked each other for being too dogmatic or, in some cases, not dogmatic enough. At the same time many rushed to disassociate themselves from the discredited Laffer curve. Monetarists objected to the unrealistic forecasts of the supply-siders, and supply-siders blamed the monetarists for causing the recession. The Fed held the supply-siders responsible for creating large deficits which held up interest rates and artificially inflated the value of the dollar, while monetarists accused the Fed of departing from their targets and embarking on a ruinous course.

As the level of the debate degenerated into ad hoc theorizing, personal attacks, and stubborn denials, it is understandable if the public failed to fully understand the economic issues involved. Many of our top economic officials at the Federal Reserve, the Council of Economic Advisors, the United States Treasury as well as columnists for the *Wall Street Journal, Business Week*, and *Newsweek* were all implicated in these economic fiascoes. This elite group of insiders responded to the failed experiments with a barrage of lies, half-truths, and faulty statistics in an effort to either shift the blame for these failures or deny that they even were failures. If anything is to be learned from these experiences, it will be necessary to separate economic facts from self-serving rationalizations.

10

Rewriting Economics

At the end of an economic or scientific experiment all that remains is the conclusion. At the completion of an experiment a scientist writes a conclusion, objectively assessing the meaning of the results and reflecting on their implications for contemporary theories. However, the luxury of being able to write one's own conclusion is not one enjoyed by economic experimenters. The experiments are too public, the impacts too widespread, and the results too controversial to be ignored by political pundits, Wall Street gurus, editorial writers, syndicated columnists, and politicians. The deluge of opinions gushing from these sources are seldom coherent, objective, or even well informed. If there is any educational value associated with the sound bites of these self-appointed commentators, it occurs more by chance than design. When opinions are gauged by their simplicity and mass market appeal, the public's desire for wisdom and insight is easily shortchanged.

Columnists and editorial writers for the *Wall Street Journal*, for example, offered their own opinions about the supply-side experiment. They were among the few that looked failure straight in the face and shamelessly pronounced it a success. Through endless tracts—often written by the experimenters themselves—the *Journal* sought to salvage whatever credibility it could for supply-side economics. While the paper's editors were clearly enamored with tax reductions for wealthy citizens and corporations, it tried in vain to convince the middle class that they too had benefited from the experiment. Given the *Journal*'s complicity in the supply-side revolution, which began with its early publication of essays by Paul Craig Roberts and Jude Wanniski, all this effort looked more like damage control than objective reporting.

It is not necessarily a bad thing that economic experimenters are denied the privilege of writing their own conclusions. Consider for example Milton Friedman who saw his prize theory, monetarism, shattered by historical events. Where any rational person would have recognized the error and acknowledged the need to revise the theory, Friedman refused. He remained stubbornly loyal to monetarism to the bitter end and, in fact, has never actually conceded defeat. Through much of the 1980s he persisted in predicting a great inflation even after he had lost his *Newsweek* column and much of his credibility. I have no doubt that if inflation should return at some time in the future, Milton Friedman will insist he was right after all, perhaps conceding that it was just a little late.

The conclusions offered by supply-siders have not been any better. When Paul Craig Roberts publicly declared that the 1982 recession was caused by David Stockman, it seemed that personal hostilities had gotten in the way of his economic judgment. Authors of economic textbooks should be excused if they omit this embarrassing comment from the chapter on supply-side economics. With commentary of this caliber, it is not surprising that the true meaning of these great economic experiments is at risk of being lost. Without a clear understanding of how badly these experiments failed, we run the danger of allowing them to be repeated.

So how does one make sense of these experiments? Obviously this is no simple task. First you have the problem that these are economic experiments susceptible to distortion by extraneous events. Even under the best of conditions, an economic experiment can be sandbagged by an oil crisis, a poor grain harvest, or international events.

The second problem is that it makes little sense to run three experiments simultaneously. No scientist would ever advise such a course, but that is exactly what happened in the early 1980s. Why did the economic experimenters allow this to happen? There is the fact that all of the experimenters started out on relatively good terms. All of them shared a strong philosophical faith in unregu-

lated markets and were united by their collective battle against
Democrats, Keynesians, and liberals. They were, after all, part of
the Reagan revolution and there was no reason for one group to
challenge another. They focused on their own priorities and were
content to leave the others alone.

There was, however, another reason why the experimenters
originally ignored each other; they saw little possibility of failure.
Each group believed in their experiment with the faith of a religious
zealot. David Stockman moved easily from his religious training to
his economic profession as if replacing one set of dogma with
another. The faith of Milton Friedman and his followers in monetarism rivaled that of any fundamentalist. These men were not
simply testing an economic theory, they were implementing the
solution to America's economic problems. If they had been a little
less confident they might have foreseen that conditions were not
ideal for their experiments. They might have realized that conducting three major economic experiments simultaneously was not
such a good idea.

In an effort to make sense out of the 1980s experiments, we
cannot ignore how they affected one another. For this purpose the
theories of the economic experimenters are not useful. In addition
to having failed, they are also too narrow. The effect of tax cuts was
not limited to saving and economic growth as supply-siders insisted. Nor was the effect of changes in the money supply limited
to inflation as monetarists claimed. The U.S. economy in the 1980s
was too complex for these simple theories. A proper understanding
of what happened to the economy in the 1980s requires a theory
capable of accounting for a wide range of unusual events. The best
theory for this purpose, surprisingly enough, is Keynesian economics.

KEYNESIAN COMEBACK

Supply-siders, monetarists, and free-floaters fought for and won
political power in the 1980s by attacking the status quo in the 1970s,
which was closely associated with Keynesian economics. They
criticized Keynesians for focusing on demand and for advocating
public policy based on demand management. They ridiculed the
Phillips trade-off, which showed that government policies could
alleviate inflation but only at the cost of higher unemployment. In

the end, through their own failures, the conservative experimenters opened the door for a Keynesian revival. The failure of the three experiments to produce anything close to what they predicted gave Keynesians a second chance.

If supply-siders, monetarists, and free-floaters were unable to account for the economic events of the 1980s, how much better did the Keynesians do? Keynesians did not deny the importance of money, but they did claim that the key to inflation was the level of economic activity. Historically, economies with high levels of economic activity have been far more prone to inflation than those saddled with chronic unemployment and excess capacity, regardless of the money supply.

When large and erratic increases in the money supply failed to ignite inflation between 1982 and 1985, the Keynesians had an answer. The economy still had too much unemployment and was producing below its capacity. Prices do not usually rise, they said, until demand exceeds the capacity of the economy to produce and this point had not yet been reached. Economic activity improved after 1982, but never quite reached full capacity; many factories and workers remained idle. Friedman's mistake was to ignore this fact. Capacity, he had argued for years, was not important and was not supposed to be related to inflation. However, after the experience of the 1980s, it was apparent that the failure of the economy to reach full employment kept inflation down despite great and sporadic increases in the money supply.

Keynesians were never so naive as to believe that full capacity was the only reason behind inflation, although they would be likely to place it at the top of the list. They also pointed out that a price shock, such as an oil crisis, is another important inflationary force. It was easy to recognize this in the 1970s when soaring petroleum prices ignited inflation in 1974 and again in 1979 and 1980. During the 1980s, petroleum prices were important again, not because they were going up, but because they were going down. Oil prices, corrected for inflation, fell sharply after 1981, falling 63 percent by 1989.[1] This fortuitous development helped contain inflation but contributed to Friedman's mistake. Friedman, of course, was well aware that oil prices were falling, he just did not think that it mattered. In monetarism, inflation was supposed to be exclusively related to the money supply, not oil prices or unemployment.

Somewhere on the Keynesian list of causes of inflation is the power of corporations and unions. Even when the economy falls short of full employment, corporations and unions are able to generate their own little inflationary spiral that can spill over into other sectors. Corporations raise prices to increase profits, and unions respond by demanding higher wages and capturing a share of their profits. While corporations and unions may have contributed to the 1970s inflation, their importance started to erode in the 1980s. Corporations, thrust into a more competitive global market, were less likely to initiate price increases, and unions were in a slump. Unions lost more members during the 1982 recession than at any other time in the previous 50 years. As a result, during the 1980s there was little danger that corporations and unions were going to interfere with the downward trend in inflation. This was once again good for the economy but bad for Milton Friedman's prognostication. In the monetarist book these things just were not supposed to matter.

While Keynesian economics easily explains Friedman's mistake, what about the success the Federal Reserve had in bringing down inflation in the first place? By clamping down on the money supply, the Federal Reserve's monetarist experiment could at least take credit for reducing inflation for consumer goods from 13.3 percent in 1979 to 3.8 percent in 1982.

But even here, Keynesian theory does a good a job of explaining what happened. Once again, there appears to be a Keynesian trade-off between inflation and unemployment. Inflation did go down, but like a teeter-totter, unemployment went up, rising from 5.8 percent in 1979 to a record 9.7 percent in 1982. The monetarist policies only succeeded because they raised interest rates so high that housing and auto sales plummeted and employees were laid off. It is a much overlooked principle of economics that unemployed workers are a potent antidote for inflation for the simple reason that they do not buy much. Monetarists mistakenly credit the Federal Reserve for reducing inflation when it is really the unemployed who make the difference and suffer the consequences.

All together, Keynesians clearly came out ahead of monetarists. Keynesians had a more plausible explanation for lower inflation from 1979 to 1982, and they explained Friedman's mistaken prediction from 1983 to 1985.

SUPPLY-SIDERS SLIP

Superficially, Keynesians and supply-siders would seem to have something in common—they both prescribe tax cuts as a remedy for a sick economy. Keynesians, of course, pioneered the technique during the Kennedy administration, but supply-siders raised the stakes and redirected the benefits to corporations and the well-to-do. Still there are other important differences. Keynesians emphasize the fact that tax cuts leave more money in people's pockets for spending, while supply-siders emphasize the fact that lower tax rates create an added incentive for saving and investing. Tax cuts are effective, according to Keynesians, because of demand-side effects and, according to supply-siders, because of supply-side effects.

When the massive tax cuts were first proposed in 1980, Keynesians were initially concerned that they were too large and could push the economy past full capacity and right back into inflation. But this was only because they were not paying enough attention to the Federal Reserve. At the same time that the tax cuts were pumping up the spending power of the wealthy, rising unemployment from the Federal Reserve's policies was deflating the spending power of the poor. Never before in history had such a massive expansionary fiscal policy, based on increasing the spending of the rich, been run against a diametrically opposed monetary policy based on reducing the spending of the average citizen. Like two massive locomotives heading toward each other at full tilt, fiscal policy and monetary policy were headed for a major collision. The fact that no economist was able to exactly pinpoint where the wreckage would end up was due to the novelty of the experiments.

This was admittedly unfamiliar ground for the Keynesians who had traditionally felt that fiscal and monetary policies should point in the same direction. In order to give the economy a boost they would typically advocate a stimulative fiscal policy, in other words, a tax deficit accompanied by a generous increase in the money supply; or to smother inflation, a budget surplus accompanied by restraint in the money supply. Throughout much of the 1950s up to the 1980s this is exactly what happened. The idea of running opposing fiscal and monetary policy was never suggested because in Keynesian theory there was no predictable advantage, one policy just offset the other.

The collision took place in 1982 and it was the monetary train that carried the day. Tight money and record interest rates overwhelmed the stimulus of the tax cuts and brought the economy to its knees, culminating in the deepest recession since the Depression. Up to this point there had been some debate among Keynesians about the potency of monetary policy. While most thought that monetary policy was quite capable of bringing on a recession, they were inclined to believe that fiscal policy was the stronger of the two forces. From the collision of 1982, Keynesians learned not to underestimate the power of the Federal Reserve, especially when it pursues a goal of low inflation at any cost.

While the remainder of the decade was less spectacular than a train wreck, the tension between fiscal and monetary policy continued. After the tax cuts, large federal deficits opened up and continued to provide a demand stimulus to the economy. The Federal Reserve, however, abandoned its monetarist experiment but continued to follow a strict anti-inflationary program. The two locomotives were now placed head to head, grinding away in opposite directions. Once again the superior power of the Federal Reserve clearly asserted itself. Whenever the huge deficits threatened to push the economy into high employment, the Federal Reserve countered by raising interest rates still further. The economy was allowed to recover from the 1982 recession, but a full recovery was never permitted. These policies ensured that the average unemployment rate for the 1980s would set a post–World War II record. By preventing a full recovery and maintaining high unemployment, the Federal Reserve believed it was eliminating any possibility of renewed inflation.

If the experimenters overlooked the conflict between fiscal and monetary policy, this was only a temporary lapse. Paul Craig Roberts had initially believed that the monetarists at the Federal Reserve would douse inflation and the supply-side tax cuts would reinvigorate the economy. This was one of the naive beliefs that characterized supply-side economics before the experiment. However, as it became clearer that the tax cuts had failed to work as planned, Roberts switched gears from blaming Stockman for the recession to blaming the Federal Reserve. This was a credible explanation for why the tax cuts failed to restore high economic growth, but it was not a supply-sider's argument; it was a Keynesian argument. Economists are in real trouble when they adopt their opponent's ideas to explain their own failures. Supply-side economics had slipped just that low.

There was another fact, however, that created even greater problems for supply-siders and that was the savings rate. Supply-siders insisted that the stimulus from their tax cut, and even the Kennedy tax cut in the 1960s, was through the supply side, not the demand side. Well, if that were true, then the savings rate should have increased. The fact that it fell in the 1980s to record levels was a problem for supply-siders. They had bet on the savings rate rising and lost big. Nor could they blame this on the other experiments since they had little to do with the savings rate.

The question remains as to why the savings rate plummeted. It could be that the wealthy were inclined to save less of their earned income because of windfall gains they made in the stock market. It is possible that the nation merely embarked on a spending binge, preferring to buy now and pay later. Whatever the reason for the lower savings rate, it was clear that the force of supply-side tax cuts was not strong enough to reverse it. To this extent the supply-siders failed. Keynesians may have been surprised by the dramatic decline in the savings rate, but unlike the supply-siders they had not bet their reputations on a prediction one way or the other.

FREE FLOATERS FOILED

The concept of free floating was discredited in the 1980s because the dollar, rather than becoming more stable during the free float, was more volatile than ever before in history. Once again the Keynesians could explain why.

With fiscal and monetary locomotives grinding away to almost a standstill, something had to give and that was the interest rate. The Federal Reserve was obviously relying on high interest rates to hold back the economic expansion. The problem was that since the federal deficit was in such a strong expansionary mode, the interest rate required to hold back the economy was unusually high. This would have been the end of the story if the United States were insulated from the rest of the world, but it was not. With interest rates in the United States out of line with other major countries, the effect on international markets was predictable.

That investors throughout the world are obsessed with short-term interest rates is a well-regarded fact. Thanks to the development of sophisticated communication networks, investors are relatively free to convert their funds into any major currency in the world in order to invest at these short-term rates. When U.S. interest rates rose relative to the rest of the world, investors were anxious to invest in the United States, requiring them to purchase dollars with foreign currency. This act raised the demand for dollars relative to other currencies, causing the dollar's value to rise.

This series of events had happened before. This time was different though because no immediate effort was made to rein in either interest rates or the dollar. As a result, the dollar rose faster and higher than it had ever done before, reaching record levels in 1985. After 1985, real interest rates in the United States fell relative to the rest of the world, and the series of events that had pushed the dollar up swung into reverse. As investors sold their dollars to invest elsewhere, the value of the dollar came down as well. This was a perfectly plausible and Keynesian explanation of what transpired in the 1980s.

How much smaller would the speculative bubble have been if the United States and other governments had intervened? The dollar still would have risen I believe, but not nearly as much. While history cannot be rerun to prove this point, there are some very good reasons to believe it is true.

The entire episode began when some investors wanted to exchange their foreign money for dollars and invest at high U.S. interest rates. As a result, demand for dollars overtook supply, and the value of the dollar rose. But unlike the textbook model, other investors did not automatically respond by selling more dollars. Instead, the results were quite perverse. The appreciation of the dollar made other investors even less interested in selling dollars. Since the goal of an investor is to own assets that appreciate in value, few of them volunteered to sell dollars while its value was rising. There was a shortage of dollars and no obvious way to alleviate it. The market failed.

If speculators had been doing their job, as Milton Friedman and the free-floaters had theorized, they would have flattened this roller-coaster ride. If they had realized that the dollar was only temporarily in short supply, they could have made fortunes selling dollars at their temporarily inflated price. This act of prescience, multiplied by thousands of investors, would have greatly increased the supply of dollars and countered the dramatic upswing. But where were these omniscient speculators when the need was so great? Evidently they were doing what everyone else was doing, attempting to profit on the immediate run-up of the dollar.

As Martin Feldstein wrote in the *Economic Report of the President* in 1984, "In the long-run, the real value of the dollar is widely expected to fall back to a level that allows U.S. firms to compete in world markets on an equal basis."[2] It was no secret that the dollar was overvalued in the long-run, but in the short-run there was a lot of money to be made on this speculative bubble. Speculators are only human, and their obsession with the short-run is well known. That they failed to prevent this speculative bubble is no surprise, except perhaps to Milton Friedman and Beryl Sprinkel.

Speculation was out of hand partly because there was no effort to suppress it. The government was on the sidelines. Prior to 1981, the government stood ready to sell dollars when just such a shortage arose, but this was prohibited by the free-floating experiment. The Treasury refused to sell dollars and break the upward spiral.

There was also evidence that "overshooting"—the hypothetical flaw unique to international financial markets—was in fact a reality. The overshooting problem arises because the immediate response of consumers to changes in exchange rates is not helpful. In the short-run, Americans actually made the dollar shortage worse. Because the automobiles, stereos, and other imports became cheaper when the dollar rose, Americans at first spent fewer dollars (not more) on imports. A compact disc player that cost $200 before, cost only $180 after a 10 percent appreciation of the dollar. American consumers, acting quite predictably, responded to the rising dollar in the short-run by selling fewer dollars, making the dollar shortage noticeably worse.

American consumers could have alleviated the dollar shortage by trading in more dollars for foreign currencies and increasing their purchases of these cheap imports. They would eventually do exactly this, but it took a year or two before the purchase of imports had increased enough to make a difference, and by then it was too late to do any good. During the delay, the dollar had climbed even higher. The name for this phenomenon became known as the *J-curve* among economists.

Speculation, overshooting, and the J-curve were all familiar ideas to economists before the free-floating experiment, but it was the experiment that provided the evidence. The fact is that international markets for money are fraught with defects, and the experiment was able to highlight these faults in a most dramatic way. The dollar was allowed to soar 48 percentage points before intervention was restored, and the dollar was shepherded back to its original level.

Keynesians, as a group, have always preferred enlightened government intervention as a solution to our economic problems rather than nonintervention for the sake of preserving free-market purity. The disastrous outcome of free floating certainly enhanced the reputation of the Keynesian approach. Although there is probably a time when most economists, including Keynesians, would advise against government intervention in international markets, the historical experience of the 1980s shows that when conditions are volatile and markets falter, nonintervention for the sake of nonintervention can be a perilous course.

EXPLAINING THE 1980s

There is little doubt that the actual course of events during the 1980s paved the way for a Keynesian revival. Clearly, even a rudimentary understanding of Keynesian theory was sufficient to explain many of the unusual developments of the 1980s. As things turned out, an understanding of more advanced Keynesian theories was even better.

A conventional Keynesian model included in almost every intermediate macroeconomic textbook written since the 1950s is called the IS-LM model, short for investment, savings, liquidity, and money. In this model, interest rates are higher when government deficits are large or the money supply is small. The fact that these two conditions coincided in the 1980s and interest rates reached record levels was a striking vindication of the theory. At the very least it seemed to justify all the effort devoted to explaining this abstract model to multitudes of marginally interested economics students over the decades.

Interest rates were certainly high in 1981 and 1982 because of the monetarist experiment, but why did they remain high after 1982? It appears that after abandoning monetarism in 1982, the Federal Reserve intentionally held interest rates high in order to limit the economic recovery. The Fed had apparently returned to a basic Keynesian principle: inflation is less likely in a slow growing economy. By slowing down economic growth, the Fed attempted to prevent any chance of reigniting inflation. With monetarism rejected, the Federal Reserve wasted no time reverting to an active interventionist role. The specific policies of the Federal Reserve remained controversial, but there was no denying that its new stance was based on active intervention, similar in this one respect to the role Keynesians had pioneered decades earlier.

The record trade deficits were also no surprise. These began with the dollar appreciation in 1981, which made imports cheaper and exports more expensive. After a delay of about two years, American consumers began to take advantage of low import prices created by the overvalued dollar. Purchases of foreign goods started out slow and then exploded in 1984. By 1985 the dollar was 48 percentage points higher than it had been in 1980, making imports too cheap to pass up.

At the same time, the overvalued dollar made U.S. exports more expensive to foreigners. The dollar price of wheat may not have changed, but the dollars foreigners needed in order to buy the wheat were much more expensive. These higher prices had the effect of retarding the growth of U.S. export sales between 1981 and 1985. With imports soaring and exports floundering, the trade deficit opened up to record levels.

What this means is that the record trade deficits and all the problems they created could be traced to the failed economic experiments. The monetarist and supply-side experiments created high interest rates; high interest rates and the free-floating experiment created the overvalued dollar; and the overvalued dollar created the massive trade deficit. The fact that record trade deficits were a side effect of the failed economic experiments should not be forgotten. These trade deficits carried an immense human cost including millions of unemployed Americans and thousands of failed businesses. This episode alone should be enough to convince even the most apathetic citizen that economic experiments and their side effects are too important to be ignored.

Keynesians did equally well in terms of the big picture. Starting in the 1930s, Keynesians focused on savings as a particularly crucial element in the economy. Some sectors save money, others borrow it, and problems occur when the two do not balance. When the country slips into a recession there is typically an imbalance between savings and borrowing. The problem is that borrowing declines as businesses cut back on investments and consumers buy fewer big-ticket items. The federal government can sop up some of the extra savings by running a deficit and borrowing money to finance the deficit. This is one way for the government to add some balance to the overall flow of money.

The problem after 1983 was that there was no recession and no extra savings, but the government ran a huge deficit anyway, creating another kind of imbalance. The deficit had to be funded, but no extra savings were available. If the government has to borrow more and the public saves less, then where do the funds come from? According to Keynesians, the difference has to be made up by borrowing from abroad, which is precisely what happened. The United States became increasingly dependent on foreign funds during the 1980s, borrowing much more than it lent overseas. In a few short years this borrowing contributed to making the United States into the largest net debtor in the world. None of this was a surprise to anyone familiar with Keynesian concepts.

There have been only three major expansions in the stock market since 1871. The unbridled euphoria of the 1920s stock market boom has never been matched, but the 1980s earned a place among the top three expansions.

To a professionally trained economist the reason for a stock market boom is simple. It is inspired by a general improvement in anticipated profitability, and this no doubt had something to do with the 1980s expansion. The massive reductions in corporate profit taxes contained in the Reagan administration's new tax codes certainly improved potential profitability. Depreciation was accelerated, tax breaks were introduced for R&D, and overall tax rates on corporate income were greatly reduced. This alone was enough to spark a buying spree on Wall Street.

Another related development was the 1981 tax cut which provided a permanent reduction in income tax liabilities for the wealthy. Every April, accountants for wealthy families could point to a sizable savings due entirely to the tax reductions of 1981. Disposing of this windfall gain created more than a few jobs for financial advisors as much of the money was probably reinvested. This annual bonus could be used to buy stocks, bonds, or other financial assets. The injection of large amounts of these additional funds into the stock market could have contributed to the stock market boom.

There are parallels here between the 1920s and 1980s. In both decades taxes were reduced for the wealthiest individuals, and in both decades the stock market boomed. In case this seems a mere coincidence, it is worth pointing out that these were not just any tax cuts or just any stock market booms. These two decades are unique with respect to the amount of tax relief they provided the rich. In the 1920s, the top tax rates were slashed from 77 percent to 25 percent, and in the 1980s they were reduced from 70 percent to 28 percent.[3] In both periods the reductions were defended by claiming that the rich would save more, invest more, and create economic prosperity for all. The decades are also unique with regard to the stock market booms. Two of the three largest stock market booms in history were recorded in these two decades. The correlation between tax cuts for the wealthy and stock market booms seems to be based on more than mere coincidence. In practice it appears that tax cuts for the rich sparked a stock market boom, making them richer still. Of course this was not what supply-siders promised, but it does appear to be what happened.

While tax cuts may be sufficient to initiate a stock market boom, they are not sufficient to perpetuate it. What is required for this is a speculative bubble. The stock market, it seems, is capable of maintaining a speculative bubble for many years. All that is required is for investors to expect a significant share of their return to come from increasing stock prices. Under these conditions it is possible for just a few years of rising stock prices to bubble into a prolonged expansion. Due to this feature of the stock market, the 1981 tax cut could have caused many more years of stock market expansion than would otherwise seem possible. If a speculative bubble has in fact carried the stock market past its "appropriate" long-term level, it will only be evident in falling stock prices in the future.

There was another, related phenomenon of the 1980s, the radical redistribution of income in favor of the wealthy. Many developments contributed to the overall polarization of income including the decline of unions, the expansion of trade, and the relocation of U.S. companies abroad. But in addition to these developments, a complete list of the causes would have to include the three failed economic experiments of the 1980s. The authors of the 1981 tax reduction should be given particular credit for their role in all this. Tax reductions had the immediate effect of shifting after-tax income toward the upper income classes, but this was only the start. If the wealthy invested their tax savings in the stock market, then they made windfall gains from the booming market. In fact, since the wealthy own most of the stocks in the country anyway, they did quite well in the 1980s.

Some wealthy investors probably used part of their tax savings to buy government bonds and benefited from high real interest rates. Instead of paying taxes, they lent the government their tax savings and received interest payments in return. This was an extremely favorable arrangement because instead of paying the government, the government paid them. Unfortunately only the highest income earners were in a position to exploit this lucrative deal.

Down at the bottom of the economic ladder, lower income classes did not fare particularly well. For them there were no tax breaks, capital gains, nor interest earnings. Instead they had to contend with higher unemployment rates, which the Federal Reserve steadfastly refused to rectify for fear of worrying investors about potential inflation. For some employed workers, high unemployment rates made it more difficult for them to demand higher wages because employers could simply threaten to replace them. Life was clearly more difficult for those at the bottom of the income distribution.

The merger boom of the 1980s was not entirely independent of the economic experiments. Corporations, like the wealthy, saved billions of dollars from the tax cuts of 1981. They were expected to use these funds productively, to buy equipment, build factories and conduct more R&D, but this was a hope, not a requirement. The fact is that many corporations began to spend a lot more money buying out each other, resulting in one of the largest merger booms in the history of the country.

The public was leery of the merger boom from the start. First it seemed to be a wasteful diversion of funds that could have been constructively invested elsewhere in the economy. It certainly did not help when a merger was followed by massive layoffs as companies attempted to "downsize" and reduce costs. Some mergers were also associated with a loss of competition; where there were once two companies competing for customers, there was now one. For consumers facing fewer choices and higher prices, this was hardly cause for celebration. The supply-side tax cuts might have been less popular if it had been clear that they would provide funds for one of the largest merger booms in history.

There was another reason for the merger boom. The antitrust division of the Justice Department adopted a laissez-faire approach to merger regulation in 1982, essentially flashing a green light for corporate acquisitions. In the late 1980s I had the privilege of hearing several economists from this Department present research papers at a professional conference, and I was impressed with their singular opposition to antitrust regulation. They presented academic papers defending mergers and acquisitions and questioning the need for government regulation. The fact that this made them and their employment superfluous was never mentioned. In any case, while the antitrust division was fully occupied proving itself expendable, businesses took the opportunity to merge and consolidate at record rates.

A DISCOVERY?

It may be that one of the most important lessons from the 1980s is related to a combination of experiments rather than one in particular. For example, it was never intended that a huge federal budget deficit would provide the demand to power economic growth while monetary policy would be used to finesse the economy past recessions, but this is exactly what happened. In a sense, this was an ingenious invention, combining familiar tools in an unorthodox alignment. In another sense it was a dangerous short-run strategy with ominous implications for the future.

The ingenious part is that the unique combination of fiscal and monetary policies exploits the strengths of both approaches. Monetary policy has the desirable feature that it can be implemented swiftly, virtually overnight with a change in Federal Reserve policy. But monetary policy also has a weakness when it comes to manipulating the economy; it has never been believed to be very effective at stimulating a stagnant economy. It may be able to slow down an economy with accelerating inflation, but as a means of avoiding deep recessions, it has never been the policy of choice.

In terms of strengths and weaknesses, fiscal policy is almost the mirror image of monetary policy. It is clearly effective in a recession, after all, it was largely responsible for putting an end to the Great Depression and reviving the economy after the 1960–61 recession. But fiscal policy can be slow, requiring Congress and the president to negotiate appropriate levels of revenue and spending. Even when Congress and the president can agree on how much to cut taxes or raise spending, they still have to decide whose taxes to cut and whose spending to raise. If a change in economic conditions requires an immediate response, fiscal policy can be frustratingly slow.

The combination of monetary policy and fiscal policy that evolved in the 1980s exploited the best of both policies. Fiscal policy provided the engine to power the economy, and monetary policy provided the brakes to adjust the speed. When a recession threatened, the Fed could lower interest rates and allow the large budget deficits to accelerate the economy. If, however, the recovery accelerated too quickly and inflation threatened, it was a simple matter for the Fed to raise interest rates and slow things down. The unique feature of this arrangement is that fiscal policy and monetary policy were set in direct opposition to each other. The boost from persistent federal budget deficits was more or less balanced by higher average interest rates.

It may be overly generous to credit the 1980s experiments with this discovery because it was admittedly accidental. If the supply-side experiment had succeeded there would have been no large federal deficit, and if the monetarist experiment had succeeded, the Federal Reserve would not have been in the business of adjusting interest rates to counter business cycle trends. What evolved out of their combined failures, however, was a discovery that fiscal policy and monetary policy could be run in opposition, providing an underlying stimulus and rapid adjustment.

As is often the case in economics, there is also a downside to this strategy. One problem is that this strategy grants control over the economy to a small group of economists and bankers who constitute the Federal Reserve Board and presidents of the regional Federal Reserve Banks. It would be more luck than design if the interests of such a narrow group should ever coincide with the interests of the broader American public. Nothing in the selection process for these positions ensures a broad representation or even accountability. Equally alarming is that under this new strategy the

Federal Reserve Board constitutes a concentration of economic power that may well be unprecedented in American history.

Another deficiency of this new strategy is that it requires a large, permanent deficit to work effectively. The costs of these deficits may make this approach quite impractical for any extended period of time. During the 1950s and 1960s, the federal deficit swung from deficits during recessions to a balanced budget or even a surplus during inflation. On average the amount of debt accumulated was never really large. However, the deficits required to conduct the counterbalance between fiscal policy and monetary policy in the 1980s were large and relentless. Over time, the funding of these deficits has greatly increased the indebtedness of the federal government, forcing greater and greater shares of public spending to go solely to interest payments on the national debt. Since huge deficits cannot be maintained indefinitely, it is a safe prediction that they will have to be reduced in the future. What will happen to the government's ability to manage the economy once the deficit is eliminated? This may well be the principal economic question of the next decade.

VINDICATION

Keynesians were much maligned during the 1970s. Their critics blamed them for all the problems of the decade, which were severe indeed: simultaneous inflation and recession, low productivity, and falling real incomes. Of course in retrospect, Keynesian macroeconomic policies do not appear to have been at fault. How could a Keynesian have prevented the oil crisis that sent oil prices and unemployment on an upward spiral? How can they be blamed for low productivity and falling real incomes when both continued after Keynesian policies were suspended in the 1980s? As unfounded as these attacks on Keynesians were, they constituted the first battle of the Reagan revolution.

The aftermath of the 1980s experiments coincided with a gradual shift back to Keynesian ways of thinking. The Federal Reserve has adopted a strong countercyclical policy, raising interest rates to slow the economy and cutting them during recessions. With fiscal policy set in perpetual expansion mode, monetary policy has proved to be far more effective than anyone would have guessed. It is no longer debated whether the government should intervene in the economy, but rather how much intervention is appropriate. In this respect, Keynesian economics was vindicated by the 1980s experiments.

11

Out of the Ashes

John Kenneth Galbraith once noted that "Henceforth it should be the simple rule in all economic and monetary matters that anyone who has to explain failure has failed."[1] That at least some aspects of the 1980s experiments were properly recognized as failures is encouraging. That some of the failures have spawned proposals for a new generation of experiments is not.

It is worth remembering that the Laffer curve once provided the primary justification for slashing tax rates for wealthy income earners. As an economic principle it may never have been very good, but as a political argument it was invaluable. The Laffer curve provided a seemingly objective rationale for cutting the taxes of a small, already privileged group. Supporters of the tax cuts could defend themselves by claiming that the tax cuts were good for the entire economy, so good in fact that there would be no real loss of tax revenue. When accused of serving the interests of wealthy individuals and corporations, tax cutters could respond that their purpose was more altruistic—to help the economic development of the entire nation. If not for the Laffer curve, it would have been difficult to deny the charges that they were simply catering to the rich.

By now the Laffer curve has become something of a historical curiosity. While still included in many economic textbooks in the

1990s, it is portrayed as something supply-siders believed during the 1980s rather than as a valid model of the U.S. economy. This is one valuable lesson that emerged from the 1980s experiment.

There is still the question as to whether supply-siders ever really believed in the Laffer curve. Were supply-siders so intent on cutting tax rates for the rich that they were willing to promote an economic theory that they knew in all likelihood was wrong? David Stockman and Paul Craig Roberts were guilty of this deception. Both claimed that they had never really believed in the Laffer curve, although they recanted only after its failure had become obvious. It is equally possible to question Laffer's confidence in the Laffer curve. Even before the experiment began, he confessed that there was "more than a reasonable probability" that he was wrong. Was this enough assurance to conduct a $750 billion experiment? It seems more plausible that the real purpose of the experiment was to cut the taxes of the rich, a true Trojan horse, just as Stockman had described it. From the outside, it looked like a legitimate economic policy, but from the inside it was a ploy to reduce the top tax rates for the highest income earners.

Irving Kristol's early observations only reinforce the characterization of supply-side economics as a Trojan horse. Although he pledged allegiance to the Laffer curve, he devoted most of his attention to speculating on its failure, not its success. He expected that even a failed tax cut would eventually accomplish the conservative goal of reducing the size of the federal government. Even if you disagree with Kristol's point of view, it is difficult to deny the accuracy of his speculations. He figured that a tax cut could open up large deficits that would have to be resolved some day. At worst, from a conservative perspective, the deficits would be eliminated by restoring the tax rates on the rich. In the meantime, large deficits could impede the growth of government spending and the wealthy would enjoy at least a temporary reprieve from high taxes.

Kristol on the other hand, was more optimistic. He believed that deficits would ultimately be eliminated, not by any supply-side miracle, but by cutting government spending. Supply-side economics was still a Trojan horse intended to reduce taxes on the rich, but for Kristol it had another covert objective: to eventually reduce the size of the federal government. This would have happened sooner rather than later if Stockman had succeeded in cutting spending during his tenure as director of the Office of Management and Budget. In this effort, Stockman failed and the deficit was passed to future administrations. President Clinton, who inherited a $255 billion deficit, responded with a small increase in the tax rate on the top income bracket from 28 percent to 39.6 percent. This, however, did not come close to restoring the top rates to 70 percent as they had been in 1980, nor did it make more than a small dent in the deficit.

Today, the prospect for major deficit reduction has never looked so good. While President Clinton and the Republican leadership in Congress lock horns over budget details, both have endorsed plans that rely primarily on spending cuts, not tax increases, to balance the budget. As this plan is implemented, Kristol's prophecy will be fulfilled. The fact that the reduction in the size of the federal government has been endorsed by a Democratic president and Democrats in Congress is an irony that even Kristol had not foreseen.

It is not uncommon for interest groups to claim that a reduction in their own taxes will benefit everyone. What was truly remarkable about the supply-side revolution is that such claims were used so effectively to reduce taxes for corporations and the rich. To this day there is no convincing evidence that the economy is performing any better under a 39.6 percent maximum tax rate than it did under a 70 percent maximum tax rate in the 1960s.[2] It could be argued that the economy is actually performing worse today under the lower tax rates since the nation is rapidly accumulating an immense debt while average unemployment rates remain high and real wage growth remains low. The supply-side tax cut may have failed to magically raise revenue, but it succeeded in permanently reducing taxes on the rich and may ultimately reduce the services provided by the federal government.

UNREPENTANT

Despite the failure of the supply-side experiment, demands by wealthy tax payers for more tax relief has not abated. A recent proposal for special, lower taxes on capital gains was included in Newt Gingrich's "Contract With America" and has gained considerable support from the Republican-dominated Congress. A capital gain occurs when an asset appreciates, such as a corporate stock or even a house, but it does not become taxable until the asset is sold and the gain is *realized*. Individuals who generate substantial amounts of capital gains are typically those with great wealth invested in stocks, bonds, and other securities. Under current laws, capital gains are taxed at 28 percent although the sale of a security can always be postponed, thereby delaying the realization and the tax indefinitely.

Recent proposals to cut the capital gains tax would reduce them from a level that is already low by historical standards. The maximum tax rate on capital gains was as high as 49.1 percent in 1977 until it was reduced to 28 percent under the Revenue Act of 1978. For a short spell, from 1981 to 1986 it fell to 20 percent, but was restored to 28 percent as a trade-off for lowering the maximum income tax rate in 1986.

The reasons given for reducing the capital gains tax have evolved from simplistic supply-side ideas. Instead of promising a free lunch, tax cut proponents are more likely to offer a lunch special. Their more modest claim is that a reduction in capital gains taxes will precipitate a great increase in realizations and hence additional tax revenue. The theory behind this is not much different from the reasons cities have given to justify offering limited amnesty on parking fines. By temporarily reducing fines, by 50 percent for example, cities expect to see enough increase in compliance to actually collect more money. In the case of capital gains taxes, if enough investors sell their stocks and realize their gains, tax revenue could actually increase.

An article in the *Wall Street Journal* by Senator Connie Mack, a Republican from Florida, noted that recent realization rates are unusually low.[3] This may be a natural result of a booming stock market or it may be that investors are holding back on realizations in anticipation of a lower capital gains tax. Whatever the reason, Senator Mack saw this backlog of capital gains as a big problem and recommended lowering the capital gains tax in order to resolve it. Proponents have yet to prove that the backlog of capital gains is a problem, but if it is, then there are more reliable ways to increase revenue from capital gains.

One alternative would be a temporary tax reduction to encourage realizations, making the process even more similar to the parking fine deal, as explained above. Another policy is suggested by the fact that the largest recent increase in realizations occurred in 1986, on the eve of an *increase* in the capital gains tax, not a decrease. If the goal is to encourage realizations then there is nothing like a scheduled increase in the capital gains tax to speed things up. Most investors would prefer to realize their capital gains before the tax rate increased. Another possibility is simply to wait until the stock market boom has run out of steam. At that point, selling will naturally replace buying and the number of realizations will increase. If all these approaches seem too uncertain, then there is always the direct way: make capital gains immediately taxable. Capital gains would then be taxed when they *accrued* rather than when they were realized. Any one of these approaches would be more likely to increase tax revenue than a simple decrease in the tax rate.

However, if the real goal is to reduce taxes on the rich then none of these alternatives is as good as Senator Mack's proposal. A permanent reduction in the capital gains tax is the surest way to increase the after-tax income of the rich. Any other justification for a capital gains tax cut begins to look suspiciously like another Trojan horse. Troy would probably not have accepted a second Trojan horse. Whether the American electorate will remains to be seen.

ANOTHER TROJAN HORSE

A capital gains tax cut is only one of the policies endorsed by advocates of lower taxes on the rich. Another is the flat tax. Although the federal income tax has taken a beating in recent years, it remains slightly progressive, that is, higher income earners pay on average higher income tax rates. A flat tax rate would go a long way in reducing whatever progressivity is left. Although there are many versions of the flat tax, the basic principle is to lower tax rates on high income earners and raise rates on middle- and low-income earners. The flat tax is a useful device if the goal is to shift the tax burden from the rich to the middle and lower classes. Multimillionaire Steve Forbes made the flat tax a central theme of his brief but unsuccessful campaign for the Republican presidential nomination in 1996. It is clear why high income earners would favor the flat tax; it is more of a mystery why anyone else would.

The selling point for the flat tax is that it would make taxes simpler, a worthy goal, as anyone who has ever filled out a tax form can appreciate. But the progressive tax rate structure is not what makes taxes complicated. It is the special tax rates for capital gains, the deferral of current taxes, and the deductions for charitable contributions, business activity, mortgage interest payments, and myriad other credits and exemptions. If the public really wants tax simplification then it means they must be prepared to eliminate these lucrative tax breaks. If, on the other hand, the public wants to shift the tax burden from the rich to the middle class, then they should adopt a flat tax rate. Tax simplification and the flat rate are in fact two very different ideas.

The fact that advocates of the flat tax have included tax simplification in their proposal is a clever political strategy, not an economic requirement. By itself, a flat tax would not be very popular. Middle-class taxpayers really do not want to pay more taxes so that wealthy families can pay less. The only hope for a flat tax was to tie it to the more popular proposal for tax simplification, and that is exactly what was done. Tax simplification may be a worthwhile goal, but not when it is used as a Trojan horse to lower taxes on the rich.

While advocates of flat taxes and capital gains tax cuts can be accused of creating new Trojan horses, there have been some efforts to patch up the original supply-side Trojan horse. Failure, it seems, is not sufficient to extinguish the passions of supply-side zealots. Congress has a renewed enthusiasm for tax cuts that would further reduce the tax burden on businesses and the wealthy. Tax cuts of $350 billion over seven years were passed by the house in 1995 but defeated in the Senate despite the support of key senators like Bob Dole and Phil Gramm. Opposing the tax cuts were many Democrats like Carl Levin from Michigan who claimed that, "Families earning less than $28,000 a year will have to pay more for taxes under this amendment while people earning more than $100,000 will get a big tax cut."[4]

The arguments for these tax cuts had a familiar ring. The tax cuts would, according to Gramm, stimulate investment, create jobs, and produce a more prosperous economy. Gramm was quoted as saying, "No poor person ever hired me in my life. If we want people to create jobs, we've got to create incentives for them to do it."[5] Senator Gramm's employer at the time was in fact the federal government, financed by taxes imposed on both the poor and the rich. That his policies seem to consistently favor the rich is perhaps a result of his mistaken view of who pays his salary.

Tax cutters did learn something, however, from the failure of the 1981 tax cut. They no longer insisted that tax cuts would pay for themselves. Even Phil Gramm had the good sense to resist this promise.

What is behind all these efforts to cut taxes for the rich? If these tax cuts do not really benefit the larger economy in any way, why promote them? Many politicians, like Phil Gramm for example, are leading advocates of this cause. For those politicians that are not already wealthy, the heavy financial demands of campaigns force them to be sympathetic to the wishes of their wealthy benefactors. Many intellectuals have also signed on to the cause. Some have found that adopting positions that favor the rich can be professionally and financially rewarding. Irving Kristol has earned a position as a fellow at the American Enterprise Institute and Milton Friedman is a senior fellow at the Hoover Institute.

LEARNING FROM MISTAKES

At some point in the 1980s, most observers of the nation's monetary policy reached the obvious conclusion that Milton Friedman's monetarism had failed. There are exceptions of course, including Milton Friedman and his ally, Robert Bartley, editor of the *Wall Street Journal*. As recently as May 1994, Bartley was repeating Friedman's favorite dictum, "Inflation is a *monetary phenomena*" and insisting that inflation certainly isn't "caused by too many people working."[6] One can only wonder how many times monetarism will have to fail to shake the faith of these two loyalists.

Since the monetarist experiment, however, U.S. monetary policy has never been quite the same. When Paul Volcker took charge of the Fed in 1979, he abandoned all concerns except one—inflation. This was a break from the past because federal law requires the Fed to pursue low inflation and low unemployment. Previous chairmen of the Fed at least voiced an interest in achieving both objectives, but Paul Volcker seldom offered even this much. His sole mission became to drive inflation down and hold it down, a goal that has been adopted by succeeding chairs and governors of the Board. Tragically, unemployment no longer appears to be a problem the Fed has much interest in.

In this regard, the United States is not much different from national banks and treasuries around the world. The German central bank has earned a reputation for being especially wary of inflation, a preoccupation that dates back before World War II and Germany's unfortunate experience with hyperinflation. The Bank of England has also focused on containing inflation as have other central banks in Europe. In fact, the goal of stopping inflation has become a preoccupation of central banks and treasuries worldwide.

The obsession with stopping inflation survived the monetarist experiment, but the means of achieving that goal did not. The Fed still periodically raises or lowers interest rates, but their guide is no longer just the money supply. They have officially returned to a more eclectic approach, looking at a variety of statistics and then pronouncing the danger of inflation as either receding or expanding. In practice, however, it appears that the unemployment rate plays a particularly important role. The Fed is much more likely to lower interest rates when unemployment rises above 6 percent and raise interest rates when unemployment is below 6 percent. While the timing and extent of the Fed's actions may be based on a variety of economic conditions, their analysts appear to be using unemployment levels as a key indicator of inflation. If you think this reasoning sounds like the Phillips curve, then you are right. The Phillips curve is back on the computers at the Fed.

Despite the fact that the Fed may be using the Phillips curve, they are not using it like the Keynesians did in the 1960s. During the Kennedy years, Keynesians were committed to achieving the lowest possible unemployment rate compatible with low inflation, a level they placed at 4 percent. Kennedy's economic advisors also advocated strong public support for the unemployed since they acknowledged that some people would suffer under this policy. Contemporary governors of the Federal Reserve Board have a different approach. They do not acknowledge that their policies are responsible for high average rates of unemployment, yet should that rate fall below 5 percent, the Fed will predictably move to raise interest rates. Another difference is that the current members of the Fed seldom voice any support for programs that assist the unemployed.

There have been dissenting voices on the Federal Reserve Board, including President Clinton's appointee, Alan Blinder, a professor of economics from Princeton University. Blinder once noted that the "Phillips curve trade-off is alive and well," an observation that offended an op-ed author for the *Wall Street Journal*.[7] This fact and

Blinder's overt concern about unemployment exposed him to a rather vicious attack by the business press. He was called "inflation's friend" by the same *Wall Street Journal* author. Blinder was perhaps not aware that it was professionally acceptable for the Fed to use the Phillips curve to set monetary policy, but not to admit its existence.

Blinder has since resigned from the Board, but his replacement will face the same obstacles he faced. Blinder and fellow Clinton appointee, Janet Yellen, did not by themselves have enough votes to sway the Federal Reserve Board composed of seven presidential appointees. Their two votes were even less important in the powerful 12 member Federal Open Market Committee (FOMC) that directs monetary policy. The FOMC includes the seven member Federal Reserve Board and five of the 12 presidents of the regional Federal Reserve Banks. Because terms for Federal Reserve Board governors are 14 years, even three presidential terms may not be enough to appoint a solid majority of the FOMC. A two-term president may appoint as few as four members to the FOMC compared to the five bank presidents selected by the banking community.

It is not surprising that as a result of this imbalance, the nation's monetary policy tends to reflect the interests of bankers more than democratically elected officials. The problem for public policy is that these interests are not always the same. Elected officials answer to the general public whose concerns include both unemployment and the risk of inflation. Bankers answer to the banking community where inflation risk is the preeminent concern.

The undemocratic nature of the nation's monetary policy was firmly established with the creation of the Federal Reserve system in 1913. It was clear to Congress that a centralized authority was needed to prevent financial disasters like what had occurred in 1907, the year that the nation's banks ran dangerously short of cash and credibility. A far more disastrous crisis was narrowly averted only after a deal was brokered by J. P. Morgan, one of the nation's most powerful bankers. The need to regulate financial institutions was urgent, but Congress also faced opposition from the banking community who feared sharing power with a central bank. The compromise struck in 1913 created a central bank to regulate the nation's banking system and granted commercial banks considerable control over that system.

The biases of the Fed were easier to overlook in the past when fiscal policy was still the primary policy tool. Yet in the past ten years, with fiscal policy locked on automatic pilot, monetary policy has taken on much of the responsibility for our nation's economic health. Ceding control of such an important public institution to the banking community makes far less sense today. At times, the demand by bankers for high unemployment seems to reflect their own narrow priorities rather than the public will. Reform is long overdue at the Fed. The place to begin is to shorten the terms of governors on the Board and to eliminate the role of regional bank presidents on the Federal Open Market Committee.

THE POUND AND THE PESO

The free-floating experiment in the 1980s dispelled the notion that a ban on all government intervention was somehow good for international currency markets, but it did not provide a blueprint of what government intervention should look like. It is not simply a question of supporting government intervention or not; the question is what type of intervention is better than none at all. How can the government save international financial markets from their own flaws without creating additional, unnecessary problems? We have in recent years seen examples of government intervention that tell us about how it should be done as well as how it should not be done.

Perhaps one of the most spectacular failures in recent times was the British effort to support the pound and to save the European Monetary System (EMS) in 1992. Europe developed the EMS in 1979 with the goal of reducing inflation and providing more exchange rate stability. In some ways, the EMS resembled a little Bretton Woods agreement, limited to European countries. Exchange rates between European countries were fixed within a narrow band, plus or minus 2.25 percent for Belgium, Luxembourg, Denmark, France, Germany, Ireland, Italy, and the Netherlands and 6 percent for Britain, Spain, and Portugal. While exchange rates were free to fluctuate within this band, central banks were obligated to ensure that the thresholds were not violated. If they were, then a formal revaluation up or down was required. In this system, the German mark became the monetary standard, much like the dollar in the Bretton Woods system.[8]

The EMS was often viewed as a precursor to a single European currency. As long as Europe was able to maintain more or less fixed exchange rates it was in fact operating as if it had a single currency. For many observers, a single currency was a logical extension of the economic integration that Europe was already undergoing. The form of such a currency system was outlined in the Maastricht Treaty in December 1991 and appeared to have a good chance of being adopted, at least until September 1992.

The prime minister of Britain in 1992, John Major, committed his government to the EMS in no uncertain terms. During the summer of that year he had taken "a vow to maintain the parity of the pound at any cost."[9] Major was one of the signers of the Maastricht Treaty and was intent on pursuing an integrated European economy with a single currency. But economic events were making all this increasingly difficult.

The problem can reliably be traced back to West Germany's decision a few years earlier to absorb and rehabilitate East Germany's economy. The cost of such a project placed a heavy burden on the national budget and without compensating tax increases, created a danger of inflation. Germany's solution was to raise interest rates, an action that set off a round of destabilizing international reactions. Quite predictably, higher interest rates in Germany attracted investors who proceeded to bid up the price of the German mark. This left other countries, especially Italy, Spain, and Britain, to watch their currencies rapidly fall toward the bottom of the exchange rate bands established by the EMS.

If the problem had been limited to Germany's interest rate policy, the system might have survived but the stakes were immediately raised by speculators who began betting against the weaker currencies. If, as they guessed, these currencies would soon be devalued, then it was time to sell them and buy German marks. Even if speculators did not own liras, pesetas, or pounds, they could borrow them, sell them while the price was still high, and pay back what they borrowed later at a reduced price. This method, described as "selling short," greatly increases the opportunities for speculators to make money on faltering currencies.

The Italian lira succumbed first to the pressure. On Sunday, September 13, 1992, Italian officials decided to devalue their currency by 7 percent, a decision that seemed only to make things worse. William Ledward, a bank economist, claimed that, "In agreeing to a 7 percent devaluation, you gave the speculators a big profit, and these people are like vampires. Once they taste blood, they have to have it again."[10]

In Britain, official resistance to the attack on the pound was tenacious. By one estimate, the British government bought 10 billion pounds in a single day.[11] It also resorted to raising its own benchmark interest rate despite the fact that unemployment was at a five-year high. The interest rate was increased from 10 to 12 percent on Wednesday morning, September 16, but by the afternoon it became clear that the markets were not responding. The prime minister had made vows during the summer to "never devalue the pound" and so the interest rate was increased again in the afternoon, this time to 15 percent. Speculators, however, were not persuaded and decided to call Major's bluff. Despite the spectacular increase in interest rates, speculators continued to exchange British pounds for German marks.

Shortly before midnight on Wednesday, the monetary committee of the European Community met to consider its options. When it reported its decision six hours later, Britain had withdrawn from the EMS, allowing the pound to float; Italy had abandoned efforts to stabilize the lira; and Spain had devalued the peseta by 5 percent. The European Monetary System was in shambles and the British government was embarrassed, having lost a high-stakes game of poker to international speculators.

It was revealed more than a month later that a single speculator had won big on the devaluation of the British pound. Hungarian-American financier George Soros reported that he had made approximately a billion dollars by acting on his hunch that the German Bundesbank favored a devaluation of the pound and lira.[12] Like other speculators, he borrowed heavily, betting everything on a devaluation. His accomplishment earned him a highly revered position among currency traders.

It is easy to conclude that Britain made a mistake defending the pound. However, rather than use this experience to condemn all government intervention in currency markets, we should recognize why this particular intervention failed. The prime minister's primary motivation in this instance was not to stabilize the pound, it was to preserve a system of semifixed exchange rates long enough to make a transition to a single European currency. By pledging to never devalue the pound, Major may have thought that he was building confidence in the pound, but in reality he was digging in his heels against overwhelming economic forces. Because the British pound was not as attractive to investors as the German mark, devaluation became increasingly irresistible. If government intervention is to be successful it must not ignore these economic realities. A government can stabilize a currency only after it has adjusted to market forces; it cannot prevent the adjustment entirely.

The British experience in September 1992 provided a valuable lesson for other countries: when governments intervene in currency markets to achieve political goals and ignore economic realities, they risk disaster. Mexico had ample time to absorb this lesson so it had no excuse for what happened in 1994. There were many reasons for Mexico to support the peso at that time; all of them were political, none economic.

One aspect of the problem can be traced to the 1960s when Mexico absorbed increasing amounts of foreign debt to finance its development. The loans, many of which were financed by large American banks, were predicated on the prospect that Mexico would become one of the great economic success stories of the developing world. By the 1980s it became apparent that this dream was not going to materialize. Oil revenues eventually subsided and the economy struggled with chronic unemployment, explosive inflation, and rampant corruption at the highest levels of government.

With the election of President Carlos Salinas de Gortari in Mexico in 1988, a major campaign was begun to attract foreign investors, promote trade, and reduce the role of the federal government. Salinas was lauded in the American business press for these reforms. Rudi Dornbusch, an economist at MIT, characterized Salinas's programs for "privatization, trade liberalization including the North American Free Trade Agreement [NAFTA], deregulation, and budget balancing" as "brilliant reforms."[13] Similar praise was voiced by Steve Hanke, professor at The Johns Hopkins University, and Sir Alan Walters, vice chairman of AIG Trading Group. According to them, "Mexico has accomplished much. It has substantially opened its economy to world trade, reduced regulation, privatized much of its state sector, reduced the fiscal deficit and finally made the Central Bank independent of government."[14]

Mexico's reality did not quite measure up to this acclaim. For starters, many of the government enterprises were sold to members of Salinas's campaign finance committee, raising questions about the integrity of privatization.[15] Another problem was that the reforms rapidly increased the role of private markets in a country already prone to economic extremes. A more volatile, private economy can be a risky experiment when you have a huge foreign debt that requires reliable servicing. What Mexico did was not unlike taking its mortgage payment to the race track. These problems were only compounded by the fact that the Salinas government stubbornly refused to devalue the peso.

The fact that the peso was overvalued was not unknown in 1994. Mexican authorities had pegged the value of the new peso to the dollar and were attempting to maintain a value of 3.3 pesos to the dollar. But according to Hanke and Walters, the peso at this rate was overvalued and would become "increasingly overvalued" because inflation rates were higher in Mexico than in the United States. A weaker peso could also have been good for Mexico in the long run. It would have made Mexico's exports more competitive and eventually discouraged imports. Hanke and Walters recommended in July 1994 that Mexico either devalue the peso by 16 percent or permit it to float freely on international exchanges.

This was sound economic advice even though it was not compatible with Salinas's political goals. Mexico was scheduled to have an election in late August and Salinas must have worried that a devaluation would not sit well with the electorate. The Partido Revolucionario Institucional (PRI), Salinas's party, had dominated these elections for a long time, not, however, without considerable effort. Salinas's own victory in the 1988 presidential election was replete with electoral irregularities. Even before he was announced the winner, reports were circulating that ballots for his opponent "were found discarded in dumpsters, burned in piles along roadsides and floating down rivers in soggy bales."[16] There was no guarantee that Salinas's handpicked successor could win an honest election, especially if the peso was devalued.

Salinas's own ambitions were also incompatible with devaluation. After his term as president, he pursued the position of director general of the World Trade Organization, fully supported by the Clinton administration. A devaluation would have cast a shadow over his legacy as a free-trade reformer, raising the question of whether or not he had fulfilled his promises to the Mexican people. There was also the danger that a Mexican devaluation would reflect badly on American politicians who had defended NAFTA, including, of course, President Clinton. Rather than risk losing the election and jeopardizing his personal ambitions, Salinas stubbornly refused to devalue the peso.

A devaluation by itself is not necessarily destructive, but the expectation of a devaluation can be catastrophic. Between August and December of 1994, confidence in the peso steadily eroded as more and more investors concluded that a devaluation was inevitable. The government stuck by its pledge to not devalue the peso and spent its precious foreign reserves buying unwanted pesos.

Shortly after taking office, Salinas's successor, Ernesto Zedillo Ponce de Leon, succumbed to the pressure and devalued the peso. It is interesting in economics how delaying a certain action only five months can create an altogether different, unique response. Following the devaluation on December 20, 1994, it was as if a dam had burst. Investors who only months earlier had converted their dollars, pounds, and marks into pesos to reap extraordinary profits in the Mexican stock market were now just as quickly trying to sell their pesos. With a shortage of buyers, however, they were forced to accept lower and lower prices.

It wasn't long before the initial tumble turned into a full-fledged panic. During the six weeks following the devaluation, the peso continued to fall, losing 45 percent of its value. Where only 3.4 pesos were required to buy a dollar prior to December 20, 1994, it required 6.3 pesos by the end of January 1995. At the same time it was reported that Mexico's international currency reserves had fallen to $2 billion, not enough to support any serious government intervention. Not only had Mexico's efforts to maintain the high price of the peso failed, they had created a free fall that they were incapable of arresting.

Once again, it would be a mistake to condemn all forms of government intervention based on the peso crisis of 1995. The Mexican government was not trying to cushion the fall of the peso, they were trying to defy the law of gravity. President Salinas exhausted Mexico's meager foreign reserves in order to win an election, save NAFTA, and increase his chance of securing a prominent international position. He not only failed to get the job with the World Trade Organization, but he ended up fleeing to the United States leaving Mexico to contend with an extraordinary financial crisis.

Government intervention cannot permanently prevent markets from changing the value of a currency. What government intervention can do is prevent these changes from getting out of hand. Without government intervention, the combination of speculation and other flaws in currency markets can create speculative bubbles or, as in the case of Mexico, a speculative collapse. If there ever was a legitimate time to intervene on behalf of the peso, it was January 1995. But by this time the Mexican government had exhausted its reserves, leaving the fate of the peso in the hands of a spooked market.

Mexicans were not the only ones concerned about the collapse of the peso. Mexico had $23 billion in debt that came due in 1995, much of which was owed to American banks and businesses including Citibank and Goldman Sachs.[17] In addition, many American companies that had invested heavily in Mexico after the passage of NAFTA faced major losses if the peso collapsed. Furthermore, the Mexican panic was beginning to spread to financial markets as far as Argentina and Poland, jeopardizing their progress toward a stronger market orientation. As a result of these events, there were powerful voices calling for the United States to intervene to save the peso.

On the other side, opposing U.S. intervention, was the American public. By some estimates, 80 percent of Americans opposed a financial bailout for Mexico.[18] Responding to this public pressure, Congress rejected the Clinton administration's proposed $40 billion in loan guarantees. The news of congressional rejection was sufficient to send the peso tumbling again.

The peso was ultimately rescued by U.S. government intervention. The Clinton administration put together a $50 billion rescue package including $20 billion in U.S. Treasury funds and $17.8 billion from the International Monetary Fund. Robert Rubin, Clinton's new Treasury secretary, was given much of the credit for leading the administration's efforts in this operation. His 26 years of experience with a prominent investment banking house evidently proved useful in negotiating this immense deal. But the fact that the banking house he had worked for was Goldman Sachs exposed him to accusations of conflict of interests. He defended himself by insisting, "I don't give one whit for the investors."[19] His transition from banker to public servant had apparently been complete.

The Clinton bailout was highly controversial. It provided valuable benefits to some large U.S. corporations and banks and only vague promises to everyone else. It did however succeed in arresting the fall of the peso. Although the peso has yet to recover or even regain much confidence, the bailout did succeed in ending the peso crash of 1995.

DOLLAR DEFENSE

In contrast to the British and Mexican experiences, the defense of the dollar in 1994 was highly successful. Starting about the beginning of the year, the dollar began a steady decline, probably related to relatively lower interest rates in the United States and the fact that the country was experiencing an economic recovery. Whatever the reason, the U.S. Treasury refused to intervene, seeing the dollar's decline as a natural response to economic conditions and perhaps even a resolution to the chronic U.S. trade deficit with Japan. A cheaper dollar would tend to make Japanese imports more expensive and U.S. exports cheaper.[20] Asked to explain the absence of government intervention in March, an administration official responded, "It is the right thing to do at the appropriate time, and an inappropriate thing to do at the wrong time."[21]

In October, Treasury Secretary Lloyd Bentsen announced that the Treasury had no intention of intervening. Two weeks later, in early November, the Federal Reserve moved aggressively to buy dollars, arresting its decline and even providing for a small increase against the yen. There were some complaints that this was a cynical attempt to boost the dollar on the eve of the 1994 elections, and there were other complaints that these actions were sending mixed messages because of the "on again, off again" nature of the intervention. In fact this was probably a model of how government intervention can stabilize currency markets.

Without the Treasury's actions it is quite likely that market inertia would have continued to punish the dollar, pushing it below its long-term level. Only government intervention could have prevented this problem in 1994. But in order to be successful, the intervention had to be properly administered. For example, the U.S. Treasury had to resist intervening too early. The dollar was probably overvalued in the beginning of 1994 and needed to be devalued. If intervention had occurred too early, then this useful adjustment would have been blocked. The United States would have found itself swimming against the economic current, much like Britain had two years earlier and Mexico would a year later. Instead, the Treasury and Federal Reserve waited until a reasonable adjustment had taken place before they intervened.

The U.S. Treasury and Federal Reserve did a few other things right as well. When they did intervene, they did so in a swift, decisive manner. They were willing to spend a large amount of money in a relatively short period of time. In today's huge currency markets, interventions that lack conviction are not likely to be taken seriously and therefore have a slim chance of succeeding. The U.S. intervention in 1994 was large enough to be taken seriously. It was estimated that $4.5 billion was spent in only two days to support the dollar.[22]

The benefits of a surprise intervention are both more subtle and more enduring. This one effectively conveyed a message to all currency speculators: beware of short-term trends because the government may step in at any time and put an end to it. In other words, the United States will not permit a short-term adjustment to snowball into a speculative bubble or a currency rout. If the surprise nature of the intervention causes speculators to think twice before they jump on a currency trend then it has accomplished something that will provide additional stability to currency markets in the future.

The intervention in 1994 was successful because it was well timed, it was decisive, and it was unexpected. Even then it could have been better if it had been coordinated with other central banks. To some observers it appeared as if the United States was acting unilaterally, without the support of other central banks. Coordinated actions are generally preferable because they signal even greater commitment to the intervention as well as the availability of even greater resources.

As the world learns more about the art of effective currency intervention, the markets are changing in such a way as to make them more difficult. Most important is the fact that foreign currency reserves held by the world's central banks are not growing as fast as currency markets themselves. The *New York Times* reported that the volume of currency trading increased about 50 percent between 1989 and 1992. In a slow day of trading, hundreds of billions of dollars worth of currency are exchanged on the world markets centered in London, New York, Tokyo, Frankfurt, and Hong Kong. A typical day of trading would come closer to $1 trillion.[23]

Foreign currency reserves held by central banks have not increased as quickly in recent years. In fact, central bank reserves today are about $1 trillion, the same magnitude as one day of trading on the currency exchanges. The concern is that if transactions on the exchanges continue to increase at current rates, they will soon dwarf official reserves, making government intervention more difficult.

If government intervention is to be effective in the future, official reserves cannot continue to lag behind the growth of the market. What can be done? Central banks could begin to accumulate more foreign reserves, buying them with their own currency. The reason this has not happened so far is that most countries are worried about inflation. Any country can use its own currency to buy more foreign reserves, but this puts more of its money into circulation, thus creating a potential for inflation. Only a coordinated exchange of currency by central banks could succeed in raising reserves without increasing currency in circulation.

An alternative method to augment the reserves of central banks was offered by John Maynard Keynes while negotiating the Bretton Woods agreement. His suggestion was to create a new monetary unit in order to supplement existing reserves. The new money would be restricted to central bank transactions and would be regulated by the International Monetary Fund. While the Bretton Woods negotiators rejected the idea, it was resurrected years later with the creation of special drawing rights (SDR) by the IMF. An allocation of SDR from the IMF was, in some ways, as good as gold because it could be used to obtain foreign currency quickly, as required for effective intervention. One possible solution to the reserve shortage is to increase the amount of central bank money, like SDR.

Any increase in central bank money would have to be carefully limited. No one would want central banks to have so much in reserves that intervention would become ubiquitous. The goal should be to preserve the ability of central banks to intervene, not necessarily augment it. Truly massive interventions can be conducted today only through the coordinated actions of several central banks and this is probably a good thing. It means that unilateral interventions of this magnitude will be discouraged.

In the past, a country facing a currency crisis would consider the option of exchange controls, limiting the conversion of currencies. While exchange controls have certain redeeming features, they have become increasingly unpopular among central bankers. If a country imposed exchange controls to slow down the exodus of capital, it would run the risk of undermining its relationship with the IMF, the World Bank, and international trade organizations. Mexico, for example, chose to suffer from a massive capital flight rather than impose exchange controls because it was unwilling to jeopardize NAFTA and support from international banks. Without effective exchange controls, it becomes essential that countries have sufficient currency reserves for effective intervention. Otherwise we may see what happens when a currency panic, like Mexico's in 1995, is allowed to become a free fall.

THE BALANCED BUDGET EXPERIMENT

There is no shortage of suggestions for economic experiments that promise to make the country more competitive internationally and accelerate economic growth. Sometimes these proposals are new and sometimes they are merely extensions of past experiments. One that has received considerable attention recently is the balanced budget amendment. There is no guarantee that a balanced budget will be mandated by constitutional amendment or by federal law but it is at least a possibility. If this should come to pass, it would mark the beginning of a major experiment.

The call for balanced budgets is not a new phenomenon. During the 1930s, advocates of balanced budgets denounced the New Deal for deficit spending, which they claimed only added to the economic crisis. Budget deficits, they asserted, undermined confidence in the currency, banking institutions, and the entire national economy. As a result, they believed that positive economic activity, such as investing, producing, and consuming, were impaired. The economic prosperity of the country, they insisted, required strict adherence to a balanced budget.

The promise of a balanced budget is to restore confidence in the economy and thus promote economic growth and prosperity. Some advocates of balanced budgets may promise more than this, but few would promise any less.

It is difficult to hear this claim without seeing another Trojan horse being wheeled down Pennsylvania Avenue into the nation's capital. Advocates of a balanced budget are often the very same people that supported the tax cuts that created the deficits in the first place. Irving Kristol advised conservatives in advance that the supply-side tax cuts, if they failed, would create large deficits. Still, rather than worry about the prospect of massive deficits, he figured they would be a useful bargaining chip in reducing the overall size of government. Similarly, Congress must have realized when they voted for the Reagan tax cuts that major deficits were a likely outcome.

This is one of those instances where it would help if the American electorate had a longer memory, one reaching back 15 years to be exact. Robert Dole and Phil Gramm, who are now leading the movement for the balanced budget amendment, were two of the elected officials that gave us the Reagan tax cuts in 1981 that created the deficits in the first place. Where was their passionate interest in balanced budgets then? Were deficits less important only because they had the opportunity to cut hundreds of billions of dollars from the tax liability of wealthy families and corporations? By the 1990s many of the tax cutters had become budget balancers. Based on their aversion to deficits, you would never guess that Robert Dole and Phil Gramm had a hand in creating them in 1981.

If the nation does eventually embark on a balanced budget experiment, it will present two serious challenges. The first is that a balanced budget would permanently mothball fiscal policy. No longer will the government be able to increase spending or cut taxes to compensate for a lack of investment or consumption in the private sector. Without this alternative, the government will have far less ability to buffer the natural booms and busts associated with business cycles. In this environment, only the Federal Reserve will have any chance of rescuing the economy from a serious collapse and this is only a chance.

In recent years, the Fed has attempted to avoid steep recessions by lowering interest rates when the unemployment rate exceeded 6 percent. For more than a decade, this policy has successfully held the unemployment rate below 7.5 percent but only because it was

assisted by immense federal deficits. The more immediate challenge for the Federal Reserve will be to avoid economic collapse
without the aid of these underlying deficits.

Based on their understanding of the Great Depression, Keynesians expect that a balanced budget will render the Federal Reserve's
policies far less effective. As unemployment began to mount during
the Depression, the Federal Reserve fought back by lowering the
discount rate to 1 percent in an effort to push interest rates lower
and stimulate investment and consumption. But even a prime
interest rate of 1.5 percent in the 1930s was incapable of resusci-
tating the economy. Keynesians concluded that you can offer
businesses and consumers low interest rates, but you cannot
guarantee that they will borrow and spend. As a result, monetary
policy was thought useful only during mild recessions and even
then, only as a complement to fiscal policy.

With a balanced budget amendment, the Federal Reserve may
be allowed another opportunity to see how effective it can be in
the face of a major economic downturn. Whether interest rates
alone can prevent the entire national economy from running
aground will be the question posed by a balanced budget experiment.

A more moderate approach to the deficit would be to restore the
balance that existed prior to the Reagan tax cuts. There is very little
reason for the budget to be in deficit during an economic expansion
and even less reason for it to be balanced during a recession. If the
Reagan tax cuts were rescinded, the government budget would be
well on its way to regaining a rational balance, without the hazards
of a balanced budget requirement.

DESIGNING THE NEXT EXPERIMENT

If there is one kind of experiment that it is best to avoid, it is the
Trojan horse. A Trojan horse is an experiment based on a theory
without logic or evidence. It generates hypotheses that are judged
for their political popularity rather than their credibility. This kind
of experiment's real goal is never publicly articulated. A code of
secrecy prevents the experimenters from explaining that their true
intentions may be to redistribute income, burden the government
with debt, eliminate public regulation, or allow one group to gain
an advantage over another. A Trojan horse is an experiment built

on deceit. The experiments of the 1980s provide a clear warning of the risks involved for a nation conducting these kinds of experiments.

It is worth being reminded that economics is different from sciences in one important way. There may be no fundamental laws of economics that transcend time and place. Economic policies that succeed in a country one year may not succeed a decade later. As long as people and institutions experience change, there can be no assurance that one set of economic principles will always apply. Even economic knowledge itself may be capable of changing the way the economy works. This fluid aspect of economic development and our limited understanding of it creates the need for experiments. In fact, it is difficult to imagine a world that has outgrown the need for economic experiments.

Notes

1 CAMELOT AND TROJAN HORSES

1. *Economic Report of the President* (1965, Jan.): 38.
2. Ibid., 63.
3. *Economic Report of the President* (1995, Feb.): 367.
4. The world was under a regime of fixed exchange rates at the time, which meant that the United States had to maintain the dollar or devalue. Since the dollar provided the basis for the entire world system, devaluation was not perceived as a realistic alternative.
5. In particular, the U.S. Treasury made a point of selling short-term securities in order to force short-term rates up but bought long-term bonds, which generally has the effect of lowering interest rates. They also attempted to increase the supply of funds available for long-term investments by raising the maximum interest rate that banks could, at the time, legally pay savers for their deposits. Higher rates for savers, it was thought, would increase the amount of savings and put pressure on long-term rates to fall.
6. *Economic Report of the President* (1965, Jan.): 289.
7. Ibid., 33–34.

2 ORIGINS OF MONETARISM

1. Milton Friedman and Rose Friedman, *Free to Choose: A Personal Statement* (New York: Harcourt Brace Jovanovich) (1979): 13.

2. Milton Friedman, *Dollars and Deficits: Living with America's Economic Problems* (Englewood Cliffs, N.J.: Prentice-Hall) (1968): 7.

3. While credit cards are used to make purchases, they must be paid off in cash or more likely checks. While it is easy to confuse credit cards with money, they are nothing more than a device for expanding credit.

4. Eugene Lerner, "Inflation in the Confederacy, 1861-65," in Milton Friedman, ed., *Studies in the Quantity Theory of Money* (Chicago: Univ. of Chicago Press) (1956): 170.

5. The impact of this restraint by banks was all but lost in a virtual flood of Confederate money.

6. Friedman (1968): 8-9.

7. Milton Friedman, *The Optimum Quantity of Money and Other Essays* (Chicago: Aldine) (1969): 47-48.

8. Ibid., 48.

9. Ibid., 2.

10. Ibid., 8.

11. Friedman and Friedman (1979): 281.

12. Friedman (1968): 171.

13. Friedman and Friedman (1979): 281.

14. Friedman (1968): 127.

15. Friedman and Friedman (1979): 254.

16. Milton Friedman, ed., *Studies in the Quantity Theory of Money* (Chicago: Univ. of Chicago Press) (1956): 26.

17. Friedman and Friedman (1979): 253.

18. Ibid., 270.

19. *Economic Report of the President* (1993, Feb.): 416.

20. Friedman (1969): 88.

21. Friedman wrote in 1968, "More important . . . for my own views—perhaps also for the profession—was a re-examination of the evidence for the Great Contraction of 1929-33." Friedman (1968): 13.

22. Based on the Dow Jones Industrial Averages. Phyllis Pierce, ed. *Dow Jones Averages, 1885-1990* (Homewood, Ill.: Business One Irwin) (1991).

23. See, for example, Christina Romer, "The Great Crash and the Onset of the Great Depression," *The Quarterly Journal of Economics* (1990, Aug.).

24. U.S. Department of Commerce, *Long Term Economic Growth: 1860-1970*, Series A29 (Washington, D.C.: GPO): 187.

25. John Kenneth Galbraith, *The Great Crash, 1929* (Boston: Houghton Mifflin) (1955): 71.

26. Milton Friedman and Anna Schwartz, *A Monetary History of the United States, 1867-1960* (Princeton: Princeton Univ. Press) (1963): 438.

27. This fact is inferred from the observation that the ratio of commercial bank deposits to reserves declined. Peter Temin, *Did Monetary Forces Cause the Great Depression?* (New York: W. W. Norton) (1976): 5.

28. This is represented by a decline in the ratio of commercial bank deposits to currency held by the public from 1930 to 1933. Ibid. (1976): 5.

29. Friedman and Schwartz (1963): 316.

30. Ibid., 438.

31. Ibid., 299.

32. Friedman and Friedman (1979): 85.

33. Friedman and Friedman (1979): 82. Even Friedman and Schwartz (1963), however, had to admit that under the best monetary policy "the contraction . . . would have ranked as one of the more severe contractions on record" (1963): 306.

34. Galbraith (1955): 190.

35. Temin (1976): 21, 25; and Friedman and Schwartz (1963): 317.

36. In this world, interest rates are "determined independently—by productivity, thrift, and the like." Friedman (1956): 15.

37. A. W. Phillips, "The Relationship Between Unemployment and the Rate of Change of Money Wage Rates in the United Kingdom, 1826–1957," *Economica* (1958, Nov.).

38. Friedman and Friedman (1979): 265.

39. Ibid., 282.

40. Friedman (1968): 25. The estimates of economic growth for this period are highly dubious. They are imputed from figures that are certainly no better than Friedman's own assessment of them, that is, a "rough guess." Friedman and Schwartz (1963): 34.

41. Friedman (1968): 26; Friedman and Schwartz (1963): 32.

42. Friedman and Friedman (1979): 271.

43. Ibid., 267.

44. Ibid., 281.

45. Friedman (1968): 15.

3 GAMBLING AT THE FED

1. This is the crude oil refiner acquisition cost for imports. U.S. Department of Energy, *Annual Energy Review, 1992*, p. 163.

2. "Straight and Narrow with Mr. Volcker," *New York Times* (1979, July 26).

3. "Nominee Pledges to Fight Inflation and Restore Confidence in Dollar," *New York Times* (1979, July 26).

4. Ibid.

5. Paul Volcker and Toyoo Gyohten, *Changing Fortunes, The World's Money and the Threat to American Leadership* (New York: Times Books) (1992): 164.

6. Leonard Silk, "A Conservative Choice," *New York Times* (1979 July 26).

7. Paul Volcker, "The Contributions and Limitations of 'Monetary' Analysis," *Quarterley Review* (1989): 35–41.

8. These so-called "managed liabilities" included large time deposits, Eurodollar borrowings, repurchase agreements, and Federal funds borrowings from member banks.

9. "Text of Fed's Announcement on Measures to Curb Inflation," *New York Times* (1979, Oct. 8).

10. Steven Rattner, "Executives Hail Fed's New Policy," *New York Times* (1979a, Oct. 15).

11. Ibid.

12. Robert Bennet, "Sharp Rise in Rates Expected," *New York Times* (1979, Oct. 8).

13. "Some in Business Hail Anti-inflation Measures," *New York Times* (1979, Oct. 8).

14. Steven Rattner, "U.S. Money Plan Called Reaction to Speculation," *New York Times* (1979b, Oct. 8).

15. Bennet (1979).

16. Andrew Brimmer, "Monetary Policy and Economic Activity: Benefits and Costs of Monetarism," *American Economic Review* (1983, May).

17. *Economic Report of the President* (1994, Feb.): 352.

18. Paul Volcker blamed the decline on President Carter's credit controls. This interpretation, however, may reflect more of Volcker's personal animosity toward controls than actual reality. For one, the controls were mild, even by Volcker's assessment, intended to raise the cost of only certain kinds of credit by a small amount. The controls raised the marginal reserve requirements for certain funds. It should also be noted that the credit controls were announced on March 14, 1980, but the recession had started in February. Volcker and Gyohten (1992): 172.

19. Volcker and Gyohten (1992): 173.

20. "Rockford and Its 19% Jobless Struggling to Survive," *New York Times* (1982, Aug. 30).

21. "Ohioans Move for Jobs,"*New York Times* (1982, Aug. 17).

22. William Serrin, "Panel on Economy Cites Social Cost," *New York Times* (1982b, Oct. 20).

23. "23.4 Million in U.S. Were Out of Work Sometime Last Year," *New York Times* (1982, July 21).

24. "Help Wanted," *New York Times*, editorial. (1982, Jan. 20).

25. Jonathan Fuerbringer, "Reagan Favors Unadjusted Figures on Jobless," *New York Times* (1982, May).

26. Robert Pear, "Cuts in Unemployment Aid May Spread to More States," *New York Times* (1982, Oct. 10).

27. "Senate Panel Votes Plan Linking Food Stamps to Mandatory Work," *New York Times* (1982, June 15); and S. I. Hayakawa, "Paid by Government to Do Nothing," *New York Times*, letters (1982, Sept. 8).

28. Cited in Brimmer (1983): 4.

29. Erich Heinemann, "U.S. Widens Currency-Trading Role," *New York Times* (1982, Dec. 13).

30. *Economic Report of the President* (1994, Feb.): 339.

31. "Pay Raises Average 3% in New Labor Accords," *New York Times* (1982, Aug. 1).

32. William Serrin, "Labor is Resisting More Concessions," *New York Times* (1982, June 13).

33. *Economic Report of the President* (1984, Feb.): 319.

34. Thomas Karier, "Accounting for the Decline in Private Sector Unionization," Jerome Levy Economics Institute working paper, no. 44 (1991, Feb.).

35. *Economic Report of the President* (1995, Feb.): 324.

36. James Griffin and Henry Steele, *Energy Economics and Policy* (New York: Academic Press) (1980): 16.

37. *Economic Report of the President* (1984, Feb.): 288.

38. There were exceptions, of course, such as the energy crises in the 1970s when inflation erupted without low unemployment. But this was to be expected since this inflation was not sparked by labor shortages but by price hikes passed on from abroad.

39. Volcker and Gyohten (1992): 176.

40. Ibid., 167.

41. Ibid.

42. In a symposium in 1989, members of the central banks of Britain, Germany, and Canada emphasized price stability as their overriding priority. "Monetary Policy Issues in the 1990s," a symposium sponsored by the Federal Reserve Bank of Kansas City: xxv.

4   A VIEW FROM THE SUPPLY SIDE

1. Paul Craig Roberts, *The Supply-Side Revolution* (Cambridge: Harvard Univ. Press) (1984): 101.

2. Ibid.

3. U.S. Department of Commerce, *Long Term Economic Growth, 1860–1970*, p. 223.

4. Jude Wanniski, "Taxes, Revenues, and the 'Laffer Curve,' " in Arthur Laffer and Jan Seymour, eds., *The Economics of the Tax Revolt: A Reader* (New York: Harcourt Brace Jovanovich) (1979): 9.

5. As Laffer and a colleague once noted, "With lower tax rates there will be less advantage to evade or avoid the payment of taxes." Laffer and Seymour (1979): 2.

6. Average tax rates for the rich fall far below this rate because of tax shelters, credits, and deductions. The 70 percent figure represents the marginal tax rate on only unsheltered income.

7. Arthur Laffer and Jan Seymour, eds., *The Economics of the Tax Revolt: A Reader* (New York: Harcourt Brace Jovanovich) (1979): 2.

8. Quoted by Paul Craig Roberts, "The Economic Case for Kemp-Roth," in Laffer and Seymour, eds., *The Economics of the Tax Revolt: A Reader* (New York: Harcourt Brace Jovanovich) (1979): 59.

9. Roberts (1984): 38.

10. Roberts (1984): 12.

11. Wanniski (1978): 125.

12. Joseph M. Jones Jr., *Tariff Retaliation: Repercussions of the Hawley-Smoot Bill* (Philadelphia: Univ. of Pennylvania Press) (1934).

13. *Economic Report of the President* (1993, Feb.): 353, 359.

14. Wanniski (1978): 160.

15. Martin Feldstein, *The American Economy in Transition* (Chicago: Univ. of Chicago Press) (1980): 2.

16. Roberts (1984): 60.

17. U.S. Department of Energy, *Annual Energy Review* (1992, June).

18. Jude Wanniski, *The Way the World Works: How Economies Fail and Succeed* (New York: Basic Books) (1978): 117.

19. John Maynard Keynes, *The Economic Consequences of the Peace* (New York: Harcourt Brace and Howe) (1971): 143.

20. U.S. Department of Commerce, *Long Term Economic Growth, 1860–1970*; Real GNP growth, p. 183; GNP deflators, p. 223.

21. Ibid., 231.

22. Joseph A. Pechman, *Federal Tax Policy* (Washington, D.C.: Brookings Institution) (1977): 298–99, cited in Wanniski (1978): 185.

23. U.S. Department of Commerce, *Long Term Economic Growth, 1860–1970*, pp. 213, 223.

24. Ibid., 289.

25. Galbraith (1955): 12, 71.

26. U.S. Department of Commerce, *Long Term Economic Growth, 1860–1970*, p. 271.

27. Wanniski (1978): 185, 200, 201.

28. *Economic Report of the President* (1993, Feb.): 441.

29. Wanniski (1978): 201.

30. Roberts (1984): 81; for the Kemp quote see Laffer and Seymour (1979): 68.

31. Walter Heller, "The Kemp-Roth-Laffer Free Lunch," in Laffer and Seymour, eds., *The Economics of the Tax Revolt: A Reader* (New York: Harcourt Brace Jovanovich) (1979): 46.

32. *Economic Report of the President* (1993, Feb.): 376.

33. Roberts describes this as one of the "strange arguments against supply-side economics." Roberts (1984): 41. Is it really strange that a chief executive of a corporation, who, after becoming a millionaire, decides to retire early? Great wealth can simply dissipate the will to work.

34. Cited by Heller (1979): 49.

35. Jack Kemp, "Vanik's Study Makes Convincing Case for Enactment of the Kemp-Roth Act," in Laffer and Seymour, eds., *The Economics of the Tax Revolt: A Reader* (New York: Harcourt Brace Jovanovich, 1979): 28.

36. Irving Kristol, "Populist Remedy for Populist Abuses," in Laffer and Seymour, eds., *The Economics of the Tax Revolt: A Reader* (New York: Harcourt Brace Jovanovich) (1979): 52.

37. Ibid., 52.

38. Ibid.

5 BUDGET BUSTERS

1. Roberts (1984): 81.

2. Ibid., 85.

3. Ibid., 86.

4. David Stockman, *The Triumph of Politics: How the Reagan Revolution Failed* (New York: Harper and Row) (1986): 49.

5. Ibid., 39.

6. Weston Kosova, "George, Why can't you be true?" *Utne Reader* (1992).

7. Stockman (1986): 50.

8. Ibid., 10.

9. Roberts (1984): 92.

10. Karen Arenson, "Tax Changes will Affect Savings and Investing," *New York Times* (1981, Aug. 4).

11. Edward Cowan, "Senate Approves Tax-Cut Bill," *New York Times* (1981, Aug. 4).

12. Stockman (1986): 96.

13. Ibid., 96.

14. Ibid., 104, 161.

15. William Greider, "The Education of David Stockman," *Atlantic Monthly* (1981, Dec.).

16. Stockman (1986): 272.

17. Roberts (1984): 214.

18. Ibid., 226.

19. The $228 billion figure comes from Jack Kemp, "Backing Off Economic Recovery," *New York Times* (1982, Aug. 17).

20. Karen Arenson, "Congress Approves Bill to Raise $98 Billion," *New York Times* (1982, Aug. 20).

21. Roberts (1984): 241.

22. "Measuring the Size of the Tax Bill," *New York Times* (1982, Aug. 17).

23. Arenson (1982).

6 THE FREE FLOAT

1. Ronald McKinnon, "The Rules of the Game: International Money in Historical Perspective," *Journal of Economic Literature* (1993, Mar.): 3.

2. Harold Barger, *Money, Banking, and Public Policy* (Chicago: Rand McNally) (1968): 489.

3. Ibid., 495.

4. Fred Block, *The Origins of International Economic Disorder* (Berkeley: Univ. of California Press) (1977): 8.

5. Barger (1968): 504.

6. Milton Gilbert, *Quest for World Monetary Order* (New York: John Wiley) (1980): 24.

7. Milton Friedman, *Essays in Positive Economics* (Chicago: Univ. of Chicago Press) (1953).

8. McKinnon (1993).

9. Friedman (1953): 183.

10. Ibid., 185.

11. Ibid., 183.

12. Ibid., 188.

7 GLOBAL SHOCK WAVES

1. Clyde Farnsworth, "U.S. May Cut Its Currency Role," *New York Times* (1981).

2. Karen Arenson, "Men in the News: Reagan Assembles His Cabinet," *New York Times* (1980, Dec. 12).

3. Information about interest rates in the United States and the world are based on data from the International Monetary Fund, *International Financial Statistics* (1993). World interest rates were calculated as a U.S. export-weighted average of government bond rates.

4. "U.S. Moves to Stabilize Currency," *New York Times* (1982, June 15).

5. "U.S. Bought 2 Currencies," *New York Times* (1982, Dec. 10).

6. Heinemann (1982).

7. *Economic Report of the President* (1994, Feb.): 386.

8. Ibid. In theory, a rising exchange rate may initially depress the value of imports. This occurs because the price reduction in dollars may initially exceed the growth in real imports. If this did occur it would have taken place in 1982 when imports were falling anyway because of the recession. By 1983 there was little evidence of this lagged response.

9. Clyde Farnsworth, "Job Losses Linked to Dollar Rise," *New York Times* (1985, Mar. 13).

10. Steven Rattner, "Regan Sees Trade Gain From Decline in Dollar," *New York Times* (1982, May 8).

11. Clyde Farnsworth, "Talking Business: With Treasury Secretary Donald T. Regan," *New York Times* (1983, Mar. 29).

12. Clyde Farnsworth, "Dollar Rise Is Defended by Regan," *New York Times* (1984, Feb. 23).

13. "Volcker's Currency Aid View," *New York Times* (1983, Apr. 29).

14. *Economic Report of the President* (1984, Feb.): 53. Feldstein's assessment of the situation was less than consistent. Only three pages earlier, the same report stated that "The value of a currency is whatever the market dictates that it should be."

15. "The Likely Effects of a Devalued Dollar," *New York Times* (1985, Sept. 24).

16. "The Soaring Dollar," *New York Times* (1984, Sept. 19).

17. *Economic Report of the President* (1984, Feb.): 62.

18. Volcker and Gyohten (1992): 181.

19. Ibid., 178.

20. Ibid., 180.

21. "President Designates Regan White House Chief of Staff, Switching Him With Baker," *New York Times* (1985, Jan. 8).

22. Peter Kilborn, "An Economic Adviser with a Different View: Beryl Wayne Sprinkel," *New York Times* (1985a, Feb. 22).

23. Volcker and Gyohten (1992): 241.

24. Ibid., 241–43.

25. Ibid., 229.

26. The interest gap was .6 in 1980, 2.2 in 1981, 2.5 in 1982, 2.1 in 1983, 3.6 in 1984, and 2.3 in 1985. Interest rate differentials were obtained from the International Monetary Fund, *International Financial Statistics* (1993), p. 99. They are based on the difference between an index of interest rates on U.S. government bonds and a comparable trade-weighted average for major U.S. trading partners.

27. Peter Kilborn, "U.S. and 4 Allies Plan Move to Cut Value of Dollar," *New York Times* (1985b, Sept. 23).

28. Nicholas Kristof, "Dollar Plunges to 16-Month Low in Reaction to 5 Nations' Accord," *New York Times* (1985, Sept. 24).

29. Michael Quint, "Dollar Sales by the Fed Larger than Surmised," *New York Times* (1985, Dec. 5).

30. Milton Friedman, "Let Floating Rates Continue to Float," *New York Times* (1985, Dec. 26).

8   THE RECKONING: A DECADE OF ECONOMIC RECORDS

1. *Economic Report of the President* (1995, Feb.): 365.

2. *Economic Report of the President* (1995, Feb.).

3. Growth in M2 bounced down from 12 percent in 1983 to 8.2 percent in 1985 only to float back up to 9.4 percent in 1986.

4. "Measuring the Size of the Tax Bill," *New York Times* (1982, Aug. 17).

5. U.S. Department of Commerce, *Historical Statistics of the United States: Colonial Times to 1970*, Washington, D.C.: GPO (1975).

6. Ibid. There is always a certain danger of relying on such old statistics but even with a large margin of error it is safe to conclude that deficits were large during the Civil War and WWI.

9   A FALLING OUT

1. Roberts (1984): 95.
2. Ibid., 188.
3. Stockman (1986): 42.
4. Ibid., 56.
5. Ibid., 38.
6. Ibid., 173.
7. Ibid., 122.
8. Ibid., 271–72.
9. Roberts (1984): 148.
10. Ibid., 181.
11. Ibid., 210.
12. Stockman (1986): 166.
13. Ibid., 166.
14. Ibid., 50.
15. Ibid., 322.
16. Ibid., 302–3.
17. Greider (1981).
18. Stockman (1986): 53.
19. Roberts (1984): 194.

20. Ibid., 28–29.

21. Ibid., 28.

22. Paul Craig Roberts, "The Economic Case for Kemp-Roth," in Laffer and Seymour, eds., *The Economics of the Tax Revolt: A Reader* (New York: Harcourt Brace Jovanovich) (1979): 60–61.

23. Paul Craig Roberts, "Why America's Piggy Banks aren't Bulging," *Business Week* (1988, June 20): 28.

24. *Economic Report of the President* (1995, Feb.): 306.

25. Norman Ture and Stephen Entin, "Why Americans Don't Save," *Consumers' Research Magazine* (1990, June): 29.

26. Stockman (1986): 304.

27. Ibid., 333.

28. Ibid., 333.

29. Ibid., 48.

30. Ibid., 405.

31. Ibid., 380.

32. "Stockman Is Criticized," *New York Times* (1982, Feb. 4).

33. Roberts (1984): 116–17.

34. Volcker and Gyohten (1992): 177.

35. Ibid., 178.

36. Milton Friedman, "Misleading Unanimity," *Newsweek* (1983b, Feb. 7).

37. Milton Friedman, "More Double Talk at Fed," *Newsweek* (1983c, May 2).

38. Milton Friedman, "The Needle Got Stuck," *Newsweek* (1983d, July 25).

39. Milton Friedman, "A Case of Bad Good News," *Newsweek* (1983a, Sept. 26).

40. Edward Mervosh, "Milton Friedman's Recession Forecast Sparks a Controversy," *Business Week* (1983, Dec. 12).

41. Milton Friedman, "A Recession Warning," *Newsweek* (1984, Jan. 16).

42. Ibid.

43. *Economic Report of the President* (1995, Feb.): 277, 345.

44. Milton Friedman, "Right at Last, an Expert's Dream," *Newsweek* (1986, Mar. 10).

45. Volcker and Gyohten (1992): 179.

46. Ibid., 180.

47. Ibid.

48. Ibid., 238.

49. Ibid., 239.

50. Ibid., 243.

51. *Economic Report of the President* (1986, Feb.): 53.

10 REWRITING ECONOMICS

1. U.S. Department of Energy, *Annual Energy Review* (1992, June).
2. *Economic Report of the President* (1984, Feb.): 53.
3. A good source on the earlier tax rates is Randolf E. Paul, *Taxation in the United States* (Boston: Little, Brown) (1954).

11 OUT OF THE ASHES

1. John Kenneth Galbraith, *Money: Whence it Came, Where it Went* (Boston: Houghton Mifflin) (1975): 303.
2. Of course only families with incompetent accountants ever paid the top rates in the 1950s or 1960s, or even the 1990s for that matter.
3. Connie Mack, "Capital Gains Taxes—A $1.5 Trillion Opportunity," *Wall Street Journal* (1995, Aug. 29).
4. David Rosenbaum, "Gramm Proposal for Deep Tax Cut Killed by Senate: Republicans Split," *New York Times* (1995, May 24).
5. Ibid.
6. Robert Bartley, "In Carter Rerun, Fed Owes Duty to Price Stability," *Wall Street Journal* (1994, May 26).
7. Richard Salsman, "Fed Nominee, Inflation's Friend," *Wall Street Journal* (1994, April 26).
8. "How Europe's Monetary System Works," *New York Times* (1992, Sept. 17).
9. William Schmidt, "Major Rejects Pressure to Oust Finance Chief," *New York Times* (1992, Sept. 18).
10. Richard Stevenson, "A Crisis in London: Finance Officials to Seek Measures to Salvage Monetary Links," *New York Times* (1992, Sept 17).
11. George Shultz, "Economics in Action," *American Economic Review* (1995, May).
12. "Big Winner From Plunge in Sterling," *New York Times* (1992, Oct. 27).
13. Rudi Dornbusch, "We Have Salinas to Thank for the Peso Debacle," *Business Week* (1995, Jan. 16).
14. Steven Hanke and Alan Walters, "The Wobbly Peso," *Forbes* (1994, July 4).
15. Andrew Reding, "It isn't the Peso. It's the Presidency," *New York Times Magazine* (1995, April 9).
16. Ibid.
17. Anthony DePalma, "Aid for Mexico Gives Economy Shot in the Arm," *New York Times* (1996, Feb. 2).
18. David Sanger, "The Education of Robert Rubin," *New York Times* (1996, Feb. 2).

19. Ibid.

20. David Sanger, "U.S. Spree Bolsters the Dollar," *New York Times* (1994, Nov. 3).

21. David Sanger, "U.S. Officials Take No Action As Dollar Continues to Slide," *New York Times* (1995, Mar. 8).

22. Sanger (1994).

23. Allen Myerson, "Currency Markets Resisting Powers of Central Banks," *New York Times* (1992, Sept. 25).

Bibliography

Arenson, Karen. 1980. "Men in the News: Reagan Assembles His Cabinet." *New York Times*, 12 December: A28.

————. 1981. "Tax Changes Will Affect Savings and Investing." *New York Times*, 4 August: A1.

————. 1982. "Congress Approves Bill to Raise $98 Billion." *New York Times*, 20 August: A1.

Barger, Harold. 1968. *Money, Banking, and Public Policy*. Chicago: Rand McNally.

Bartley, Robert. 1994. "In Carter Rerun, Fed Owes Duty to Price Stability." *Wall Street Journal*, 26 May: A14.

Bennet, Robert. 1979. "Sharp Rise in Rates Expected." *New York Times*, 8 October: D1.

"Big Winner From Plunge in Sterling," 1992. *New York Times*, 27 October: D9.

Block, Fred. 1977. *Origins of International Economic Disorder: A Study of United States International Monetary Policy from World War II to the Present*. Berkeley: University of California Press.

Brimmer, Andrew. 1983. "Monetary Policy and Economic Activity: Benefits and Costs of Monetarism." *American Economic Review: Papers and Proceedings* 73, no. 2 (May): 1–12.

Cowan, Edward. 1981. "Senate Approves Tax-Cut Bill." *New York Times*, 4 August: 67–68.

DePalma, Anthony. 1996. "Aid for Mexico Gives Economy Shot in the Arm." *New York Times*, 2 February: A1

Dornbusch, Rudi. 1995. "We Have Salinas to Thank for the Peso Debacle," *Business Week*, 16 January: 20.

Economic Report of the President, various years: 1965–1995, Washington,
D.C.: U.S. Government Printing Office.

Farnsworth, Clyde. 1981. "U.S. May Cut Its Currency Role." *New York
Times*, 5 May: D13.

————. 1983. "Talking Business: With Treasury Secretary Donald T.
Regan." *New York Times*, 29 March: IV-2.

————. 1984. "Dollar Rise Is Defended by Regan." *New York Times*, 23
February: IV-7.

————. 1985. "Job Losses Linked to Dollar Rise." *New York Times*, 13
March: IV-17.

Feldstein, Martin. 1980. *The American Economy in Transition*. Chicago:
University of Chicago Press.

Friedman, Milton. 1953. *Essays in Positive Economics*. Chicago: University
of Chicago Press.

————, ed. 1956. *Studies in the Quantity Theory of Money*. Chicago:
University of Chicago Press.

————. 1968. *Dollars and Deficits: Living with America's Economic Problems*. Englewood Cliffs, N.J.: Prentice-Hall.

————. 1969. *The Optimum Quantity of Money and Other Essays*. Chicago:
Aldine Publishing.

————. 1983a. "A Case of Bad Good News." *Newsweek*, 26 September:
72.

————. 1983b. "Misleading Unanimity." *Newsweek*, 7 February: 56.

————. 1983c. "More Double Talk at the Fed." *Newsweek*, 2 May: 72.

————. 1983d. "The Needle Got Stuck." *Newsweek*, 25 July: 72.

————. 1984. "A Recession Warning." *Newsweek*, 16 January: 68.

————. 1985. "Let Floating Rates Continue to Float." *New York Times*,
26 December: I-27.

————. 1986. "Right at Last, an Expert's Dream," *Newsweek*, 10 March: 8

Friedman, Milton, and Anna Schwartz. 1963. *A Monetary History of the
United States, 1867–1960*. Princeton: Princeton University Press.

Friedman, Milton, and Rose Friedman. 1979. *Free to Choose: A Personal
Statement*. New York: Harcourt Brace Jovanovich.

Fuerbringer, Jonathan. 1982. "Reagan Favors Unadjusted Figures on
Jobless." *New York Times*, 16 May: 33.

Galbraith, John Kenneth. 1955. *The Great Crash, 1929*. Boston: Houghton
Mifflin.

————. 1975. *Money: Whence it Came, Where it Went*. Boston: Houghton
Mifflin.

Gilbert, Milton. 1980. *Quest for World Monetary Order: The Gold-Dollar System and Its Aftermath*. New York: John Wiley and Sons, A Twentieth-Century Fund Study.

Greider, William. 1981. "The Education of David Stockman." *Atlantic Monthly*, December: 27–54.

Griffin, James, and Henry Steele. 1980. *Energy Economics and Policy*. New York: Academic Press.

Hanke, Steven, and Sir Alan Walters. 1994. "The Wobbly Peso." *Forbes*, 4 July: 161.

Hayakawa, S. I. 1982. "Paid by the Government to Do Nothing." Letters, *New York Times*, 8 September: A26.

Heinemann, Erich. 1982. "U.S. Widens Currency-Trading Role." *New York Times*, 13 December: D1.

Heller, Walter. 1979. "The Kemp-Roth-Laffer Free Lunch," In Arthur Laffer and Jan Seymour, eds., *The Economics of the Tax Revolt: A Reader*. New York: Harcourt Brace Jovanovich: 46–49.

"Help Wanted." 1982, Editorial, *New York Times*, 20 January: A26.

"How Europe's Monetary System Works." 1992. *New York Times*, 17 September: D8.

International Monetary Fund. 1993. *International Financial Statistics*, Washington, D.C.

Jones, Joseph M., Jr. 1934. *Tariff Retaliation: Repercussions of the Hawley-Smoot Bill*. Philadelphia: University of Pennsylvania Press.

Karier, Thomas. 1991. "Accounting for the Decline in Private Sector Unionization." Jerome Levy Economics Institute Working Paper no. 44, February.

Kemp, Jack. 1979. "Vanik's Study Makes Convincing Case for Enactment of the Kemp-Roth Act." In Arthur Laffer and Jan Seymour, eds., *The Economics of the Tax Revolt: A Reader*. New York: Harcourt Brace Jovanovich: 28.

———. 1982. "Backing Off Economic Recovery." *New York Times*, 17 August: 27.

Keynes, John Maynard. 1971. *The Economic Consequences of the Peace*. New York: Harcourt, Brace and Howe.

Kilborn, Peter. 1985a. "An Economic Adviser With a Different View: Beryl Wayne Sprinkel." *New York Times*, 22 February: IV-1.

———. 1985b. "U.S. and 4 Allies Plan Move to Cut Value of Dollar." *New York Times*, 23 September: A-1.

Kosova, Weston. 1992. "George, Why can't you be true?" *Utne Reader*, November-December: 69–72.

Kristof, Nicholas. 1985. "Dollar Plunges to 16–Month Low in Reaction to 5 Nations' Accord." *New York Times*, 24 September: A1.

Kristol, Irving. 1979. "Populist Remedy for Populist Abuses." In Arthur Laffer and Jan Seymour, eds., *The Economics of the Tax Revolt: A Reader*. New York: Harcourt Brace Jovanovich: 50–52.

Laffer, Arthur, and Jan Seymour, eds. 1979. *The Economics of the Tax Revolt: A Reader*. New York: Harcourt Brace Jovanovich.

Lerner, Eugene. 1956. "Inflation in the Confederacy, 1861–65." In Milton Friedman, ed., *Studies in the Quantity Theory of Money*. Chicago: University of Chicago Press: 163–75.

"The Likely Effects of a Devalued Dollar," 1985. *New York Times*, 24 September: IV–1.

Mack, Connie. 1995. "Capital Gains Taxes—A $1.5 Trillion Opportunity." *Wall Street Journal*, 29 August: A14.

McKinnon, Ronald. 1993. "The Rules of the Game: International Money in Historical Perspective." *Journal of Economic Literature* 31 (March): 3.

"Measuring the Size of the Tax Bill." 1982. *New York Times*, 17 August: IV–16.

Mervosh, Edward. 1983. "Milton Friedman's Recession Forecast Sparks a Controversy." *Business Week*, 12 December: 28.

"Monetary Policy Issues in the 1990s." A symposium sponsored by the Federal Reserve Bank of Kansas City: xxv.

Myerson, Allen. 1992. "Currency Markets Resisting Powers of Central Banks." *New York Times*, 25 September: A1.

"Nominee Pledges to Fight Inflation and Restore Confidence in Dollar." 1979. *New York Times*, 26 July: A1.

"Ohioans Move for Jobs." 1982. *New York Times*, 17 August: A18.

Paul, Randolf E. 1954. *Taxation in the United States*. Boston: Little, Brown and Company.

"Pay Raises Average 3% in New Labor Accords." 1982. *New York Times*, 1 August: A31.

Pear, Robert. 1982. "Cuts in Unemployment Aid May Spread to More States," *New York Times*, 10 October: 28.

Pechman, Joseph A. 1977. *Federal Tax Policy*, 3rd ed. Washington, D.C.: Brookings Institution.

Phillips, A. W. 1958. "The Relationship Between Unemployment and the Rate of Change of Money Wage Rates in the United Kingdom, 1826–1957." *Economica* (November): 283–99.

Pierce, Phyllis, ed. 1991. *The Dow Jones Averages, 1885–1990*. Homewood, Ill.: Business One Irwin.

"President Designates Regan White House Chief of Staff, Switching Him With Baker," 1985. *New York Times*, 9 January: I1.

Quint, Michael. 1985. "Dollar Sales by the Fed Larger than Surmised." *New York Times*, 5 December: IV–1.

Rattner, Steven. 1979a. "Executives Hail Fed's New Policy," *New York Times*, 15 October: D1.

———. 1979b. "U.S. Money Plan Called Reaction to Speculation." *New York Times*, 8 October: A1.

———. 1982. "Regan Sees Trade Gain From Decline in Dollar," *New York Times*, 8 May: 32.

Reding, Andrew. 1995. "It isn't the Peso. It's the Presidency." *New York Times Magazine*, 9 April: 54–55.

Roberts, Paul Craig. 1979. "The Economic Case for Kemp-Roth." In Arthur Laffer and Jan Seymour, eds., *The Economics of the Tax Revolt: A Reader*. New York: Harcourt Brace Jovanovich: 57–61.

———. 1984. *The Supply-Side Revolution: An Insider's Account of Policymaking in Washington*. Cambridge, Mass.: Harvard University Press.

———. 1988. "Why America's Piggy Banks aren't Bulging." *Business Week*, 20 June: 28.

"Rockford and Its 19% Jobless Struggling to Survive." 1982. *New York Times*, 30 August: A10.

Romer, Christina. 1990. "The Great Crash and the Onset of the Great Depression." *The Quarterly Journal of Economics* (August): 597–624.

Rosenbaum, David. 1995. "Gramm Proposal for Deep Tax Cut Killed by Senate: Republicans Split," *New York Times*, 24 May: A1.

Salsman, Richard. 1994. "Fed Nominee, Inflation's Friend." *Wall Street Journal*, 26 April: A22.

Sanger, David. 1994. "U.S. Spree Bolsters the Dollar." *New York Times*, 3 November: D1.

———. 1995. "U.S. Officials Take No Action As Dollar Continues to Slide." *New York Times*, 8 March: A1.

———. 1996. "The Education of Robert Rubin." *New York Times*, 2 February, section 3: 1.

Schmidt, William. 1992. "Major Rejects Pressure to Oust Finance Chief." *New York Times*, 18 September: D5.

"Senate Panel Votes Plan Linking Food Stamps to Mandatory Work." 1982. *New York Times*, 15 June: B8.

Serrin, William. 1982a. "Labor is Resisting More Concessions," *New York Times*, 13 June: A29.

———. 1982b. "Panel on Economy Cites Social Cost," *New York Times*, 20 October: A20.

Shultz, George. 1995. "Economics in Action: Ideas, Institutions, Policies." *American Economic Review: AEA Papers and Proceedings* 85, no. 2 (May): 1–8.

Silk, Leonard. 1979. "A Conservative Choice." *New York Times*, 26 July: A1.

"The Soaring Dollar." 1984. *New York Times*, 19 September: I26.

"Some in Business Hail Anti-inflation Measures," 1979. *New York Times*, 8 October: D6.

Stevenson, Richard. 1992. "A Crisis in London: Finance Officials to Seek Measures to Salvage Monetary Links." *New York Times*, 17 September: 1.

Stockman, David. 1986. *The Triumph of Politics: How the Reagan Revolution Failed*. New York: Harper and Row.

"Stockman Is Criticized," 1982. *New York Times*, 4 February: D20.

"Straight and Narrow with Mr. Volcker." 1979. Editorial. *New York Times*, 26 July: A18.

Temin, Peter. 1976. *Did Monetary Forces Cause the Great Depression?* New York: W. W. Norton.

"Text of Fed's Announcement on Measures to Curb Inflation." 1979. *New York Times*, 8 October: D6.

Ture, Norman, and Stephen Entin. 1990. "Why Americans Don't Save." *Consumers' Research Magazine* (June): 29.

"23.4 Million in U.S. Were Out of Work Sometime Last Year." 1982. *New York Times*, 21 July: A19.

"U.S. Bought 2 Currencies." 1982. *New York Times*, 10 December: D19

U.S. Department of Commerce. 1975. *Historical Statistics of the United States: Colonial Times to 1970*. Bureau of the Census, Washington, D.C.: U.S. Government Printing Office.

U.S. Department of Commerce. *Long Term Economic Growth: 1860–1970*, Washington, D.C.: U.S. Government Printing Office.

U.S. Department of Energy. 1992. *Annual Energy Review*. Washington, D.C.: U.S. Government Printing Office (June).

"U.S. Moves to Stabilize Currency." 1982. *New York Times*, 15 June: D1.

Volcker, Paul. 1989. "The Contributions and Limitations of 'Monetary' Analysis." *Quarterly Review*, Federal Reserve Board of New York, 75th Anniversary Issue: 35–41.

Volcker, Paul, and Toyoo Gyohten. 1992. *Changing Fortunes, The World's Money and the Threat to American Leadership*. New York: Times Books.

"Volcker's Currency Aid View." 1983. *New York Times*, 29 April: IV–1.

Wanniski, Jude. 1978. *The Way the World Works: How Economies Fail and Succeed*. New York: Basic Books.

———. 1979. "Taxes, Revenues, and the 'Laffer Curve.' " In Arthur Laffer and Jan Seymour, eds., *The Economics of the Tax Revolt: A Reader*. New York: Harcourt Brace Jovanovich: 7–12.

Index

About the Author

THOMAS KARIER is Associate Dean and Professor of Economics at Eastern Washington University. Since 1989 he has served as research associate for the Jerome Levy Economics Institute in Annandale, NY, where he has published several policy briefs on contemporary economic policy. He has published in several journals and is the author of *Beyond Competition: The Economics of Mergers and Monopoly Power* (1993).